Biblical Creationism

What Each Book of the Bible Teaches
about Creation and the Flood

Henry M. Morris

Baker Books

A Division of Baker Book House Co.
Grand Rapids, Michigan 49516

Copyright © 1993 by Henry M. Morris

Published by Baker Books
a division of Baker Book House Company
P.O. Box 6287, Grand Rapids, MI 49516-6287

Fourth printing, April 1997

Printed in the United States of America

Library of Congress Cataloging-in-Publication Data

Morris, Henry M.
     Biblical creationism : what each book of the Bible teaches about creation and the
flood / Henry M. Morris.
          p. cm.
     Includes bibliographical references.
     ISBN 0-8010-6298-5
     1. Creation—Biblical teaching.   2. Creationism.   I. Title.
BS651 .M733 1993
231. 7'65—dc20   93-13462

Scripture references are taken from the King James Version of the Bible

For information about academic books, resources for
Christian leaders, and all new releases available from
Baker Book House, visit our web site:
               http://www.bakerbooks.com/

Contents

Foreword

It is not often that a son is privileged to write the foreword for a book written by his father, especially when the father has become recognized as the foremost author in his field. I am, therefore, deeply grateful and immensely pleased to be able to share my comments relative to this compendium of all the creation passages in God's Word, as well as the passages dealing with the flood and the other great events in the first eleven chapters of Genesis.

The biblical doctrine of creation has come under much attack, by friends as well as enemies, during the past three decades, in reaction to a widespread modern revival of true creationism. Apparently, the issues touch nerves deep inside the soul. Evidently, the credibility of the scientific case for creation has embarrassed those who have embraced or compromised with evolutionary theories. Thousands are becoming aware of the empty claims of evolutionism and are flocking to creation seminars being held all over the world.

The Scriptures clearly emphasize a recent, direct, fiat creation of the universe by an omnipotent and omniscient God. Books by my father and other creationist scientists have also convinced many people that this plain teaching of Scripture is supported by all true facts of science. No book has as yet, however, identified and discussed every passage in Scripture on creation, the flood, and other primeval events. That is the unique contribution of this book. It also analyzes corresponding material in other ancient books.

In addition, this book gives exegesis of all the more difficult sections, furnishes deep expository dividends, and yields rich spiritual insights. It should prove to be a classic for generations to come, should the Lord delay his coming, and will become a resource for pastors, teachers, and lay leaders throughout the Christian family.

The gospel without the promise of the coming eternal kingdom has no hope (Mark 1:14, 15). The gospel without the fact of Christ's substitutionary atonement and bodily resurrection has no power (1 Cor. 15:3, 4). The gospel without the assurance of a Creator-God has no foundation (Rev. 4:11; 14:6, 7). This book will embolden those whose faith has been undermined by evolutionary dogma and will enrich those who have not yet been exposed to the preaching of "all the counsel of God" (Acts 20:27).

May God add his own blessing to *Biblical Creationism,* a book which seeks to expound and magnify that act of God which speaks most eloquently of his "invisible things . . . even his eternal power and Godhead" (Rom. 1:20).

Henry Morris III

Acknowledgments

My oldest son, Dr. Henry Morris III, was kind enough to review the manuscript for me, and even to write a foreword for the book. He is a keen student of the Bible, author of the book *Explore the Word,* and has served many years as pastor and Christian college administrator, as well as businessman. I appreciate his words of commendation.

I also wish to thank Dr. Richard Bliss and Dr. John Morris, both of whom are Institute for Creation Research scientists, for reviewing the manuscript and for their helpful comments. Rebecca and Don Barber typed and prepared the manuscript. Dan Van't Kerkhoff and his editorial colleagues at Baker Book House, as always, did an excellent job of editing and publishing. I am grateful to all of these gracious people, but even more to the Lord for his wonderful Word and for the privilege of learning from it.

Introduction

T he purpose of this book is to make a complete survey of all the biblical passages which mention the creation or other events of primeval world history, in order to develop a comprehensive understanding of this foundational doctrine. Although it is often misinterpreted, and more often ignored, there is no doctrine more important, for creation is the basis of all reality. That is why God placed it first in the Bible—"In the beginning God created the heaven and the earth" (Gen.1:1).

I also have a personal reason for doing this. When I was a young Christian engineer, struggling with the dogma of evolution versus biblical revelation, I kept trying to find some means of harmonizing the creation account with the day-age theory (with the days of creation representing the geological ages), then the gap theory (with the ages of geology pigeonholed between Gen.1:1 and Gen. 1:2), or some other theory, but none of these compromise systems seemed to work for either science or Scripture.

I had become convinced that the Bible was the Word of God, inspired and inerrant in every word. That being the case, it seemed that such a vital doctrine as creation should be clearly set forth in Scripture, leaving no doubt whatever as to its nature and meaning. I proceeded then to go through the Bible verse by verse, to record and organize every verse dealing with creation and related topics. The conclusion from this study was that not one of the compromise theories was biblical. The Bible taught clearly and explicitly that all things were made by God in a six-day week of natural days. There was no room for evolution or the long geological ages at all. Furthermore, the flood was worldwide in extent and cataclysmic in effect, destroying all men and land animals except those in Noah's ark. This also should be clearly evident from the

data of science and history, if true. This literal "interpretation" is the
only one which satisfies all the biblical data, and so is the only one presented in this book and advocated by scientists of the Institute for Creation Research.

This interpretation meant that the scientific data which supposedly
had proved evolution and a great age for the earth had been badly misinterpreted. I soon came to realize that all the scientific data can, indeed,
be understood better in terms of recent creation and the global deluge.
That conviction remains firm today, almost fifty years later.

In this book, therefore, I want to go through all the Scriptures once
again, setting forth chronologically the complete biblical doctrine of
creation, with all its implications and applications. I hope such a study
will convince Christians everywhere, as it did me long ago, that they
must abandon all these compromise theories, and return to the simple
Genesis record of supernatural, six-day creation. The only other honest alternative would seem to be to abandon our professed belief in biblical inspiration and authority altogether.

I will not try to deal with science in this book, only with Scripture.
We can be confident that the scientific data will correlate with Scripture all right, because the same God who wrote the Word made the
world! If Christians who believe the Bible will take the Word of God
as it stands, determine once for all what it teaches on this most basic of
all issues, and then set about to organize the scientific data in that context, they will find everything makes good sense, to both mind and
heart. There are many books now available discussing the scientific evidence for creation and the flood (see Appendix C for a representative
listing), but there is more than enough Biblical evidence alone to fill
this book. In addition to the many biblical passages dealing with creation and related events, Appendix A summarizes the references to Genesis 1–11 that are found in the key extra-biblical books associated with
the Bible.

In setting forth the biblical references to creation and the other great
events of earth's earliest ages, I have followed a chronological approach.
This is the order in which these revelations were conveyed by God to
man in his Word. In a sense, this will be like thinking God's thoughts
after him, and so should be an effective—perhaps the optimum—way
to develop a comprehensive biblical doctrine of creation. We shall try
to understand each succeeding revelation in the sense that those to
whom it was first given understood it. It was as essential for them as for

us and since they did not have (nor need) any modern scientific theories to help them understand what God was saying to them, then neither do we.

There are so many references throughout Scripture on these themes that it is impracticable to give detailed expositions of each. Many of them, in fact, are so clear that no exposition is necessary. I have, however, tried to discuss all the key passages, so as to set forth as clearly as possible the full biblical doctrine of creation and its major applications. I have tried to understand and expound (where necessary) each reference in the way the original hearers or readers would have understood it, which generally means in the literal sense. This may occasionally require reading "between the lines," so to speak. In so doing, however, I have tried never to interpolate in any way which would question or contradict the revealed Scriptures. My fundamental premise is the inerrant authority and perspicuity of the whole Bible, and my goal is to develop on that premise a comprehensive system of truly biblical creationism.

1

The Genesis Record of Creation

Genesis 1:1–2

The Book of Genesis (i.e., "Beginnings") is the foundation book of the Bible, upon which all the rest is built. The most important chapter in Genesis is the first chapter, the basis of all the later chapters, and of all the thirty one verses in this first chapter of Genesis, the very first verse is the one upon which all the others depend. "In the beginning God created the heaven and the earth" (Gen. 1:1).

This simple declarative statement can only have come by divine revelation. Its scope is comprehensively universal, embracing all space (heaven), all time (beginning), and all matter (earth) in our space/time/matter cosmos. It is the first and only statement of real creation in all the cosmogonies of all the nations of past or present. All other creation myths begin with the universe already in existence, in watery chaos or in some other primordial form. Evidently man, with unaided reason, cannot conceive of true creation; he must begin with *something*. But Genesis 1:1 speaks of creation *ex nihilo;* only God could originate such a concept, and only an infinite, omnipotent God could create the universe.

This revelation was given initially by God himself to the very first man and woman and has been transmitted down through the ages to all their children. God either wrote it down with his own finger on a table of stone, as he later did the tablets of the law (Exod. 31:18), or else he revealed it verbally to Adam, who recorded it. It was vital that Adam and Eve, along with their descendants, should know about their own origin, as well as that of their earthly "dominion," if they were to be responsible stewards thereof. The original transcriptions of later sections of Genesis are denoted by their *toledoth* subscripts ("These are the generations of . . . ," followed by the writer's name),[1] but the events of this incomparable first chapter could only have been known to God himself. Therefore it is terminated with the subscript: "These are the generations of the heavens and of the earth when they were created" (Gen. 2:4). No human author is named, so it surely originated directly from the One by whom "they were created." We should read and believe it exactly as it stands, without trying to "interpret" it to fit some theory of men.

This concluding statement must refer back to Genesis 1:1, for no other verse in this first chapter of Genesis mentions the creation of the heavens and the earth. This fact assures us that the mighty event of cosmic creation, as declared in Genesis 1:1, was included in the events of that unique first week of earth history, as the very first act of the series of divine acts recounted in that chapter. Adam surely would have treasured and guarded that first precious creation tablet all the days of his life.

When God (Hebrew *Elohim,* actually a plural noun, suggesting already the uni-plural nature of the Godhead) first created the heaven and the earth, there were no stars or planets in the heaven (these came later, on the fourth day), nor was the "earth" material yet formed or ready for habitation. It was "without form, and void." This "earthy" material was not yet energized, for "light" (i.e., the whole spectrum of electromagnetic energy, as we call it today) had not yet been activated. There was a watery matrix everywhere, with the "earth" (that is, the "dust of the earth," as it is called later—or perhaps, in modern terminology, the particles that would function as "matter") suspended therein.

This condition is summarized in Genesis 1:2. "And the earth was without form, and void; and darkness was upon the face of the deep [or, in the presence of the deep]." There is no suggestion here to Adam or to his descendants that this state had resulted from some kind of judgment of a previous world; it was simply the elemental state of the space/time/matter universe as it sprang into being from the omnipotent Word of its Creator.

But then "the Spirit of God moved upon the face of the waters." The inference of uni-plurality drawn from the name of God *(Elohim)* is strengthened by this revelation that God is an energizing Spirit as well as omnipotent Creator. The word for "moved" refers to a back-and-forth motion, like wings fluttering or vibrating. The Spirit's omnipresent vibrating movements, pervading the omnipresent waters, energized the created cosmos and prepared it for further divine organization. God is to be revealed next as speaking, as well as creating and moving. Thus he is the divine Word as well as infinite Creator and activating Spirit.

The Six Days of Creation

The tremendous events of creation week were undoubtedly first revealed by God to Adam in the Garden of Eden. They began with the *ex nihilo* creation of the universe by God on the first day and concluded with the creation of man and woman on the sixth day. The man and woman were then placed in charge over all the earth, as stewards under God's ownership (Gen. 1:26–28).

Adam surely would have noted the emphasis on the divine Word in God's account of creation week. At least sixteen times he would have read of God speaking. God spoke to create, he spoke to identify, and he spoke to bless. Adam would have recognized also that the account was presented as an actual chronological history of the events of that wonderful week, with no hint whatever that God did not mean exactly what he said. Each verse in the account began with the conjunction of sequence—"and" (Hebrew *waw*). There was no suggestion of allegory, or overlap, or gap, or of anything except straightforward history. The conjunction "and," indicating chronological sequence, actually was used some sixty times in the creation narrative.

The account was given in terms of the events of seven sequential days— six days of work, one day of rest. Adam surely knew what a "day" was, but if there might be any question, God defined the word for him. "God called the light Day, and the darkness he called Night. And the evening and the morning were the first day" (Gen. 1:5). The same terminology was used for each of the five days following, so there should be no uncertainty whatever that God intended the account to say that the creation of all things had taken place in six literal days. It would certainly have been so understood by Adam and his descendants in those early generations who first read the divine account. The fact that each day was bounded by an evening and morning, and each modified by an ordinal number, further stressed that these days were literal days. These usages would be carefully maintained by God in all the rest of Scripture.

The particular events of the six days involved three specific events of *ex nihilo* creation, marked by the use of the Hebrew word *bara* ("create"), a verb never used to describe the work of anyone other than God the Creator. These three events were the creation of the physical universe, the creation of the entity of conscious life, and the creation of the spiritual nature ("the image of God") in man: "In the beginning God created the heaven and the earth" (Gen. 1:1); "God created . . . every living creature that moveth" (Gen. 1:21); God created man in his own image . . . ; male and female created he them (Gen. 1:27).

From these three basic created entities, comprising the physical, biological, and spiritual components of the creation, God "made" and "formed" (Hebrew *asah* and *yatsar*) the many systems of the cosmos, as summarized below.

First Day: Activating and energizing the newly created physical universe (Gen. 1:1–5).

Second Day: Making the firmament (that is, the atmosphere) to form the great hydrosphere of the earth, divided into two great water masses, one above and one below the atmosphere (Gen. 1:6–8).

Third Day: Forming the lithosphere and plant biosphere of the earth, massing the "earth" material created on Day One into great continental rock systems, supporting and separating various interconnected "seas" and bodies of "dry land," with a luscious blanket of plant material (which was also constructed of the "earth" elements, but with marvelously coded reproductive provisions—the "seed is in itself") covering the lands and consisting of grasses, herbs, and trees (Gen. 1:9–13).

Fourth Day: Constructing the vast astrosphere surrounding the earth (sun, moon and stars) and placing these "lights" throughout the infinite space of heaven that had been created on Day One, these also being made of the same "earth" matter created on Day One, their purpose being to serve for measuring time ("for seasons and for days, and years") and for "signs" (the meaning of which would be divulged later) (Gen. 1:14–19).

Fifth Day: Forming multitudes of animals for the atmosphere and hydrosphere, each containing the newly created entity of conscious life (Gen. 1:20–23).

Sixth Day: Forming animals for the lithosphere and plant biosphere, also made of the "earth" matter physically and "life" entity biologically, including "beasts of the earth," "cattle," and "creeping things," plus human beings who, in addition, were implanted with the specially created "image of God" and then placed in dominion over all the rest of the works of God made in the six days (Gen. 1:24–31). Note that even the animals that have since become extinct—such as dinosaurs—were made on the fifth and sixth days of the creation week.

Seventh Day. Acknowledging the completion of his work in creating and making all things, and therefore "resting," "blessing," and "sanctifying" this day in commemoration thereof (Gen. 2:1–4a).

As Adam and Eve first heard (or read—assuming God had written it down for them on a tablet and had taught them to read as well as speak) the account of creation, they must have been awed by the vast complexity and majestic beauty of the creation over which they had been placed in charge. They would have noted that each reproducing entity (whether plant or animal) would be reproducing "after its kind," for God used this phrase no less than ten times in his account. They also were instructed to "be fruitful, and multiply, and [fill] the earth" (Gen. 1:28), for they would need a large progeny to exercise their dominion effectively.

In order to "subdue" the earth, as they were directed, they would have to learn all about its systems and processes (thus developing what we now call "science"), then to organize and utilize this knowledge in productive ways that would both benefit others and honor their Creator ("technology"), and then to disseminate this information and its products to everyone ("business," "education," "communication," "transportation," etc.). God said five times that different aspects of his work were "good" and then finally, after it was all complete, pronounced it all "very good" (Gen. 1:31). This divine evaluation could be received and then detailed by man in works of music, art, and literature, glorifying and praising God for all he had done in creating and making all things.

There was an abundance of food for both men and animals provided by God in the fruits, herbs, and grasses of the plant biosphere (Gen. 1:29–30), so there would have been no need for any "struggle for existence." Since everything was "good," there was nothing evil—no disease, no competition, no lack of harmony, no deterioration, and, above all, *no death* of "living creatures."

The grasses, herbs, and trees were capable of reproducing their own kinds, in order to provide food for men and animals, but these were not living creatures (Hebrew *chay nephesh*), and so could not "die" when used for food. Neither men nor animals were intended to die at all. Once they had "filled the earth," as instructed by God, to its optimum capacity, it would be assumed that either they would cease reproducing or else (perhaps) be transported to other suitable "earths" to fill them as well. Adam would not have needed to speculate on such questions: his immediate mandate was to fill the earth and subdue it.

Each day's work was concluded with an "evening," and no more work was done until the next "morning" came. This would be man's pattern as well. He would work during the "day," or "light" period, then rest until the next morning. Similarly, since God had "rested" after six days of work, man also would "rest" every seventh day, for God had "sanctified" (or, "set apart") one day in seven for this purpose. This would be a *sabbath* (literally, "rest") day—no doubt one devoted to communicating with God and honoring him as Creator and Lord of all man's dominion.

It is particularly important to note that God's work of both "creating" and "making" all things had ceased; he would henceforth *conserve* and *sustain* what he had created and made, but these processes would be quite distinct from those he had used during creation week. In his work of exercising dominion over the earth, Adam would need to learn much about God's processes of maintenance, but these "natural" processes could never teach him about God's "supernatural" processes, for these had ceased. Adam was completely dependent on God for knowledge about the creation period, and *that* was what God told him about in what we now know as the first chapter of Genesis.

It would not be long before some of Adam's descendants would seek to displace God's record of supernatural creation in six days with some speculative theory of naturalistic creation over long ages, but they would inevitably be blocked by the impossibility of converting processes of conservation—such as now control the universe—into processes of creation which could produce a universe.

The Book of Adam

The first section of Genesis concludes with the unique statement: "These are the generations [Hebrew *toledoth*] of the heavens and of the earth when they were created" (Gen. 2:4a). The second section is attached to it with the initial interlocking phrase: "In the day that the

LORD God made the earth and the heavens . . ." (Gen. 2:4b). It then gives the main events in the lives of Adam and Eve and concludes with the second of the Genesis *toledoth* notations: "This is the book of the generations of Adam" (Gen. 5:1).

It seems certain that Adam knew how to write, for this section is called a "book," and no one but Adam could have known about all the events of this section. For him to be able to name the animals, as God commanded, and to subdue the earth, he must have had extraordinary intelligence and skill. He had come directly from the Creator's hand and was "in his image"—thus surely capable of accurate, rapid analytical reasoning and precise verbal and written communication. Therefore we can regard this "book of Adam" as being a precisely accurate accounting of the events it describes.

It was written from Adam's viewpoint, of course, reflecting both his experiences in the Garden of Eden and, later, outside of the garden, though still near it. Adam did not recount the earlier events of creation week, these having been outside of his own experience and already outlined by God in his previous account. Adam began by keying his record in to the conclusion of God's record, then gave a summary description of the environment into which he was "born" early on the sixth day of that creation week. He spoke of God almost exclusively as "the LORD God" (*Jehovah Elohim*), whereas the previous tablet spoke only of "God" (*Elohim*). There was no need to mention the animals until later, when the Lord brought them before him. He mentioned only that God had made and then planted the vegetation himself, since there was no provision for either rain or humans to cultivate from seeds. Except for the special garden which God planted and then told Adam "to dress it and to keep it" (Gen. 2:15), the earth's plant life must grow unattended by man until the human population could multiply to sufficient numbers.

Adam also described the primeval hydrologic system as typified by the river which "went out of Eden" and which, after leaving Eden, separated "into four heads" and then provided water for four different lands (Gen. 2:10–14). Since there was no "rain upon the earth" but only a daily "mist" which condensed upon "the whole face of the ground" (Gen. 2:6), it seems evident that such artesian-fed rivers existed at other points over the earth, emerging through "fountains" from a "great deep" of pressurized waters in great subterranean reservoirs. The latter must have been made by God on the second day of creation week, to receive the greater portion of the "waters under the firmament," the remainder constituting the network of "seas" on the surface of the earth. Presumably the rivers flowed into the seas, whence they seeped back by some mechanism into the subcrustal waters again.

The production of rain could, it seems, only have been inhibited by a very stable atmosphere, with neither global circulation nor nuclei of condensation to translate evaporated waters from the seas aloft to the lands and then to cause condensation and precipitation. This situation could most likely have been maintained by the global canopy of "waters above the firmament," set there by God on Day Two of creation week. Such a canopy, if at least partially in the vapor state, would have both permitted the stars to be seen on the earth and also served as a thermal blanket, maintaining a generally uniform, equable temperature everywhere, retaining and distributing incoming solar radiations throughout the atmosphere. In turn, the uniform temperatures would have precluded air mass movements from seas to lands or from equator to poles, as at present, so that water evaporated during the day would merely have condensed as mists in the same general regions each night. In some such way, the earth's "very good" climate was maintained at comfortable temperatures and humidities everywhere and throughout the year, supporting an abundance of plant life in every land.

All of this had been designed and made by God on Days Two, Three, and Four of creation week. The world was created in a fully functional state from the beginning. The fruit trees already were bearing fruit, the grasses and shrubs already blanketing the earth, the soils filled with needed nutrients to maintain this growth, the rocks laced with deposits of gold, iron, and other metals, as well as precious stones (Gen. 2:12; 4:22). The light from the stars could already be seen on the earth, and Adam and Eve were created as a full-grown man and woman. Animals also were made full-grown, able immediately to begin to "multiply in the earth." To judge such a full-grown creation as impossible or unscientific is equivalent to saying God could not create, and this would be equivalent to atheism. The historical record (in fact, divinely inspired record) says that this was how it was, and that should be sufficient!

Adam also described how God formed his own body and, later, that of Eve, (this particular information, of course, must have been imparted to Adam by God in later discourse with Adam). Adam's body was carefully and lovingly formed directly by God's own hands (not, like the animals, merely by the divine spoken Word) out of the "dust of the ground," the basic elements of earth matter from which all physical systems had been made (Gen. 2:7). Then Eve's body was formed by God out of the materials in Adam's side (not necessarily a "rib," as translators have assumed), probably both flesh and blood, as well as bone (Gen. 2:21–23). They were most certainly *not* formed by any evolutionary process from a population of hominids, as modern pseudo-intellectuals have deceived themselves into believing.

Before God formed Eve, however, he "introduced" Adam to the animals he had formed earlier in the day. Adam was to exercise dominion over them, so God told him to name them, giving each a name appropriate to the individual characteristics of each. The animals brought to him by God included "all cattle . . . the fowl of the air, and . . . every beast of the field" (Gen. 2:20)—that is, those animals that would live near him and might be possible candidates for companionship or usefulness to man. Not included were the fish of the sea, the beasts of the earth, or the creeping things. Furthermore, only the created "kinds" of these animals were included, not the multitudes of genera, species, and varieties that later proliferated from them.

In view of the limited number of relevant kinds of cattle, field animals, and birds and, in view also of Adam's giant intellect in comparison with our own, as well as divine guidance and instruction, this project would not have occupied more than about half a day. An additional purpose of the assignment was to show Adam that he needed a companion that would be like him, an "help meet for him." So God proceeded to form Eve from Adam's side and then to give her to him as his wife.

The basic human institution of marriage, making "one flesh" of husband and wife in lifelong union, is thus directly founded on the special creation of the first man and woman, for each other and for God. This would be the pattern, and norm, for all the descendants of Adam and Eve as well.

God told Adam and Eve to "be fruitful, and multiply" (Gen. 1:28), and no doubt implanted genuine love for each other, in all its dimensions, in their minds and bodies, so it would not have been overly long before Eve conceived a child (Gen. 4:1). It was not to be the joyous occasion it could have been, however, for before the actual conception, the greatest tragedy of history intervened.

Adam told the sad story of his fall in simple, yet poignant, words. The temptation came through the serpent, the most "subtil" of the beasts of the field named by Adam. At this point in time, Adam and Eve had evidently not been informed about the invisible angelic creation, nor of the rebellion of their leader, Satan, who aspired to usurp God's reign over his creation. He had been cast out of heaven to the earth, where he would be allowed to tempt Adam and Eve also to rebel against God. Being a powerful spirit being, he was able to possess and control the body of the brilliantly shining serpent.

Whether the serpent in the primeval creation was able actually to speak in human language is a matter of uncertainty. Eve did not appear to be surprised, but perhaps this was her first direct contact with one of the animals. Another reasonable interpretation would involve telepathic or hypnotic communication, with Satan using the serpent as the object to induce a state of transfixed attention in the unsuspecting woman. To the naive young bride, the evil spirit in the serpent could communicate in such a clear way that she would assume it was the serpent speaking. Similar demonic communications have occurred on various occasions throughout history. In any case, whatever the exact mechanism may have been, Eve reported it to Adam as an actual conversation with the serpent, and he then recorded it as such. The end result, of course, was that Adam and Eve both ate of the forbidden fruit of the tree of knowledge of good and evil, first doubting God's word and finally disobeying his explicit commandment. As God had warned (Gen. 2:19), they died as a result. They first died spiritually, in the sense that their fellowship with God was instantly broken. They also *began* to die physically, the law of decay starting to work in their bodies, and this process would finally take them back to the dust from which their bodies had been formed.

It was not only Adam and Eve who died. The principle of death which began to operate in their bodies had infected their reproductive systems, along with everything else, and has since been transmitted to all their descendants, so that "in Adam all die," as the apostle Paul would acknowledge thousands of years later (1 Cor. 15:22). As a matter of fact, the curse of death affected everything in Adam's dominion. God said to Adam, "Cursed is the ground for thy sake" (Gen. 3:17). The very elements of the earth were brought under God's judgment. The serpent also was "cursed . . . above every beast of the field" (Gen. 3:14), indicating that all the animals also came under the curse, as a part of Adam's dominion. Their bodies, like that of Adam, had been made out of the "dust of the ground." The very elements of matter—"the ground"—were thus included in God's curse, thereby affecting everything in the physical universe. Because of Eve's key involvement, the process of reproduction was especially affected, so that what would have been a pleasant and painless experience would henceforth become an experience of unique travail and suffering (Gen. 3:16), not only for Eve but also for all her daughters in the times to come.

As for Adam, and all his sons, they must henceforth struggle against a resisting "ground," now under God's curse, just to provide a living for their families. God's command to "subdue" the earth took on a new intensity of meaning, as "the whole creation" began to "groan and travail in pain together" under its "bondage of corruption" (Rom. 8:22, 21).

This principle of decay and death would come eventually to be recognized as a universal law of nature, with ramifications and applications in every area of life and study. Its most important effect was the entrance of death into the world. There was no death in either human life or animal life until sin entered the world, a fact extremely important to remember in attempting to construct any kind of supposed pre-Adamic history of the earth.

Because their fellowship with God had been destroyed, Adam and Eve were banished from the beautiful Paradise that had been planned as their home. Although the garden still existed, at least for a time, people were no longer allowed to go there, where they might partake of its life-sustaining Tree of Life.

In spite of their awful loss, however, Adam and Eve left the garden with God's gracious promise of a coming Savior in their minds and hearts. This promise, given even before the curse, was addressed *to* the serpent (and to the malignant spirit using its body), but it was *for* Adam and Eve and their descendants. "I will put enmity between thee and the woman, and between thy seed and her seed; it shall bruise thy head, and thou shalt bruise his heel" (Gen. 3:15).

This primeval promise was faithfully recorded by Adam, even though he probably did not fully understand it. The "serpent" who had occasioned their fall would himself eventually be crushed by one of their human descendants, one who would uniquely be of the woman's "seed," rather than that of the man. This, in turn, would have to mean that, although human, the promised "seed" must also be divine—the God/man, or God in human incarnation.

Although they could not understand fully, this time they *believed* God's word, and God responded to their faith by providing a covering for their nakedness before him and before each other. This clothing entailed the very first *death* (physical death, that is) in the world. Innocent animals, probably two sheep, must be put to death, shedding their blood, so that God could make from their skins "coats" for the guilty pair. This was the very first "sacrifice," substituting the death of an innocent creature for the deserved death of a guilty sinner. Although Adam did not record anything more about it, God must have given him some such explanation, for it served as the type and pattern for multitudes of later sacrifices in human history.

This book of the generations of Adam also tells the sad story of Cain and Abel, the two oldest sons of what eventually would become a large number of sons and daughters (Gen. 5:4). Even before they left the garden, Adam had named his wife Eve (meaning "life giver"), because he was confident, by faith, that she would, indeed, be "the mother of all living" (Gen. 3:20).

But Cain, her first son, eventually became the world's first murderer, and Abel her second son, was the first martyr and the first person to experience physical death. This experience brought home to Adam and Eve in a very painful way the stark reality of sin and death which had entered God's "very good" world through their disobedience. The regular practice of substitutionary animal sacrifice, as illustrated by Abel's offering, had already made this point to Adam's family (by this time they probably had other sons and daughters in addition to Cain and Abel), but the tragic loss of the two oldest brothers must have been to them a bitter reminder. They must have longed for the coming of the promised Redeemer, and when Seth was born in place of Abel, there is some intimation that Eve may have hoped he would be the one (Gen. 4:25). In one sense he was, since he became the one in Adam's family through whom the promise would eventually be fulfilled.

Adam and Eve evidently kept in touch with Cain also, even after God banished him from their home in the land of Eden, for Adam's book records Cain's activities and his posterity to the sixth generation after Adam (i.e., Cain, Enoch, Irad, Mehujael, Methusael, and Lamech). The account mentions several significant innovations brought into human history by Cain and his descendants—including urbanization, agriculture, ranching, musical instruments, metallurgy, and metal-working. All of this presupposes ability in reading, writing and arithmetic, at least, as well as construction, animal husbandry, and other skills (note Gen. 4:16–22). By no means were these early generations of people illiterate ape-men.

Both Cain and Seth had to marry one of their sisters, of course (or, possibly, nieces), for there was no other way for Adam's progeny to begin to fulfill God's command to multiply. Much later, as such close marriages became both unnecessary and harmful, they would be prohibited.

Adam had many sons and daughters (Gen. 5:4—Josephus, the Jewish historian shortly after the time of Christ, cited a tradition that Adam had thirty sons), and evidently all lived hundreds of years, so the population did multiply rapidly. For some reason, Adam did not record the names of his descendants through Seth (except for Enos, Seth's son), leaving that for Noah to do in the next tablet of the series. Possibly Seth and Enos took care of that until they could turn the records over to Lamech, Noah's father.

It seems likely that Adam and his sons (as Cain and Abel had done) continued to meet with God occasionally (perhaps on each Sabbath day), through the medium of sacrifice, at the entrance to the Garden of Eden. This privilege somehow ceased after a while, and they had to communicate with God thereafter only through prayer, along with the sacrifices. This is probably the meaning of the closing statement in Adam's tablet: "And to Seth, to him also was born a son; and he called his name Enos: then began man to call upon the name of the LORD [i.e., Jehovah or Yahweh, the name of God associated more with self-revelation and redemption than with his mighty power in creation]. This is the book of the generations of Adam" (Gen. 4:26–5:1a).

In this chapter I have summarized the chief events in the Genesis creation record, as contained in the first two *toledoth* tablets—"the generations of the heavens and of the earth" and "the book of the generations of Adam" (Gen. 2:4a; 5:1a). I have not attempted a verse-by-verse commentary on these foundational chapters of the Bible, since I have already done this in my complete commentary on the whole book, *The Genesis Record.* I have tried to emphasize especially, however, those portions dealing directly with the creation and events related thereto, in light of their significance both for the people of Adam's generations (when they were first written) and also for us today.

The Genesis creation record is real history, not some esoteric allegory. It is an account of real people, real places, real events, at the very dawn of the history of God's created universe. This literal understanding of these primeval days is, as we shall see, completely supported by all later references to them in the Bible, God's revealed Word.

2

The Lost World

The Generations of Noah

The next *toledoth* portion of Genesis, which many conservative expositors (including myself) assume was written on a stone or clay tablet by Noah, begins with Genesis 5:1b and ends with Noah's testimony at Genesis 6:8: "Noah found grace in the eyes of the LORD," and then his concluding signature: "These are the generations of Noah" (Gen. 6:9a).

It begins with the same device Adam used in beginning his own *toledoth* tablet—that is, using terminology that keys the record back in with the previous records. Noah's account starts by referring to both earlier tablets: "In the day that God created man, in the likeness of God made he him; male and female created he them" (Gen. 5:1, thus quoting Gen. 1:27). Then, alluding to Genesis 4:25: "And Adam . . . begat a son in his own likeness, after his image; and called his name Seth" (Gen. 5:3).

Noah's record is in two main parts. The first consists essentially of the genealogical (and chronological) data extending from Adam to himself and his sons. The second is a description of the terrible moral and spiritual deterioration that had developed in the world, especially after Adam, Seth, and Enos died, followed by God's decision to send a great flood to destroy the antediluvian civilization.

From our point of view today, one of the most remarkable aspects of Noah's record is the great longevity of the antediluvian patriarchs (the average lifespan of those recorded—except for Enoch—was 912 years), but Noah recorded it as simple, matter-of-fact history. In his day, such long life spans were obviously the norm, so they required no special explanation, as would have been the case if the account had been written originally by Moses or some later scribe.

We could wish that more details of the events of those far-off days had been given by Noah, but somehow he chose to record nothing but the patriarchal genealogy and chronology. Even the remarkable translation of Enoch into heaven without dying receives only the barest mention (Gen. 5:22–24).

A few points of interest are worth noting. There were just ten antediluvian patriarchs, in the line of the promised Seed—Adam, Seth, Enos, Cainan, Mahalaleel, Jared, Enoch, Methuselah, Lamech, and Noah. Adam lived 930 years (Gen. 5:5), evidently including his brief time in the Garden of Eden, and he lived until Lamech, the father of Noah, was 56 years old. Adam, thus, lived to know all these men except Noah, and Noah was born in time to know all of them except Adam, Seth, and Enoch. Methuselah lived 969 years (Gen. 5:27), longer than anyone else in the line. In fact, he outlived his own son and did not die until the very year of the great flood. In any case, Noah did record that all of his direct ancestors, even though they each lived a long, long time, finally died (except for Enoch, whom he had known only by name and testimony). He must have known about Enoch's strong witness against the ungodly world of his day, for this tradition survived even beyond the time of Christ (Jude 14,15). Perhaps one reason Noah did not write more details about the life of his ancestors was that they had already written about these matters, so he needed only to record the genealogy, and then to write more fully about the wickedness of his own generation. Then, for reasons known only to God, these biographies were not preserved (except, possibly, for some of the traditions in such apocryphal books as Enoch, Jubilees, etc.[1]), and we now have only Noah's sketch of this period.

Noah did write, of course, of the terrible moral deterioration that came to its climax in his days, evidently triggered by the mysterious unions of the "sons of God" with the "daughters of men," along with the dreadful "giants in the earth" which resulted from these demonic intrusions into the human family. Up to this point, there had been no mention in the earlier records of the demonic spirits, or fallen angels, who had joined Satan in his rebellion against God. Not even Satan himself had been mentioned, although he had used the serpent's body to bring about the fall of Adam and Eve.

Therefore, when these demons did come to the earth and begin to interfere in human relations, Noah knew they were not descended from other men and women, so he could merely assume (correctly, as a matter of fact) that they had been created by God, so he called them "sons of God." Their behavior was not godly, however, as they began to take possession of the bodies of the rebellious men of that period (just as their master, Satan, had been able to use the body of the serpent back in Eden to tempt Eve) and then to tempt the beautiful (but ungodly) "daughters of men" into godless unions. If Satan could possess and use the body of a serpent to tempt Eve, it is no marvel that his wicked spirits could possess and use the bodies—and voices—of men to woo and win her great great granddaughters.

Then the children born of these corrupt marriages, with demon-possessed fathers and beautiful but vain and self-centered mothers, could hardly grow into anything but monsters of wickedness and violence. The parents were, no doubt, excellent physical specimens and would thus also bear children of exceptional strength and stature. More than this, however, must have been involved in actually generating giants. The Hebrew word so translated is *nephilim*, meaning literally "the fallen ones," probably referring to the fallen angels, or demons. That it was understood also by the ancient Hebrews to mean "giants" is evident from its translation by them into the Greek Septuagint version of the Old Testament by the Greek word *gigantes*. The most likely implication from all this is that these children were also demon-possessed, and that the superhuman intelligence of the evil spirits controlling them and their fathers enabled them to develop giantism in size as well as wickedness.

In any case, the net result of this demonic intrusion of Satan and his angels into the lives of the antediluvians was the most terrible irruption of evil and wickedness the world has ever known. Noah wrote that "the wickedness of man was great in the earth, and that every imagination of the thoughts of his heart was only evil continually" (Gen. 6:5).

Many commentators in modern times have proposed the rationalistic interpretation that "the sons of God" and "daughters of men" were actually merely "the sons of Seth" and "daughters of Cain," and that their unions were simply mixed marriages of believers and unbelievers. Such an idea, while more amenable to our modern naturalistic environment, is certainly not the obvious meaning of the text—Noah could easily have said "sons of Seth" if that were his intent. Such a more-than-human state of global evil, violence, and giantism, capable of being remedied only by a worldwide hydraulic cataclysm, must have had a more sinister cause than believers marrying unbelievers! Noah may not, in his day, have known very much about the invisible world of angels and demons, but he obviously recognized that this terrible state of universal evil could only be explained by a supernaturally evil cause.

Noah recorded two occasions on which God actually spoke concerning this situation, presumably to Noah himself. So far as the record goes, these were the first direct words from God in the long centuries since he had spoken in judgment to Cain (Gen. 4:9–15). God had surely spoken to Enoch, for "Enoch walked with God: and . . . God took him" (Gen. 5:24), but we have no record of what he said. Perhaps he spoke to Lamech before his son Noah was born, for Lamech had prophesied concerning Noah's future ministry (Gen. 5:29).

In any case, God finally spoke again in grave words of warning: "My spirit shall not always strive with man, for that he also is flesh: yet his days shall be an hundred and twenty years" (Gen. 6:3). And then, later: "I will destroy man whom I have created from the face of the earth, both man, and beast, and the creeping thing, and the fowls of the air; for it repenteth me that I have made them" (Gen. 6:7).

This is the second specific reference in the Bible to the Holy Spirit. In the first (Gen. 1:2), he was revealed as energizing and activating the created cosmos. Here, he is revealed as "striving" with man, no doubt with respect to man's increasingly blatant rebellion against his Creator. This is the first clear glimpse we have in Scripture of this loving ministry of God the Holy Spirit, as he seeks to convince men and women to forsake their rebellion and return to their Creator. At the same time, we also learn that God's patience has limits, and judgment must come eventually when men persist in their rebellion.

Finally the 120 years of grace were gone, and the time for judgment came. During this period, no doubt, Noah had been building the ark and also trying to call men to repentance before it was too late. However, he said little about himself or his deeds. Instead he closed his own account with the simple testimony: "But Noah found grace in the eyes of the LORD. These are the generations of Noah" (Gen. 6:8, 9a). He had said very little about his ancestors, merely recording their names, their birth dates, and their dates of death, and this was all he would say about himself. In this very first mention of grace in the Bible, he acknowledged simply that, in a world wholly given to wickedness, he was saved from the coming judgment simply by the grace of God. His sons, in the next tablet, would say much more about him, but he would only say that he had found grace in the eyes of the Lord. And then, no doubt weary from his six hundred years of struggle for righteousness in a violent world (Gen. 7:11), including perhaps a long period in building the great ark, as well as a hundred years of constraining his sons to obey God in such a godless environment (Gen. 5:32), Noah simply signed his name to his brief survey of the first 1,656 years (calculated by adding the appropriate time periods in Gen. 5), and laid his tablet aside, with the previous tablets handed down from Adam, for storage and safekeeping in the ark through the flood that was about to come.

Noah's Ark and the Worldwide Flood

Shem, Ham and Japheth were born into Noah's family after he was five hundred years old (Gen. 5:32). It seems reasonable that he may have had other sons and daughters (the other sons listed in the genealogy were born when their respective fathers were anywhere from 65 to 187 years of age) but, if so, they must all have perished in the flood.

In any case, these three sons (with their wives) *did* prove loyal to their father and his God, no doubt helping him in the construction of the ark. Then it was they who assumed responsibility for taking up the record where he had left off. They described the preparations for the flood, then their experiences in the ark during the year of the flood, their father's prophecy concerning the respective destinies of their descendants, and finally the death of their father, 350 years after the flood. They signed off their tablet with the simple statement: "Now these are the generations of the sons of Noah" (Gen. 10:1a).

The three sons keyed their account to the preceding tablets by referring back to their father. He had closed his record by claiming only that he had found grace in the eyes of the Lord. His sons, however, who had closely watched his deeds and listened to his counsel for almost a hundred years, were not so reticent. "Noah was a just man," they wrote in their opening, "and perfect in his generations, and Noah walked with God" (Gen. 6:9b). Quite a testimony that was—coming from his three faithful sons!

They summarized again the corrupt condition of the world, which they themselves had seen firsthand. They noted also that "the earth was *filled* with violence" (Gen. 6:11), a statement which at least implies that the earth had been filled with people. Men indeed had managed "to multiply on the face of the earth" (Gen. 6:1), as God had commanded in the beginning (Gen.1:28), but the end result was that "all flesh had corrupted his way upon the earth" (Gen. 6:12).

Then followed an extensive communication from God to Noah, giving instructions for building the ark and caring for the animals. Presumably Noah repeated the message to his sons, for they would be helping in these projects, and so it was they who recorded it for future reference.

God made it clear that the flood would cause "the end of all flesh," and that it would "destroy them with the earth" (Gen. 6:13). These statements made it clear that the flood would have to be a worldwide flood, not a local flood, to accomplish such ends. Therefore, a huge ark must be constructed to preserve representatives of all the created kinds of animals for the future world. Such an ark would have been completely unnecessary if the flood were merely a regional inundation. Noah and the animals could easily have migrated to another region in that case.

The dimensions of the ark were given in terms of cubits, with the relative proportions such as to assure optimum stability in riding out the coming floodwaters. If we assume a reasonable value for the cubit (probably eighteen inches), we find that the ark could easily carry two of each kind of land animal in less than half its capacity. Again God emphasized that the flood would be universal—"a flood of waters upon the earth, to destroy all flesh, wherein is the breath of life, from under heaven; and everything that is in the earth [that is,the land] shall die" (Gen. 6:17).

The ark was to be made watertight with some kind of "covering" (same Hebrew word elsewhere translated "atonement"), which most translators have rendered "pitch." Whatever this was (perhaps some kind of resinous plant material), it was not a petroleum-based "pitch" (a different Hebrew word), as was used much later by Moses' mother for the much smaller "ark" in which she placed her infant son (Exod. 2:3) to shield him from Pharaoh's death edict.

The ark was to provide space for two of every "kind" of land animal (fowls, cattle, crawlers—Gen. 6:20), as well as food for all of them and living quarters for Noah and his family (eight people altogether). The ark was big enough to care for many more people, but apparently no one else accepted the invitation until it was too late.

Noah's preaching of a coming flood must have seemed ridiculous to the antediluvians, for there had never been such a thing in all history. There was no rain in their world (Gen. 2:5), and their rivers were all well controlled, with sources in steady artesian springs (Gen. 2:10), so God's warning through Noah of a coming flood of waters which would destroy that world was dismissed as foolishness, and they went right on in their ungodly life styles.

There was no need for Noah and his sons to set out on expeditions finding and trapping animals for the ark, since God had told Noah they would all "come unto thee, to keep them alive" (Gen. 6:20). In that primeval world, with fairly uniform climates everywhere, as well as essentially uniform distribution of land and water areas, all kinds of animals could live in each region, so the ones sent by God to the ark would not have to travel far when the time came.

Shem, Ham, and Japheth faithfully recorded all these events, but they were evidently most of all impressed with the godly example of their father. They had begun their account by mentioning his righteousness, his spiritual wholeness and his close walk with God. He must have endured intense ridicule from the people around him as he proceeded with his "foolish" building project and his unwelcome preaching, but he kept right on, and his sons and their wives observed his unquenchable faith. Four times they recorded that Noah did everything God directed him to do (Gen. 6:22; 7:5, 9, 16). Therefore, when the time came, even though it meant leaving the people and the life and the world they had known for an unknown and very uncertain future, they chose to follow Noah into the ark (Gen. 7:13). They believed him when he told them that God had said: "Come thou and all thy house into the ark; for thee have I seen righteous before me in this generation" (Gen. 7:1). The importance of a father's example is a timeless lesson here. Noah's faithful righteousness resulted in the salvation of his family as well as himself.

His sons then proceeded to keep a graphic record of the great flood and their own experiences in the ark. The land animals went in, two by two, into the ark, one male and one female of each created kind (a broader term than our modern concept of "species," perhaps approximating in most cases the taxonomic "family"). The relatively small number of "clean" kinds were each represented by seven animals, probably because God intended a broader range of species and varieties to develop from these after the flood, and also because it was from these that the animals best suited for direct human use (for sacrifice, for clothing, for food, for labor, etc.) would come.

After all had been settled in their intended "rooms" (Gen. 6:14), small or large as needed and designed, and been well fed, they soon began to sleep—probably even to hibernate. Most or all of the animals had been created with genetic potential for both migration and hibernation if and when weather conditions should warrant, and these had evidently been directed by their Creator first to migrate to the ark and then to relax into a state of hibernation as the sky began to darken and the temperature to fall as the flood was about to break on the earth.

All of this apparently took seven days (Gen. 7:4, 10) and finally Noah and his family went in just as the rains began (Gen. 7:13), and the Lord himself shut the door (Gen. 7:16). In . . . "the same day were all the fountains of the great deep broken up, and the windows of heaven were opened. And the rain was upon the earth forty days and forty nights" (Gen. 7:11, 12).

The description of the flood was, of course, written from the viewpoint of those in the ark, but they could observe what was happening outside through the ark's peripheral window (Gen. 6:16). It was a terrible scene, like nothing before or since in all the world's history. For the first time, rain fell from the darkened skies, and it fell in great torrents, as though from giant sluiceways opened in heaven. Evidently the vast water vapor canopy surrounding the earth ("the waters above the firmament" placed there on the second day of creation week) was now condensing and plummeting to earth, as there could be no other way of accounting for an intense global rainstorm enduring for forty days without ceasing.

At the same time (or even slightly before this), great bursts of water erupted from the hitherto well-regulated fountains of the great subterranean deep. The steady flows in the antediluvian rivers quickly began to overflow their banks as they received both the enlarged flows from the shattered artesian springs and also the run-off from the heavenly sluicegates. The subterranean eruptions undoubtedly brought up other materials also with the gushing waters—volcanic lavas, perhaps, from the hot mantle, as well as volcanic dust. The dust particles blown up into the sky may even have served as condensation nuclei to trigger the precipitation of the vapor canopy, aided too by the uprushing air currents accompanying the eruption.

Sea-floor fountains probably also burst open, producing submarine lavas as well as tsunami waves traversing the water surfaces. Those watching in the ark could not see phenomena like this, however, nor any other aspect of the tremendous geologic activities that must have been taking place beneath the flood waters.

They could see what was happening on the surface, of course, and this they recorded: "the waters increased, and bare up the ark." Then, as they continued to rise, "the waters prevailed exceedingly upon the earth; and all the high hills, that were under the whole heaven, were covered. . . . And all flesh died that moved upon the earth . . . all in whose nostrils was the breath of life, of all that was in the dry land, died. . . . and Noah only remained alive, and they that were with him in the ark" (Gen. 7:17, 19, 21, 22, 23).

No mention was made of the fish and other marine animals, but many of these (though certainly not all) must have perished also, in the submarine upheavals. Also unobserved, under the waters, great quantities of sediments were undoubtedly being eroded, transported, and deposited, together with tremendous numbers of trees and other plants uprooted from the antediluvian forests, hills and plains. Animals, too, sometimes in great numbers, were being trapped and buried in onrushing sediments.

The ungodly men and women of that age, all over the world, surely tried desperately to escape the waters—fleeing to higher ground, riding on makeshift rafts, or whatever they could do. Not many would be caught in the sediments, of course, but they all eventually were overtaken and drowned. Their bodies would float on or near the surface until eaten by scavengers or until the waters finally abated; there they would eventually decay and return to dust.

Their cities and towns also were obliterated. Probably none of their buildings were of very substantial construction, for the climates had always been mild and pleasant, and they had never experienced storms or earthquakes or other phenomena requiring more than the flimsiest of housing. Thus their entire civilization, however advanced it may have been, was quickly destroyed, leaving few traces. There would be much of the antediluvian plant life, and considerable remains of the animal life, caught by the sediments and buried, eventually to be fossilized, but very little evidence of the human life that God had said he would "destroy . . . from the face of the earth" (Gen. 6:7).

The geological effects of the flood necessarily must have been tremendous, but these could not be observed by those writing the account, and so would have to remain for future scientific study to recognize. The surface phenomena, however, were profoundly impressive in their own right. Noah and his family could see that, within the first forty days and nights of torrential rainfall, "the mountains were covered" (Gen. 7:20) by at least fifteen cubits of water, so that the ark, with its height of thirty cubits half submerged due to the weight of its occupants, could float freely over the highest of them. They could also see that "every living substance was destroyed which was upon the face of the ground" (Gen. 7:23). Actually "living substance" is only one word in the original, meaning simply "that which is standing." In other words, everything standing on the lands of the pre-flood world, whether living or nonliving, plant or animal, anything constructed by man or under his dominion, was "destroyed." The great flood, with its accompanying outpourings from the great deep and torrents from the skies, changed the face of the earth in the most drastic way imaginable. It was necessarily accompanied by great volcanic eruptions and gigantic earth movements, then followed by drastic climatic changes. Whatever the pre-flood geologic and geographic structure may have been, it was all totally different after the flood. The occupants in the ark could not see all this taking place, of course, but the floodwaters must necessarily have been accompanied by such changes.

The rains and eruptions were continuous for forty days and nights, and then evidently continued intermittently for another 110 days. Finally they stopped, but then great winds began to blow, resulting presumably from the temperature changes induced by the collapse of the earth's vapor blanket. "After the end of the hundred and fifty days the waters were abated. And the ark rested . . . upon the mountains of Ararat" (Gen. 8:3, 4).

"Ararat" is the same as "Armenia" in the Hebrew, and the ark had grounded on the highest peak in the great mountain ranges of Armenia, as is evident from the fact that it took another two and a half months of dropping sea level before those in the ark could see the tops of any of the other mountains (Gen. 8:4, 5). The only way this could happen, of course, would be for additional earth movements to take place that would restore at least partial isostatic equilibrium to the distorted and displaced crust of the earth. Somehow new continental structures and mountains would have to rise up, accompanied by the opening of new ocean basins into which the floodwaters could drain. How this was accomplished—whether by divine miracle or by natural tectonic read-justments—may remain to be determined by future studies. It was simply a matter of thankful observation to those who had been in the ark for five long months already, and were destined to be there for seven months more, before they could leave.

Finally, after they had spent over a year in the ark, the ground had dried sufficiently for them to leave the ark. The returning dove had found that plant life had begun to grow on the land again, presumably from seeds or cuttings carried by the waters until deposited on the earth's surface, so Noah knew the animals could find food to eat as they scattered out from Ararat, the whole world before them. The ark was left high on Mount Ararat, very near the geographic center of the earth's new land areas, to be preserved possibly as a witness to future generations.

The world was drastically different from the "very good" world they had known before. Barren and cold, rugged and forbidding, it seemed only a devastated remnant of what it once had been. But the wickedness of its inhabitants had been vanquished, and the God of Noah was there with them—that was the main thing!

The Rainbow Covenant

After the animals were gone and Noah's family had come down from the mountain, the first thing they did was to build an altar and offer sacrifices of thanksgiving and prayer, as they faced an uncertain future. In response, "the LORD said in his heart, I will not again curse the ground any more for man's sake" (Gen. 8:21). This clearly harked back to his original judgment against man, when he told Adam: "Cursed is the ground for thy sake" (Gen. 3:17). But it also referred to the flood, for he then said: "Neither will I again smite any more every thing living, as I have done." The original curse had seemed to be greatly increased in rate and intensity during the flood, but this would not happen again. "While the earth remaineth, seedtime and harvest, and cold and heat, and summer and winter, and day and night shall not cease" (Gen. 8:22). That is, even though the decay principle (climaxed by death) was still operational, it would never be intensified again as it had been during the flood, when everything in the dry land had died. All earth's processes, controlled as they were by the seasonal and diurnal cycles, would operate essentially uniformly from then on.

Then, "God blessed Noah and his sons" (Gen. 9:1), a fact duly noted by the three sons in their account. The original mandate to Adam was repeated: "Be fruitful, and multiply, and [fill] the earth." The dominion mandate was then amplified in a slightly different form. Not only was man to have dominion over the animals, but the animals would fear man, and man was authorized now even to eat the flesh of animals (Gen. 9:1–3). Originally, both men and animals were allowed only plant products as food but here, for the first time, meat eating was authorized, presumably both for men and for those animals whose metabolism might require protein materials no longer sufficiently available in the plants growing in the depleted soils of the post-flood world.

One very important addition was made by the Lord to the original Adamic mandate. "Whoso sheddeth man's blood, by man shall his blood be shed: for in the image of God made he man" (Gen. 9:6). Thus capital punishment was not only authorized, but commanded, by God for the crime of murder. This commandment implicitly established the institution of human government, replacing the patriarchal system which evidently had been ordained for the antediluvian economy, but which had deteriorated almost into anarchy.

The establishment of governmental responsibility among human populations in effect also authorized many new types of honorable vocations—government, law, police, military, and various other forms of social service—in addition to science, technology, business, education, and others already authorized. Approval of meateating did include one significant restriction: "Flesh with the life thereof, which is the blood thereof, shall ye not eat" (Gen. 9:4).

God then amplified his previous promise never again to destroy all life on earth by making what he called an "everlasting covenant between God and every living creature of all flesh that is upon the earth" (Gen. 9:16), saying there would never again "be a flood to destroy the earth" (Gen. 9:11). The new rainbow (Gen. 9:13–15) that appeared in the sky would serve as a token of the covenant. There had been no rain before the flood, and in fact a rainbow could not occur at all, since rainbows require the presence of liquid water droplets rather than water vapor. With the canopy now dissipated, a worldwide flood would also have become essentially impossible. Even a severe and prolonged rainfall (as in a monsoon, for example) eventually must end, leaving a rainbow behind, reminding us once more that a worldwide flood will never occur again.

Shem and his brothers probably knew little of the meteorological factors involved, but they would need and appreciate this sign, for in the centuries following the flood, there would necessarily continue to be many severe local floods and other geophysical disturbances as the earth was adjusting to its new hydrological and tectonic balances. The rainbow would repeatedly reassure them that the great worldwide flood (Hebrew *mabbul*, a word used only in connection with *that* flood) would never be repeated. God's covenant applied, of course, only to the *mabbul*, not to local floods. The frequent occurrence of local floods in the present world would give the lie to his promise if the Genesis flood had been only a local flood, as many latter-day skeptics would allege.

The narrative of the three sons was then summarized and apparently terminated for a time, as they concluded with their signatures. "And the sons of Noah, that went forth of the ark, were Shem, and Ham, and Japheth" (Gen. 9:18a). Apparently much later, however, an appendix was inserted, possibly by Shem and Japheth, noting that "Ham is the father of Canaan" (Gen. 9:18b).

Noah's Prophecy on His Sons

They then went on to add the record of the sad experience that led to a famous Noahic prophecy many years later. First they noted again that "these are the three sons of Noah: and of them was the whole earth overspread" (Gen. 9:19). By this time the three families had multiplied and begun to spread out from Ararat, but all were descendants of the three sons. The *mabbul* had indeed accomplished its purpose of destroying antediluvian man from the face of the earth, and the post-diluvian population of the world has all come from Noah's three sons.

The reason for this special mention of Canaan was made clear in the narrative that followed, describing the event that would lead to a partial disintegration of this first family after the flood. They had initially settled somewhere in the vicinity of Mount Ararat, where the three brothers began to raise their own families.

Many years had evidently passed when the incident of Noah's drunkenness and unwitting exposure took place, followed by Ham's apparent pleasure at this evidence of his father's fall from his pedestal of righteousness (Gen. 9:20–23). Shem and Japheth, on the other hand, gently covered their father with a garment without even looking at him.

While Noah's drunkenness was a wrongful act on his part, Ham's carnal delight at this revelation of his godly father's brief lapse was a far greater sin. It evidenced a fatal weakness in his own character, at the very least a lack of respect for his father and of reverence toward his father's God.

Such an attitude would inevitably affect his own children, both by heredity and by his example; in fact, Noah had probably already detected a similar attitude in Ham's son, Canaan. Accordingly, God led him to pronounce a blessing on Shem and Japheth, but a curse on Ham through Canaan.

Both the blessing and curse were actually prophecies, and therefore particularly attributable to divine inspiration. Presumably Noah cursed Canaan rather than Ham because he could not bear to pronounce a curse on a beloved son who had endured so much with his father before and during the flood. Perhaps also he felt it appropriate to note that, just as Ham had grieved his father, so Ham would be grieved by *his* son. As a matter of fact, however, it should be remembered that this Noahic curse was not rendered by him as an imprecation but as a divinely given prophecy. Noah could see enough in the characters of his three sons (or if not Noah, then God did) to predict the general characteristics of their descendants.

Canaan—including, presumably, all Ham's descendants—was destined to be "a servant of servants" to his brethren, Japheth would be "enlarge[d]," and Shem would be "blessed" in his God (Gen. 9:25–27). All mankind would share various measures of physical, mental, and spiritual attributes, but Ham's descendants would be characterized mainly by their physical contributions to the world, Japheth's descendants by their intellectual achievements, and Shem's descendants by their spiritual interests, with Japheth eventually coming also to share in the latter. Shem and Japheth would be servants to God and man with their spiritual and mental contributions to the corporate life of the world in their stewardship thereof under God, whereas Ham would be a servant of these servants as well as a steward of God, providing the physical substructure (agriculture, navigation, construction, business, etc.) upon which the intellectual and religious superstructure of the world could be erected. The word "servant" in these verses, incidentally, does not mean "slave" in the Hebrew, but "steward."

It seems likely that Shem and Japheth wrote this particular segment, because the above incident reflected badly on Ham, perhaps even resulting in his estrangement from the rest of the family. The three had worked together in narrating the ark-building project, their experiences during the flood, and God's post-flood covenant of the rainbow, but it was important that the record of Noah's prophecy—and, finally, his death—also be preserved, so Shem and Japheth added that to the record of the three sons.

Noah finally died 350 years after the flood, at the age of 950 (Gen. 9:28–29). Only Jared and Methuselah had lived longer. The drastically changed world environment would soon result in rapidly declining longevity for all post-flood mankind.

At last the two sons finished their record, and signed it for all three: "Now these are the generations of the sons of Noah, Shem, Ham and Japheth" (Gen. 10:1a). Ham had already left, and Japheth would soon move away too, leaving Shem alone to carry on with the future record.

3

Before Abraham

The Generations of Shem

Shem, the "spiritually-minded" son of Noah, probably stayed in the general vicinity of Ararat, even after father Noah died. Ham eventually migrated into Egypt, and Egypt later became known as "the land of Ham" (e.g., Ps. 105:23). In fact, the word "Egypt" in the Bible is a translation of the Hebrew *Mizraim,* the latter being the name of one of Ham's sons (Gen. 10:6). Japheth presumably eventually moved northward, his name later being recognized as the patriarchal ancestor of the Greeks, with his sons generally identified with other tribes in the north. Both, however, settled first, for a while, in the land of Shinar (Gen. 11:2).

Shem, however, seems to have stayed closer to their post-flood home near Ararat and to have given his name to later "Semitic" tribes and languages. It was also Shem who took the responsibility of preserving the patriarchal tablets and then adding to them. He, in fact, kept up with many of the descendants of his two brothers, as well as his own descendants, recording their names in what has come to be known as "the Table of Nations" (Gen. 10).

He did not live as long as his ancestors, but he did make it to age 602 (Gen. 11:10, 11) and outlived his father, Noah, by 152 years (compare Gen. 9:28; 11:10, 11). In his genealogical lists (i.e., the Table of Nations), he recorded the names of some of the descendants of Japheth to the third generation, some of Ham's descendants to the second generation, and some of his own descendants to the fifth generation.

Shem began his tablet by simply continuing the previous tablet, for which he had also been largely responsible. He and Japheth had concluded their earlier record with: "Now these are the generations [Hebrew *toledoth*, meaning essentially "genealogical histories"] of the sons of Noah, Shem, Ham, and Japheth." Shem then tied his additional record to this by: "and unto them were sons born after the flood" (Gen. 10:1). He then immediately continued with "the sons of Japheth" (Gen. 10:2), later with "the sons of Ham" (Gen. 10:6), and finally with "Unto Shem also . . . were children born" (Gen. 10:21).

After first listing the sons of Japheth (Gomer, Magog, Madai, Javan, Tubal, Meshech, and Tiras), as well as the sons of Gomer and Javan (Gen. 10:2–4), Shem noted that "by these were the isles of the Gentiles divided in their lands; every one after his tongue, after their families, in their nations" (Gen. 10:5).

The reference to "after his tongue" indicates this was not written until after the confusion of tongues and scattering of the people at Babel (Gen. 11:9), an event described later by Shem. The term "isles" can possibly also be under-stood as "coasts," and the term "Gentiles" (used here for the first time) is the same word as "nations."

The sons of Ham were Cush (identified later as Ethiopia), Mizraim (Egypt), Phut (Libya), and Canaan, father of the tribes in the land of Canaan encountered by the Israelites later in their exodus from Egypt. Cush was the father of Nimrod, and Shem noted that Nimrod had been the "mighty one in the earth" who founded the city of Babel, as well as other cities, "in the land of Shinar" (Gen. 10:8, 10). Nimrod became proverbial as "the mighty hunter before the LORD," a phrase implying a confrontational aspect rather than one of fellowship. It is possible, though uncertain, that his reputation as a "mighty hunter" was acquired through ruthless slaughter of the beasts that were multiplying more rapidly than the human population after they all left the ark. He later also founded Nineveh, which became the capital of Assyria (Gen. 10:11).

After listing the sons of Mizraim and Canaan, Shem then summarized Ham's descendants thus: "These are the sons of Ham, after their families, after their tongues, in their countries, and in their nations" (Gen. 10:20). Note again the emphasis on families, tongues, countries (same word as "lands"), and nations.

Then Shem proceeded to list his own descendants. Elam eventually became Persia, Asshur became Assyria, Lud became Lydia, and Aram became Syria. Most important, however, was Arphaxad, the grandfather of Eber (from whose name came the term "Hebrew") and great grandfather of Peleg, from whom would eventually come Abraham and the chosen nation. It is even possible (if there are no gaps in the genealogical listing in Genesis 11) that Shem lived long enough to know Abraham, though Shem made no mention of any of Peleg's descendants in his own tablet (leaving this to the next tablet, authored by Abraham's father, Terah).

Again he summarized his own descendants by noting that "these are the sons of Shem, after their families, after their tongues, in their lands, after their nations" (Gen. 10:31). Realizing that his repeated references to tongues and nations, needed explication, he proceeded to explain the origin of different tongues and nations in the latter part of his record. First, however, he added a comprehensive summary statement to his Table of Nations, writing: "These are the families of the sons of Noah, after their generations, in their nations: and by these were the nations divided in the earth after the flood"(Gen. 10:32).

This was the second time Shem had referred to the nations and lands as being "divided." He had also included a cryptic note in reference to Peleg: "Unto Eber were born two sons: the name of one was Peleg: for in his days was the earth divided" (Gen. 10:25). In this verse the Hebrew for "divided" is a somewhat different word than in the other two instances (Gen. 10:5, 32), so perhaps a different kind of "division" was in view in reference to Peleg. Is it possible that an actual physical splitting of the lands took place in the days just before Peleg's birth (hence the name given him by his father)? Or was this "division" really the same as the dividing of the nations linguistically and tribally, as seems most evident in the other two references? Or could both have taken place together?

It is not possible to be dogmatic here, but it does seem that any such mighty geophysical event as the splitting and subsequent spreading apart of a great continent would warrant more than one very uncertain reference in the Word of God. Hence it seems probable that Peleg was so named because of the dividing of the nations at Babel.

The Dispersion from Babel

Shem proceeded then to explain how this division came about, recording the remarkable event at Babel as the climax and conclusion of his narrative. Before the flood and for some time thereafter, there had been only one human language, both written and oral—"of one language and of one speech" (Gen. 11:1). As the families of Japheth and Ham, as well as at least some of the Shemites, began to migrate away from the Ararat region, they eventually settled on "a plain in the land of Shinar" (Gen. 11:2).

This region is the same as "Sumer," later known also as "Mesopotamia" ("between the rivers"). The plain was fertile and it must have seemed almost like the beautiful world they had known before the flood, so they named the two rivers that traversed the plain "Tigris" and "Euphrates," after the rivers they had once seen flowing out of the land of Eden (Gen. 2:14). For similar sentimental reasons, Ham had named one of his sons Cush, and Shem had named one of his sons Asshur (after the primeval lands of Ethiopia and Assyria, also mentioned by Adam in Gen. 2:13, 14). It is clear that the flood, as described by the three sons, was such a devastating cataclysm that the primeval geography no longer existed. The Garden of Eden was gone, and so were the original Tigris and Euphrates rivers, and the first regions called Assyria and Ethiopia (Cush). The post-flood world was barren and rugged, so when the people finally found a region that looked somewhat like the world they remembered, they settled there, and gave the rivers the same ancient names.

By this time, Nimrod had emerged as "a mighty one in the earth" and had either been chosen as the king of all the "Shinarians" or had acquired the position by force. As Ham's grandson, he (probably also his father, Cush) probably resented the curse predicted by Noah on his family and resolved to lead a rebellion against God. As noted in Genesis 10:10, he centered his kingdom at the city of Babel, refusing to follow God's command to "replenish the earth" (Gen. 9:1, 7). "Let us build us a city and a tower, whose top may reach unto heaven; and let us make us a name, lest we be scattered abroad upon the face of the whole earth" (Gen. 11:4).

In this declaration, Nimrod was not actually proposing to reach heaven with a tower; he was anything but stupid. The words "may reach" are not in the original Hebrew. What Nimrod undoubtedly had in mind was a tower *unto* the heavens —that is, a tower with a shrine at the summit dedicated to the heavens and to the worship of the "host of heaven," the angels. Many later ziggurats in Babylonia and elsewhere around the world were so constructed and dedicated, and this first great tower was probably the prototype of all of them.

This temple tower of Nimrod's would be the focal point of the cultural, political and religious life of his kingdom. Evidently, practically the entire human population at the time, only a century or so after the flood, was concentrated here in this one area, prepared to follow Nimrod's leadership in establishing a one-world government and a religious system involved in worshiping the creation rather than its Creator. No doubt Nimrod was subtle enough not to propose a blatant rebellion against God, but rather to suggest that by honoring the beautiful starry heavens, with the various stars and constellations which had been given as "signs" (Gen. 1:14) of God's great promises, the people would be worshiping God. After all, God was invisible and far away, but they could *see* these signs and their symbolical representations (signs of the Zodiac) emblazoned on the temple walls and ceilings, so these could serve as aids to their faith.

They would eventually be taught also that these heavenly bodies actually were where the angelic "host of heaven" resided. Therefore, when they observed the stars, they were really seeing the "gods," who could influence and control their own lives on earth. In some such manner, the primeval stellar message of God's great gospel promise of the coming Redeemer (Gen. 3:15) would be gradually corrupted into astrology, and thence into a polytheistic pantheism.

Gods and goddesses soon would be conceived as residing not only in the stars but also in other components of the creation—trees, rivers, animals, and so on. The actual presence of the demonic spirits following Satan in his rebellion against God would, furthermore, easily convert these beliefs into various forms of animism, spiritism and idolatry, with actual communication between evil spirits and those men and women who would yield to such influences.

Such a blasphemous project as this undertaking of King Nimrod could only have originated in the mind of Satan himself, who had been at war with God ever since his first rebellion after his creation. He had succeeded in causing Adam and Eve to fall into sin and later had almost succeeded in corrupting the whole world at the time of Noah. Now, once again, he was trying to get this new generation of men to rebel against God, using Nimrod as his willing tool.

Shem may not have known much about Satan and his plans at this point, since there had been as yet no specific revelation from God about him, so far as we know. But he did know about the demonic corruption of mankind before the flood, and he could see something similar developing at Babel. Furthermore, somehow God had actually revealed something to him about the councils of the Godhead concerning this development, for he was able to record the words of God himself. "The LORD said, Behold, the people is one, and they have all one language; and this they begin to do: and now nothing will be restrained from them, which they have imagined to do. . . . let us go down, and there confound their language, that they may not understand one another's speech" (Gen. 11:6–7).

God had promised never to destroy all flesh again, but he could prevent them from a *united* rebellion, and this he proceeded to do in the most effective way. If they could not communicate, they could not cooperate. Therefore, "the LORD did there confound the language of all the earth: and from thence did the LORD scatter them abroad upon the face of all the earth" (Gen. 11:9).

With the announcement of this awful judgment on the entire population of Babel, Shem apparently felt he should write no more, so he ceased with his signature, saying simply: "These are the generations of Shem" (Gen. 11:10a).

There are a number of further important inferences, however, from his record. In his Table of Nations, as he summarized the descendants of each of the three sons, he indicated in each case that they had been divided by their respective tongues, families, nations, and lands (or countries). This would suggest strongly that each family unit at Babel was given its own language, then found its own land and settled on it, and there finally became a distinct nation. Since there are seventy nations listed in the Table, this suggests in turn that there were seventy family units in the population at Babel. Each unit presumably contained at least ten members by this time, so the total population, a little over a century after the flood may have been about seven hundred or more. This assumes no significant gaps in the genealogical chronologies of Genesis 11 at least up through the generations at Babel. If such gaps do exist, the population could have been greater, of course.

It should also be noted that, although the people must have realized that this event, like the flood, was a supernatural judgment from God, there was no great turning back to God as a result. The various family/nation units now had different languages, but they still carried the apostate religious system of Nimrod with them into their new lands.

Thus, the complex of astrological, pantheistic, polytheistic, spiritistic, humanistic evolutionism which Nimrod introduced at Babel was carried into all the nations of the world with the great dispersion.

There was surely at least one exception, however. Neither Noah nor Shem were participants in the rebellion at Babel, so it seems reasonable that *their* language was not changed. Shem's tablet, therefore, would have been written in the same language as those of the antediluvian patriarchs. This would support the conviction of the ancient Israelite scribes that Hebrew was the original language, a belief further supported by the fact that the names of the antediluvian patriarchs, as well as the later patriarchs leading to Abraham, all have specific meanings only in the Hebrew language.

If there were seventy original languages and nations, that particular number could not be assumed to stay constant. The law of decay would apply to language as well as other aspects of human life. Both nations and languages would proliferate, but the net result would inevitably be deterioration of each—physically, morally, spiritually, linguistically, every other way—except for such infusions of new spiritual and moral energy into the world as God might introduce through his Holy Spirit from time to time.

Shem survived long enough to transmit his own tablet and those of his predecessors to his eighth-generation descendant, Terah, the father of Abraham, who would write the next tablet. Shem concluded his record with the traditional formula: "These are the generations of Shem" (Gen. 11:10a).

The Brief Tablet of Terah

How it was that Terah came to take over the responsibility of preserving and extending the patriarchal record from Shem we do not know exactly. Shem had, in his Table of Nations, kept the records at least up through the time of Eber, with his two sons Joktan and Peleg (whose name, meaning "division," most likely was given in commemoration of the dividing of the tribes at Babel). He had even listed all the sons of Joktan, although Joktan was not to be in the line of succession to Terah and Abram (Shem may have thought he was at the time).

Peleg was in the third generation after Shem, whereas Terah was in the eighth generation. One significant implication appears here. Many writers have suggested the possibility of long gaps in this record, primarily in order to accommodate the expanded chronologies of secular archaeologists, who seem always to be looking for ways to push back the date of the beginning of human history as far as they can.

The fact that Shem must have given the patriarchal tablets to Terah, however, is a strong argument against the idea that very many generations might be missing from Terah's record. According to the record as it stands, the line of succession ran from Shem to Arphaxad to Salah to Eber to Peleg to Reu to Serug to Nahor to Terah (Gen. 11:10–24), so that Terah was in the eighth generation from Shem. If the ages of the patriarchs at the births of their respective sons are accurate and complete as they stand in the traditional text, then Shem lived 280 years after the birth of Terah, so he had ample opportunity to meet him and discuss the tablets with him. This period might be compatible with a gap of a few generations, but certainly not enough to accommodate the chronology favored by evolutionary anthropologists and archaeologists.

There may be two reasons why the tablets were given to Terah instead of Abraham. Terah was seventy years old when Abraham (originally Abram) was born, and Shem may have wanted to transmit his records to Terah before that time, not knowing how long he might live. Secondly, if Shem had waited until Abraham were sufficiently mature for Shem to trust him with this responsibility, Abraham may already have departed for Canaan and been unavailable.

Therefore, even though Terah would not have been as good a candidate as Abraham for this duty, Shem may have felt he had no other option at the time. As it turned out, Terah's record was very brief and factual, consisting solely of the genealogy (with supplementary chronological data) from Shem to Terah and his three sons (Gen. 11:10b–27a). He included no spiritual content at all.

Terah's record does contain important chronological data, however, which yield a total of 101 years from the flood to Peleg's birth (perhaps approximately the time of the Babel judgment) and a total of 292 years from the flood to the birth of Abraham. It is also very obvious that the longevity of mankind began a sharp decline after the flood. The antediluvian patriarchs (not including Enoch) had lived an average of 912 years, with Noah himself reaching age 950. Shem, however, died at 602 and Terah at 205, with the declining lifespans following a sort of exponential decay curve in between.

If any significant generations have been omitted, they would most likely have been between Eber and Peleg, when the lifespan suddenly dropped from 464 to 239 years. If several generations have, for some unknown reason, been omitted here, then Genesis 11:16 might read, for example: "And Eber lived four and thirty years, and begat [the great grandfather of] Peleg."

On the other hand, a more likely reason for the sharp drop in longevity was the traumatic change in living conditions following the dispersion at Babel, to which Peleg and his contemporaries must have been subjected. From living in a large, prosperous community and a fertile region of beauty and plenty, each family unit had been compelled to migrate suddenly to a new frontier. With only a small family group in each settlement, having to live by hunting and gathering for many years, beset by harsh environmental conditions and other difficulties, it would not be surprising if such a stress-filled life style would mean a shorter life for those suddenly subjected to it.

The most striking feature of these data, of course, is the gradual decrease in longevity from about nine hundred years to about two hundred years, in only about nine generations. The necessary conclusion is that this change was somehow caused by the convulsive changes in the earth—its geography, its climate, its soils, its greenhouse-like atmosphere, and other aspects—brought about by the great flood. In addition to the direct effects of the more rigorous environment, an increased incidence of harmful heritable changes in human (and animal) reproductive systems would be expected to result under an atmosphere without the protective vapor canopy that formerly ameliorated living conditions.

And, of course, the tablets of both Shem and Terah provide the sad record of declining morality and spirituality that soon followed the worldwide cleansing bath of the deluge. The resulting division of the descendants of godly Noah into separate languages, then tribes and nations, prevented both anarchy and a unified global rebellion, but nevertheless men drifted further and further away from God, carrying the Babel system of evolutionary pantheism with them around the world wherever they traveled. The system of national governments failed just as the antediluvian system had failed, and the time came for God to raise up a special nation to transmit his revelation and prepare for the promised Redeemer.

Even Terah was influenced to some extent by the pantheistic idolatry around him where he lived in Ur of the Chaldees (Gen. 11:28; note
the later comment in Josh. 24:2). He closed his record thus: "And Terah
lived seventy years, and begat Abram, Nahor, and Haran. Now these
are the generations of Terah" (Gen. 11:26–27a). Terah's son Abram,
however, was destined for greatness in God's plan of the ages.

4
Creation in
the Books of Moses

From Abraham to Moses

With the failure and dispersion of the nations, the history of mankind began a new phase, God preparing a special nation through which to communicate his revelation to the world. In the remainder of the Book of Genesis we have the histories of Abraham, Isaac, Jacob and Joseph, as transmitted in the *toledoth* records of Ishmael (Gen. 25:12), Isaac (Gen. 25:19), Esau (Gen. 36:1, 9) and Jacob (Gen. 37:2). Quite probably Abraham and Joseph also contributed indirectly to these records, even though their names are not attached specifically to one of them.

In any case, the records were somehow transmitted to Moses. My purpose in this chapter is to discern any references to the creation or other events of primeval history in these remaining chapters of Genesis and the other books of the Pentateuch.

The first specific reference is in Genesis 13:10: "And Lot lifted up his eyes, and beheld all the plain of Jordan, that it was well watered everywhere, before the LORD destroyed Sodom and Gomorrah, even as the garden of the LORD, like the land of Egypt. . . . " This was still in the early centuries after the flood, and quite possibly Shem and Ham were still living. The world's desert regions today—including the lower Jordan and Dead Sea areas—were at that time still "well watered" and fertile, supporting the large populations of Sodom, Gomorrah, and the other cities of the plain. It reminded Shem, apparently—perhaps also Ham, who may have at least passed through the area on his way to Egypt (which was also well watered then)—of "the garden of the LORD," which they had observed afar off, or at least heard about, when they lived in the world before the flood. This comparison had been told to their descendants, including Abraham. Consequently, this passing reference to the garden of God is a testimony to the real existence of Eden in the primeval world.

In Genesis 14 are references to Shinar (where Nimrod had founded Babel) and its current king Amraphel (v. 9), who some have suggested might have been Hammurabi, as well as Elam (v. 1). In this chapter also is the enigmatic encounter with "Melchizedek king of Salem" and "priest of the most high God" (vv. 18–20). Whether this unique personage was Shem, or Job, as some have suggested, or a pre-incarnate theophany of Christ (as others—including myself—have maintained) or merely some local chieftain, he certainly still knew the true God of creation, even though most of the nations by this time had capitulated to some form of evolutionary paganism. Abraham recognized this and gave him tithes of his spoils of battle.

What is called the Abrahamic Covenant was made by God in Genesis 15:18–21, promising Abraham's seed all the land from the Nile to the Euphrates, even though it was then occupied mainly by descendants of Ham through Canaan. Herein is an implicit claim by God that, as Creator, the lands all belong to him, and he can give them to whomever he chooses (see also Gen. 17:1–8).

In Genesis 18:25 Abraham specifically recognized his God as "the Judge of all the earth," even though the nations around him were by this time worshiping many nature gods. In a theophany, the Lord and two angels had just met with him (Gen. 18:1, 2, 33), again confirming the promises.

Angels are named as such for the second time in the account of the fiery destruction of Sodom and Gomorrah (Gen. 19:1, 15), appearing as men (Gen. 19:5, 16). There is a previous reference to the "angel of the LORD" (Gen. 16:7, 9, 10, 11) meeting with Hagar in the wilderness and giving her the remarkable prophecy concerning her expected son Ishmael and his descendants (Gen. 16:11–13). It is probable that this also was a theophany, for she recognized that it was the Lord who had spoken to her (16:13).

It is worth noting also that Abraham (first of all at Bethel—Gen. 12:8), as well as Isaac and Jacob, continued the practice of his father Noah in building sacrificial altars whereby to worship God, evidently still remembering the Edenic promise of a coming Savior, as well as God's provision of an "atonement" (or "covering") for Adam and Eve, through such animal sacrifices.

At the great offering (in type) of Isaac on Mount Moriah (where later Christ, the Lamb of God, would be offered), God promised Abraham that He would "multiply [his] seed as the stars of heaven, and as the sand which is upon the sea shore" (Gen. 22:17). This is a remarkably scientific notation concerning the innumerable stars of heaven, made at a time when men could see only about five thousand stars at most.

Again Abraham clearly acknowledged the God of creation when he called him "the LORD, the God of heaven, and the God of the earth" (Gen. 24:3). Abraham's God was no mere "tribal god," as evolutionists allege.

Isaac and Jacob also shared this concept of God. Jacob, in particular, was given the remarkable vision of the ladder reaching from earth to heaven, with angels ascending and descending on it (Gen. 28:12), wherein God confirmed his covenant with Abraham to him also (rather than Esau, or Ishmael, or the sons of Abraham by Keturah).

Abraham, Isaac, and Jacob and his sons, especially Joseph, were subject to many temptations to worship nature gods. They lived among the Canaanites, then the Egyptians, surrounded by the polytheistic evolutionary pantheism that had swept around the world with the dispersion from Babel. Yet they continued to believe and worship the true God of creation, with his promises of coming redemption, praying only to Him and offering animal sacrifices to him in token of their faith that he would forgive their sins and save their souls. In his dying prophetic blessing on his twelve sons, the patriarch Jacob said that "Shiloh," a name for the promised Redeemer, would "come; and unto him [would] the gathering of the people be." Then he spoke of "a serpent by the way," followed quickly by his testimony of faith: "I have waited for thy salvation, O LORD" (Gen. 49:10, 17, 18). Although these statements were in the context of his prophecies on Judah and Dan, respectively, they do reflect also the primeval protevangel of Genesis 3:15, concerning the promised Savior who would someday crush the serpent and bring salvation and restoration.

While there is not much material in Genesis 12–50 referring specifically back to the great events of Genesis 1–11, it is all built naturally on the foundation of those events. Furthermore, there is nothing whatever that would contradict or question any of those events. In view of the worldwide rebellion against the God of heaven at Babel, carried around the world by the dispersing tribes, this in itself is a strong testimony to the historicity of all those events.

One incidental confirmation may also be noted in the continually declining longevity of the patriarchs after the flood. Noah lived 950 years, Shem 602 years, Terah 205 years, Abraham 175 years, Isaac 180 years, Jacob 147 years, and Joseph 110 years (Gen. 9:29; 11:10–11; 11:37; 25:7; 35:28; 47:28; 50:26, respectively). These figures show clearly that the flood was a cataclysmic global event, changing the environment of life so drastically that it resulted in an exponential decay of longevity from around 900 years to around 70 years (Ps. 90:10) in the period from Noah to Moses. Also this indicates that the period from Noah to Moses could not have been very much greater than the 900 or so years assigned to it by the traditional Hebrew text. The lifespan was halved, for example, in the 300 or so years between Joseph and his great great grandfather Terah, but it had declined even more rapidly from Noah to Terah.

Israel in the Wilderness

The Book of Genesis is generally considered one of the books of Moses, for he compiled and edited it from the older, eyewitness, *toledoth* tablets. These had been transmitted down through the line of the patriarchs, probably being kept safe by one of the tribes (either Judah or Joseph) during their Egyptian exile and captivity, until finally Moses acquired them when he assumed national leadership.

The later books of the Pentateuch (Exodus, Leviticus, Numbers, Deuteronomy), however, record events during Moses' lifetime, and were written directly by him. Their primary purpose is to narrate the early history of Israel—in Egypt and the wilderness—on its way to the promised land, and especially the giving of the so-called Mosaic laws. There are relatively few references to the earlier history of the world, but these few are all fully consistent with what had already been recorded in Genesis.

The first was when Moses met God at the burning bush (Exod. 3:2).

There, God introduced himself as the God of Abraham, Isaac, and Jacob (Gen. 3:6), and also as the eternally existing one, I AM THAT I AM (Exod. 3:14). He continued to be the God of these fathers, for they were still living, even though they had died physically long ago. He proved to Moses that He was the Creator, by creating a living serpent out of Moses' rod (Exod. 4:2–4). The later counterfeit miracle of the Egyptian magicians was presumably a demonically induced illusion (Exod. 7:11–12), for only God can create life.

The great miracles performed in Egypt by God through Moses, as described in Exodus 7 through 14, were clear proof to the Egyptians that their sizable pantheon of nature gods and goddesses could not in any way compete with the God of Israel. He was the Creator of all things, including the natural forces and systems and evil angels with which they had sought to replace the true God of creation. These were mighty miracles of creation, and the "enchantments" of the Egyptian sorcerers were no match for them. God created blood in the river, frogs, lice, flies, a deadly disease on the Egyptian cattle, terrible boils, hail mixed with fire, locusts, thick darkness and finally death on all the Egyptian firstborn sons. All of these fell only on the Egyptians, not on the Israelites.

Furthermore, he created an anti-gravitational force of some kind to hold up the waters of the sea as two walls, making a path for the children of Israel on which they could pass through the sea (Exod. 14:21–22). No one but the Creator of energy and matter could control his creation in such ways. The evolutionary gods of the Egyptians were utterly helpless in the face of the God who is real! "Who is like unto thee, O LORD, among the gods?" sang Moses after their great deliverance (Exod. 15:11).

God performed many other miracles of creation for the children of Israel during their forty years in the wilderness. There was the pillar of cloud by day and fire by night (Exod. 13:21), the healing of the noxious waters of Marah (Exod. 15:25), the provision of the great multitude of quails and then the daily provision of manna (Exod. 16:13, 35), the miraculous supply of water (Exod. 17:6), the budding of Aaron's rod (Num. 17:8), the healing of the serpent bites (Num. 21:8–9), the speaking of Balaam's ass (Num. 22:28–30), the forty-year preservation of their clothing and shoes (Deut. 29:5), and many other mighty acts of miraculous creation. None but the Creator could do such things.

God also gave them victories over their enemies, who had seemed so much stronger that they were afraid to go against them at first. There were giants in the land, the Anakim (Num. 13:33). This tribe, as well as others—the Zamzummims and the Emims (Deut. 2:10, 20; note also Gen. 14:5)—included many giants. Before the flood, Noah had written that "there were giants in the earth in those days," and then Moses had evidently inserted the parenthetical editorial comment, "and also after that" (Gen. 6:4). As noted before, these antediluvian giants had evidently resulted from widespread demonic possession of the rebellious men and women of that age, culminating finally in God's judgment through the great flood. Moses' inserted comment suggested that demonic influence was probably involved also in the giantism among the Canaanite tribes, for these tribes also were worshiping a host of false gods. Nevertheless, when the time came, God gave the Israelites victory over them.

This, in fact, was certainly at least one of the reasons why God told the Israelites to destroy the Canaanites. They had so yielded themselves to occultism and wickedness in general that they were much like the antediluvians, for whom there had been no remedy except extermination. Moses soberly warned his people against becoming contaminated with such pantheistic nature worship when they came in contact with these people in the land. "Take ye therefore good heed unto yourselves . . . lest ye corrupt yourselves, and make you a graven image . . . and lest thou lift up thine eyes to heaven, and when thou seest the sun, and the moon, and the stars, even all the host of heaven, shouldest be driven to worship them, and serve them, which the LORD thy God hath divided unto all nations under the whole heaven" (Deut. 4:15, 16, 19).

Included in this warning against any compromise with evolutionary paganism (and there are many more such warnings in Scripture) is an incidental confirmation that this type of religion did originate at Babel, as we have inferred, because it was there from whence "the LORD thy God [had] divided unto all nations under the whole heaven" this anti-creationist system of belief and worship. And it was because of this that he called the people of Israel into existence, to be a witness and opponent against this system. It was this division also to which Moses referred shortly before his death. "Remember the days of old, consider the years of many generations . . . When the most High divided to the nations their inheritance, when he separated the sons of Adam, he set the bounds of the people according to the number of the children of Israel. For the LORD's portion is his people; Jacob is the lot of his inheritance" (Deut. 32:7–9).

In this remarkable statement is not only an explicit confirmation that all nations are descended from Adam but also that the separation of the nations (referring undoubtedly to the dispersion at Babel) and the resulting seventy original nations listed in Genesis 10, the Table of Nations, was somehow divinely ordained to correspond with the seventy original children of Israel as they entered Egypt to form a cohesive national entity among the other nations of the world (see Gen. 46:27).

Note also the strong witness for God given in Moses' valedictory to Israel just before his death. "Know therefore this day . . . that the LORD he is God in heaven above, and upon the earth beneath: there is none else." "Behold, the heaven and the heaven of heavens is the LORD's thy God, the earth also, with all that therein is." "For the LORD your God is God of gods, and LORD of lords, a great God, a mighty, and a terrible . . ." (Deut. 4:39; 10:14, 17).

Finally, in his blessing of the tribes, he invoked for Joseph "the chief things of the ancient mountains, and for the precious things of the lasting hills," for these were now almost a thousand years old, since their formation after the flood. But then, in contrast, even to such a long time, he said: "The eternal God is thy refuge, and underneath are the everlasting arms" (Deut. 33:15, 24). The mountains were ancient by this time, but God is eternal! The hills are lasting, but his arms are everlasting!

Creation and the Law

The most definitive and important reference to creation in the Pentateuch, apart from the creation record itself, is found in the Ten Commandments. The fourth commandment is as follows.

Remember the sabbath day, to keep it holy. Six days shalt thou labour, and do all thy work: but the seventh day is the sabbath of the LORD thy God: in it thou shalt not do any work, thou, nor thy son, nor thy daughter, thy manservant, nor thy maidservant, nor thy cattle, nor thy stranger that is within thy gates: for in six days the LORD made heaven and earth, the sea, and all that in them is, and rested the seventh day: wherefore the LORD blessed the sabbath day, and hallowed it (Exod. 20:8–11).

The observance of the "sabbath day" (that is, rest day) was not instituted by this commandment, for it had been practiced by mankind ever since the actual week of creation, when "God blessed the seventh day, and sanctified it: because that in it he had rested from all his work which God created and made" (Gen. 2:3). In fact, God had previously arranged the miracle of the manna to occur on a weekly cycle. "And [Moses] said unto them, This is that which the LORD hath said, To morrow is the rest of the holy sabbath unto the LORD. . . . Six days ye shall gather it; but on the seventh day, which is the sabbath, in it there shall be none. . . . the LORD hath given you the sabbath . . ." (Exod. 16:23, 26, 29).

The Lord himself had worked six days, then rested on the seventh, setting thereby a permanent pattern for the benefit of mankind. "The LORD hath given you the sabbath"! Man is physiologically so constructed that he needs a day of rest and worship at least one day in seven, but as in other things, he tends to forget God's plan in this as well. Therefore, when God prepared a special nation for himself, he emphasized this truth by his forty-year-long provision of heavenly food for them on this weekly basis. Then, he wrote its observance into their very law, as the concluding commandment of the four dealing specifically with their relation to God. The six remaining commandments dealt with their behavior toward other people.

The unique importance of these Ten Commandments is underscored by the fact that—out of all the Bible—this portion was written directly by God himself! Note carefully Moses' testimony.

> Six days may work be done; but in the seventh is the sabbath of rest, holy to the LORD: whosoever doeth any work in the sabbath day, he shall surely be put to death. . . . It is a sign between me and the children of Israel for ever: for in six days the LORD made heaven and earth, and on the seventh day he rested, and was refreshed.
>
> And he gave unto Moses, when he had made an end of communing with him upon mount Sinai, two tables of testimony, tables of stone, written with the finger of God (Exod. 31:15, 17–18).
>
> And the tables were the work of God, and the writing was the writing of God, graven upon the tables (Exod. 32:16).

All of the Scriptures are divinely inspired, but the Ten Commandments were divinely *inscribed!* If any portion of the Bible should be believed, therefore, *this* should be believed—and taken to mean exactly what it says, more than all the rest.

And the fourth commandment says, as plainly as words could ever express a thought, that God made *everything* in six natural days. This should forever settle the vexed question of the age of the earth, at least for those who really believe in the divine inspiration and inerrancy of the Bible.

The basis of man's work week—six literal work days plus a literal rest day—is explicitly said to be God's work week. The same words are used ("day," from the Hebrew *yom*, "days" from the Hebrew *yamim*) for man's days and God's days, and everything is completely parallel. If God's days are not the same as man's days, then God seems unable to communicate to man. If he intended to say the world had been created over vast ages of time (as the pagans around the Israelites all believed in their pantheistic systems), there were a number of ways in which this thought could easily have been expressed in the Hebrew language; but if his purpose was to stress the fact that the whole creation had been accomplished in six literal days, there is no better or more explicit way to say *this* than in the words which God carefully wrote with his own finger on a table of stone!

Although the words *yom* and *yamim* (like "day" and "days" in English) can refer indefinitely to "time" or "times" if the context so indicates, the frequent occurrences of these words in the Hebrew Old Testament (over 1000 times for *yom*, 700 for *yamim*) never *require* the indefinite meaning, and almost always clearly are used in the definite sense (that is, either for twenty-four-hour periods or the daylight portions of twenty-four-hour periods). They are *never* used to refer to definite periods of time (e.g., geological ages), with specific beginnings and endings, unless those periods are literal days.

It is, therefore, as certain as definite words can be used to express definite meanings, that God's Word has told us—in both Genesis and Exodus—that he created and made everything in the cosmos in six literal days. Although men in both ancient and modern times have rejected this revelation, the fact remains that this is what God has said! If we are going to call Him a liar, we must be willing to face the consequences of blasphemy.

The principle of the sabbath was established not only for man's good, but also for the animals and (in terms of years) even for the earth itself. "Six years thou shalt sow thy land, and shalt gather in the fruits thereof: but the seventh year thou shalt let it rest and lie still; that the poor of thy people may eat: and what they leave the beasts of the field shall eat. In like manner thou shalt deal with thy vineyard, and with thy oliveyard" (Exod. 23:10, 11).

There are also a few other references in these books of the law to events in primeval times. The ceremonial law, centered around the different animal sacrifices atoning for sin, finds its primeval rationale in the sacrifice of Abel and—even before that—in God's provision of animal skins to cover the nakedness of Adam and Eve. Noah also built an altar and offered sacrifices right after the flood and, at that time, God stressed the important truth—both biological and spiritual—that the blood in living flesh represented its life (note Gen. 9:4–6). This is now reemphasized in the law, as the key element in the Levitical sacrifices.

> For the life of the flesh is in the blood: and I have given it to you upon the altar to make an atonement for your souls: for it is the blood that maketh an atonement for the soul. . . . For it is the life of all flesh; the blood of it is for the life thereof: therefore I said unto the children of Israel, Ye shall eat the blood of no manner of flesh; for the life of all flesh is the blood thereof: whosoever eateth it shall be cut off (Lev. 17:11, 14).

The distinctions between men and animals were reinforced in the law, as well as the integrity of the divine provision for reproduction and marriage. Further, the sin of following other "gods" and the anti-creationist religions of Satan and the rebellious angels were also proscribed in the law. In addition to the Ten Commandments (outlawing idolatry, blasphemy, pantheism, polytheism, idolatry, and adultery), note the following warnings and exhortations in the Mosaic laws:

> Thou shalt not suffer a witch to live. Whosoever lieth with a beast shall surely be put to death. He that sacrificeth unto any god, save unto the LORD only, he shall be utterly destroyed (Exod. 22:18–20).

> And they shall no more offer their sacrifices unto devils, after whom they have gone a whoring (Lev. 17:7). None of you shall approach to any that is near of kin to him, to uncover their nakedness (Lev. 18:6). And thou shalt not let any of thy seed pass through the fire to Molech. . . . Thou shalt not lie with mankind, as with womankind: it is abomination. . . . Defile not ye yourselves in any of these things: for in all these the nations are defiled which I cast out before you (Lev. 18:21, 22, 24). Neither shall ye use enchantment, nor observe times. . . . Ye shall not make any cuttings in your flesh for the dead, nor print any marks upon you. . . . Do not prostitute thy daughter, to cause her to be a whore. . . . Regard not them that have familiar spirits, neither seek after wizards, to be defiled by them (Lev. 19:26, 28, 29, 31). If a man also lie with mankind, as he lieth

with a woman, both of them have committed an abomination: they shall
surely be put to death. . . . And if a man lie with a beast, he shall surely
be put to death: and ye shall slay the beast. And if a woman approach unto
any beast and lie down thereto, thou shalt kill the woman and the beast
. . . (Lev. 20:13, 15, 16). A man also or woman that hath a familiar spirit,
or that is a wizard, shall surely be put to death (Lev. 20:27).

The above are just a few of the passages in the law dealing with such
matters, establishing as capital crimes in the specially chosen holy nation
of Israel any practices that would undermine the knowledge or worship
of the true Creator, that would blur the created distinction between
men and animals or that would corrupt the divinely created plan for
human multiplication through the monogamous marriage relationship.
Although these may not be regarded as capital crimes in Gentile nations,
they do still represent flagrant disobedience to God's purposes for
mankind in the creation, and should certainly be avoided by all who
would honor his will even today.

There is a brief reference in the law also to God's intended system
of permanence for his created "kinds" of plants and animals. "Thou
shalt not let thy cattle gender with a diverse kind: thou shalt not sow
thy field with mingled seed" (Lev. 19:19). Also: "Thou shalt not sow
thy vineyard with divers seeds: lest the fruit of thy seed which thou hast
sown, and the fruit of thy vineyard, be defiled. Thou shalt not plow
with an ox and an ass together" (Deut. 22:9,10). While new varieties
could arise (or be intentionally bred by selection) within each created
kind, God clearly intended each to reproduce strictly "after its kind,"
so new kinds cannot evolve nor should they be generated.

Finally, there is a beautiful reference to man's creation in Moses'
review of God's unique dealings with Israel. "Ask now of the days that
are past, which were before thee, since the day that God created man
upon the earth, and ask from the one side of heaven unto the other,
whether there hath been any such thing as this great thing is, or hath
been heard like it?" (Deut. 4:32). The nation of Israel was such a unique
creation of God that the only work comparable was that of the primeval
creation of man. Israel did not slowly develop into a nation over many
millennia, just as man did not evolve over many ages. There had been
a *day* when God created man upon the earth—the sixth day of his creation week, to be precise—and nothing comparable had happened until
God came down at Sinai.

5

The Witness of Job

Job's Vision of Satan in Heaven

The book of Job contains more references to the creation and the other events of primeval history than any book of the Bible except Genesis. This is not surprising, since Job lived in the days of Genesis, probably about the time of Abraham, or even earlier. Job shows some knowledge of the events described in the books of Adam and Noah in particular, though he was not in the direct line from Shem to Abraham and probably had not seen the actual writings. On the other hand, he makes no mention of the nation of Israel or the laws of Moses or even of Abraham, so it is almost certain that Job's story took place before Moses and possibly before Abraham. That Job himself was the author of the book is indicated both by his expressed desire to write such a book (Job 19:23, 24) and by the fact that only he could have known the events of the story.

He could only have written of the events taking place in heaven, however (Job 1:6–12; 2:1–7), by a direct revelation or vision from God, given after the restoration of Job at the end of the book. In these remarkable verses are found the Bible's first direct references to Satan, although his influences have been evident many times, especially in the temptation of Eve, in the demon possession of the antediluvians, and in the career of Nimrod.

In spite of the Edenic curse on the serpent, Satan is seen as still having access to God in heaven, in the presence of all the holy angels, the unfallen "sons of God." He is also shown as the inveterate enemy of God and the people of God. Just as he had tempted Adam and Eve to sin when they were yet sinless, he now is tempting Job, who is said three times (Job 1:1, 8; 2:3) to be "a perfect and an upright man." Twice God himself testifies that "there is none like him in the earth."

We learn also from Job's vision that, in the heavenly economy, the angels ("sons of God") regularly come before the Lord, evidently to report on their activities and to receive further instruction from God. These are the first references to the "sons of God" since the mention of the rebellious "sons of God" in the days of Noah (Gen. 6:2, 4), and these references in Job confirm the previous inference that the latter were, indeed, angelic beings.

Satan not only has at least occasional access to God's presence in heaven, but he still—despite the curse—also has access to men and women on earth, just as he did in the Garden of Eden. He can still exercise his two-tiered attack on God's plan for those created in God's image, tempting them to sin on earth, and accusing them before God in heaven. He also can exercise great control over both the forces of nature (sending fire and wind to destroy men and animals, as in Job 1:16, 19) and the minds of ungodly men (leading the Sabeans and Chaldeans to attack the servants of Job—Job 1:15, 17). His behind-the-scenes activities go far to explain many of the events in both the ancient world and the modern world. But there is one more all-important truth we learn from Job's vision. Satan can test and injure men on earth only to the extent that God allows. Just as he allowed the tempting of Eve, so he allowed the testing of Job, and in both cases he had a long-range purpose that would eventually bring greater blessing to those being tested and greater honor to the sovereign Creator.

Job is not given any further direct insight into Satan's behind-the-scenes manipulation of his troubles, but a reading of Job's account makes it clear that Satan is still very much involved in testing Job. He fails in his efforts to break Job's faith by attacking his possessions, and then he also fails in his efforts to cause Job to sin by destroying his health. But he obviously does not abandon his efforts, for the rest of Job's long narrative details Satan's invisible war against his mind and soul.

Actually, we do encounter one more strong, direct indication of the influence of Satan, in the attacks of Job's friends on his character. As the chief spokesman of these friends, Eliphaz testifies of the influence of a mysterious "spirit" on his thinking and his approach in counseling Job (Job 4:15–21).

This spirit is certainly not from God, for the spirit says nothing about the grace and love of God, stressing only God's inaccessibility to mortal men. He acknowledges that God is their "maker" (v. 17), but then sarcastically refers to their bodies as mere "houses of clay, whose foundation is in the dust" (v. 19), clearly an allusion to the formation of man's body from the dust, followed by God's curse sending it back to the dust (Gen. 2:7; 3:19), "crushed before the moth."

The spirit speaking to Eliphaz, perhaps a demonic angel or perhaps even Satan himself, bitterly complains against God concerning their fall: "Behold, he put no trust in his servants; and his angels he charged with folly" (v. 18).

The bitterness of this evil spirit against God is reflected in his cynicism toward mankind, even the best among men. This traumatic night encounter apparently sets the tone, then, for the approach taken by Job's three friends, led by Eliphaz, in their attempt to deal with Job and his problems.

Creation and the Fall in the Book of Job

In a tone seemingly influenced by the message of the cynical spirit who visited him in the night, Eliphaz reflects the somber effects of the Genesis curse, saying: "Although affliction cometh not forth of the dust, neither doth trouble spring out of the ground; yet man is born unto trouble" (Job 5:6, 7). He does, however, acknowledge the creative and providential work of God. "[God] doeth great things and unsearchable; marvellous things without number: who giveth rain upon the earth, and sendeth waters upon the fields" (Job 5:9, 10). Eliphaz and his associates had an inadequate conception of God's grace, but they were still creationists, recognizing the infinite power of God as Creator and Sustainer.

Job, even more cogently, testifies of the creation, speaking explicitly of God's creation of the stars on the fourth day as "signs." "[God] alone spreadeth out the heavens" (Job 9:8). Note that he did not have to use a "big bang" to spread out the heavens, as modern cosmologists speculate. He did it *alone!* Neither did he scatter them randomly. "[He] maketh Arcturus, Orion, and Pleiades, and the chambers of the south.

Which doeth great things past finding out; yea, and wonders without number" (Job 9:9–10). Not only the stars, but also man was directly created by God. Clearly thinking in terms of the formation of Adam's body by God, Job says: "Thine hands have made me and fashioned me together round about . . . Remember, I beseech thee, that thou hast made me as the clay; and wilt thou bring me into dust again?" (Job 10:8, 9). The last question echoes the very words of God's curse on sinful man (Gen. 3:19).

In another classic passage, Job notes the purposeful creation of the various kinds of animals. These did not evolve by random processes, nor were they capriciously produced at the whim of various nature gods. "But ask now the beasts, and they shall teach thee; and the fowls of the air, and they shall tell thee: or speak to the earth, and it shall teach thee: and the fishes of the sea shall declare unto thee. Who knoweth not in all these that the hand of the LORD hath wrought this? In whose hand is the soul of every living thing, and the breath of all mankind" (Job 12:7–10).

But Job also recognizes human frailty and the effect of Adam's fall. "Man that is born of a woman is of few days, and full of trouble. He cometh forth like a flower, and is cut down . . . Who can bring a clean thing out of an unclean? not one" (Job 14:1, 2, 4).

In his second diatribe, Eliphaz again lapses into the unwitting deception taught him by the evil spirit: "What is man, that he should be clean? and he which is born of a woman, that he should be righteous? Behold, he putteth no trust in his saints [that is, his sanctified ones, the angels]; yea, the heavens are not clean in his sight. How much more abominable and filthy is man, which drinketh iniquity like water?" (Job 15:14–16). Job later apparently refers to the primeval fall of the rebellious angels, but he correctly recognizes it as a divine judgment rather than God's pettiness in not allowing them to continue their rebellion in heaven. "Shall any teach God knowledge? seeing he judgeth those that are high" (Job 21:22).

Job later again refers to God's creation of the heavens and his placement of the stars and their signs there. The heavens (i.e., space) were created in the beginning (Gen. 1:1), and the stars placed *in* the heavens later (Gen. 1:16). "By his Spirit he hath garnished the heavens; his hand hath formed the crooked serpent. Lo, these are parts of his ways: but how little a portion is heard of him? but the thunder of his power who can understand?" (Job 26:13–14).

Job recognizes that he is a sinner, but he has regularly offered sacrifices (Job 1:5) for himself and for his family, in accordance with the ancient revelation to Adam and Abel and Noah and others concerning the way to receive atonement and forgiveness. He acknowledges that he *is* a sinner, even though he is unable to think of any specific unconfessed sins he has committed, so he cannot understand why it seems as though God is ignoring his cries. "I have sinned," he confesses, "and why dost thou not pardon my transgression, and take away mine iniquity?" (Job 7:20, 21).

Nevertheless, he still maintains his faith, for he knows and believes God's Edenic promise of a coming Savior (Gen. 3:15). "For I know that my redeemer liveth, and that he shall stand at the latter day upon the earth . . . yet in my flesh shall I see God" (Job 19:25, 26).

At the very end of Job's dialogue with his three friends, he again indicates his awareness of the creation events, even mentioning Adam's secretiveness. "If I covered my transgressions as Adam, by hiding mine iniquity in my bosom: did I fear a great multitude . . . ? Oh that one would hear me! behold, my desire is, that the Almighty would answer me . . ." (Job 31:33–35).

Job concludes with these words: "If my land cry against me, . . . let thistles grow instead of wheat, and cockle instead of barley. The words of Job are ended" (Job 31:38, 40). This clearly is an invocation of God's primeval curse on the ground (Gen. 3:17, 18).

Following the conclusion of Job's dialogue with his three friends, however, the young theologian Elihu has quite a bit to say. He is very opinionated concerning his own supposed insights into God's ways, but he also clearly believes in the ancient records of creation and the fall. "The Spirit of God hath made me, and the breath of the Almighty hath given me life. . . . I also am formed out of the clay" (Job 33:4, 6). Later, Elihu refers to the curse. "If [God] set his heart upon man, if he gather unto himself his spirit and his breath; all flesh shall perish together, and man shall turn again unto dust" (Job 34:14, 15).

Twice Elihu calls God "my Maker" (Job 35:10; 36:3). He recognizes also that God is the eternal one: "Behold, God is great, and we know him not, neither can the number of his years be searched out" (Job 36:26). God is also omnipotent and omniscient. "Behold, God exalteth by his power: who teacheth like him?" (Job 36:22). "Touching the Almighty, we cannot find him out: he is excellent in power, and in judgment" (Job 37:23).

These many references to the heavens, to angels, to the creation of the universe, life, animals, and men, and then to the fall and the curse, with the entrance of death into the world, and finally to forgiveness through sacrifice, with faith in the promised coming Redeemer, all indicate that Job and his friends were still monotheists and, even without the actual written narratives, knew well the great truths of God's primeval revelation.

The Flood and the Dispersion

In addition to Job's knowledge of the Creator and his creation, he also discusses the great flood and the events following the flood that had transpired before his own time. These would correspond to the record in Genesis 6–11, but there is no indication that Job had access to these documents. Nevertheless, what he *did* know correlates well with the actual revelation in these early chapters of Genesis.

In his first answer to Bildad, Job describes the cataclysmic violence of the earth upheavals accompanying the flood. "[God] removeth the mountains, and they know not: which overturneth them in his anger. Which shaketh the earth out of her place, and the pillars thereof tremble. Which commandeth the sun, and it riseth not; and sealeth up the stars. Which . . . treadeth upon the waves of the sea" (Job 9:5–8). At the initiation of the flood, all the "fountains of the great deep" cleaved open, and the geophysical balances in the earth's crust were forever changed. The invisible water vapor canopy condensed into great banks of thick clouds and, for the first time in earth history, the inhabitants could see neither sun nor stars for at least forty days and forty nights. Soon the only things to be seen on earth were the great "waves of the sea." The rushing waters eroded all the hills and mountains of the pre-flood lands, depositing them as great sedimentary layers in the pre-flood sea basins. "Behold, he breaketh down, and it cannot be built again [e.g., the pre-flood cities]: he shutteth up a man, and there can be no opening [possibly referring to God closing the door into the ark, Gen. 7:16]. Behold, he withholdeth the waters, and they dry up [perhaps a reference to the waters stored in the pre-flood canopy and the subterranean deep]: also he sendeth them out, and they overturn the earth" (Job 12:14, 15).

Shortly following this graphic account of the great cataclysm, Job seems to refer to the formation of the various nations after the dispersion at Babel. "He increaseth the nations, and destroyeth them: he enlargeth the nations, and straiteneth them again" (Job 12:23). As the tribes scattered from Babel, many nations began to be formed, but some of these soon were destroyed (by disease, wild animals, etc., but mainly by tribal warfare), and others superseded them. Many degenerated into what now are called "primitive" tribes. "He taketh away the heart of the chief of the people of the earth, and causeth them to wander in a wilderness where there is no way. They grope in the dark without light, and he maketh them to stagger like a drunken man" (Job 12:24–25). Later, Job even notes that some of these became "cave men." "For want and famine they were solitary; fleeing into the wilderness in former time desolate and waste. Who cut up mallows by the bushes, and juniper roots for their meat. They were driven forth from among men, (they cried after them as after a thief;) to dwell in the clifts of the valleys, in caves of the earth, and in the rocks. Among the bushes they brayed; under the nettles they were gathered together. They were children of fools, yea, children of base men: they were viler than the earth" (Job 30:3–8).

Job makes still other references to the effects of the flood. "Surely the mountain falling cometh to nought, and the rock is removed out of his place. The waters wear the stones: thou washest away the things which grow out of the dust of the earth: and thou destroyest the hope of man" (Job 14:18–19).

While such a description might apply in a small way to present-day hydrologic action, it would certainly be most fitting in the context of the great flood—especially in its result, that of destroying the hopes of pre-flood man. They had hoped, no doubt, to get rid of God, but they were destroyed instead.

In this context, there seems also to be a reference to the end of the flood, with its divine promise that there would never be such a flood again, that "day and night shall not cease" as long as the earth remains (Gen. 8:22). Job says: "He hath compassed the waters with bounds, until the day and night come to an end," even though, during the flood itself, "the pillars of heaven tremble and are astonished at his reproof. He divideth the sea with his power, and by his understanding he smiteth through the proud" (Job 26:10–12).

Continuing later, Job goes on to say: "He putteth forth his hand upon the rock; he overturneth the mountains by the roots. He cutteth out rivers among the rocks; and his eye seeth every precious thing. He bindeth the floods from overflowing; and the thing that is hid bringeth he forth to light" (Job 28:9–11).

Even Eliphaz makes reference to the flood, when he says: "Hast thou marked the old way which wicked men have trodden? Which were cut down out of time, whose foundation was overflown with a flood: which said unto God, Depart from us: and what can the Almighty do for them?" (Job 22:15–17). Here, however, he uses the words "a flood," with the Hebrew word normally denoting a "local" flood. The account of the worldwide flood, however, as given in Genesis 6–9, always uses the unique Hebrew word *mabbul,* always with the sense of the definite article—"*the* flood." This word is never used for anything but the global deluge of Genesis 6–9. One wonders if Eliphaz is subconsciously anticipating modern uniformitarians who, with their "local flood theory" of Genesis, are unwilling to recognize that sin was ever so universal as to justify a universal flood.

Thus, in the book of Job—especially in the discourses of Job himself, but also implicit in the discussions of his three friends plus that of young Elihu—it is obvious that the writer was familiar with the great events of the ancient world, from creation to the fall to the flood to the dispersion. It is also obvious that, although he did not have at hand the actual tablets recording what we now call Genesis 1–11, all the references to these events are fully consistent with the actual records. This goes far to confirming the mutual historical accuracy of all these writings. But only now we come to the most remarkable document of all— the four-chapter monologue of God himself!

The Divine Monologue of Creation

Chapters 38 through 41 of the Book of Job consist entirely of the direct words of God himself, all dealing with creation, the flood, and God's providential care of his creation. In addition to confirming the Genesis record, this matchless monologue gives amazing insight into the heart of God and much additional information concerning earth history. The monologue is constructed around a framework of about seventy-seven rhetorical questions, all challenging our understanding of God's creation.

Verses 4 through 7 of chapter 38 all deal directly with the original

creation. "Where wast thou when I laid the foundations of the earth?
. . . When the morning stars sang together, and all the sons of God
shouted for joy?" The obvious answer, which Job or anyone else would
have to give, is that we existed then only in the mind of God. This
should be enough to convince any right-thinking person that the only
way we can know about the actual creation of the world is for God to
tell us. He was there; we were not. It is presumptuous in the extreme
for either ancient pantheists or modern uniformitarian scientists to try
to develop an evolutionary explanation for the origin of the world. God
had already given, through Adam, a complete explanation of origins—
the origin of everything, from the cosmos itself to men and women.

God does reveal one additional truth about origins to Job that he did
not tell Adam. When the solid foundations of the earth were laid by
God—evidently on the third day of creation week, when the solid material of the earth emerged out of solution or suspension in the primeval
deep—all the angels, the "sons of God" who had been created probably on the first day, "shouted for joy." These angels of God were also
called "the morning stars," even though the stars themselves were not
created until the fourth day. In view of the close connection throughout Scripture of the starry "host of heaven" with the angelic "host of
heaven," it seems likely that the stars may actually have been created *for*
the angels, as their residences, or at least their respective bases of operation. At this time, *all* the sons of God—even including Satan—were
evidently still subservient to God. The rebellion of Satan and his legions
took place sometime after that first creation week, for everything was
"very good" and "sanctified" up to that point (Gen. 1:31; 2:3).

The next several verses deal with the flood and its aftermath. "Who
shut up the sea with doors, when it brake forth, as if it had issued out
of the womb? When I made the cloud the garment thereof, and thick
darkness a swaddlingband for it, and brake up for it my decreed place,
and set bars and doors, and said, Hitherto shalt thou come, but no further: and here shall thy proud waves be stayed?" (Job 38:8–11). When
the "fountains of the great deep [were] broken up" to initiate the great
flood (Gen. 7:11), they were immediately followed by the liquefying
of the vast "waters which were above the firmament" (Gen. 1:7), with
the vapors turning quickly into dense clouds and torrential rains, with
thick darkness covering the face of the earth. When the assigned mis-
sion of the deluge was complete, God readjusted submarine topogra-
phy in such a way that it could never return, as he promised Noah.

Most of the remaining verses of chapter 38 deal with God's providential ordering of the earth's physical structure and activities for our present world, tremendously altered as it had been from the pre-flood world. The rhetorical questions in this section (vv. 12–38) are, in a sense, a kind of rebuke to Job and his friends—as well as to us—for not having taken God's original dominion mandate seriously enough to be able to answer them. Since they all deal with what we would now call scientific matters, they seem to constitute a sort of science examination, which mankind should have been able to pass by Job's time (at least two thousand years after the creation), and certainly by our time. Yet many of them are still unanswered today, though science has now progressed far enough for us to perceive something of the remarkable scientific insights hidden away in this ancient book.

Verses 12–15, for example, deal with the rotation of the earth, a fact presumably still unknown to men in Job's day. Verse 16 mentions the "springs of the sea," a phenomenon discovered scientifically just in recent decades. And so on. There are both remarkable scientific insights and also questions yet unanswerable. For a more extended discussion, the reader may wish to consult my book *The Remarkable Record of Job* (Baker, 1989).

One item of particular interest in connection with our attempt to learn more of the world's post-flood history during the time represented in Genesis 9–11 (before Abraham) is the following divine question: "Out of whose womb came the ice? and the hoary frost of heaven, who hath gendered it? The waters are hid as with a stone, and the face of the deep is frozen" (Job 38:29–30). Job lived in the area now known as Arabia, and the people of that latitude today have certainly never seen "the face of the deep frozen," hiding its waters "as with a stone."

God speaks here of a great sheet of ice slowly moving down, as if emerging from a womb, even covering the sea and hiding the waters below. This has come from the "the hoary frost of heaven," but men before Noah's time did not even know about rain. The appearance of snow in lower latitudes and tales of a great sheet of ice in the more northerly regions must have been awe-inspiring to the tribes as they moved out from Babel. It is significant that the Book of Job has more references to ice and snow than any other Bible book. It is hard to avoid the conclusion that God is here speaking of the great ice sheet in northern Eurasia and other regions of middle latitude that characterized the so-called Ice Age after the flood. People before the flood had never even imagined such a thing as snow, let alone great ice caps, for the antediluvian vapor canopy greenhouse effect maintained a pleasantly warm climate everywhere all through the year. The very mention of such phenomena here testifies both to the antiquity of the Book of Job and also to its divine origin.

The last three verses of Job 38 and all of Job 39 deal with God's providential care of his animal creation. Again there is an implied rebuke to mankind, even to righteous Job, for failing to understand and care for the animals, over whom man had been placed in dominion, both in Eden, then again after the flood.

A number of the animals mentioned in these verses are hard to identify in the modern world. This is especially true of the so-called unicorn (Job 39:9–12), but the same is also true of a number of others. The translators of the various Hebrew words involved have differed among themselves as to what modern animals they represent, with the result that different translations show different animals in many cases. The same problem is encountered in connection with the various animals mentioned in the Pentateuch.

The reason translators have so much trouble equating modern animals to the biblical animals is that many of the latter are now extinct, and so have no modern equivalents. Modern translators have this difficulty simply because they ignore biblical geology and chronology in deference to the standard system of evolutionary geology and chronology. Consequently they have no appreciation of the great numbers of animals that have become extinct since the worldwide flood of the Bible and the subsequent Ice Age caused by it.

The Bible teaches plainly that *all* the animal kinds that ever lived were created on the fifth and sixth days of creation week. Therefore, they were all contemporary with man in the early days, even the early centuries after the flood. After all, Noah had preserved every created kind of land animal on the ark. After the post-flood dispersion, however, many of these became extinct, being unable to adapt to the drastic environmental changes in the world after the flood. Possibly also many were hunted to extinction by man (Nimrod, in fact, acquired his great leadership role by being known as a mighty hunter).

Two of these now-extinct animals are described in detail by God in the 40th and 41st chapters of Job. An animal called "behemoth" is called "chief of the ways of God" (Job 40:15, 19). And an animal called "leviathan" is said to be so fearsome that "upon earth there is not his like" (Job 41:1, 33). The behemoth is a land animal, that "lieth under the shady trees" and "drinketh up a river" (Job 40:21, 23). The leviathan is a sea animal that "maketh the deep to boil like a pot: he maketh the sea like a pot of ointment" (Job 41:31).

The best that modern expositors have been able to do is to call behemoth an elephant and leviathan a crocodile. But such identifications are impossible. For example, behemoth "moveth his tail like a cedar" and leviathan is a fearsome monster whose "breath kindleth coals, and a flame goeth out of his mouth" (Job 40:17; 41:21). Whatever these extinct animals may have been, they were *not* elephants and crocodiles!

The most likely conclusion is that they were what modern paleontologists have called dinosaurs (and what ancient historians called dragons). Behemoth was the greatest of all land dinosaurs and leviathan the greatest of marine dinosaurs.

They were real animals, not mythical animals, and some at least were still living in Job's day, for he had seen them and knew what God was talking about. In fact, their fearsome strength and frightening aspect may well have been intended by God at this point to picture to Job the terrible foe he has been unknowingly wrestling with during his ordeal. They may well remind him of the old serpent of Eden, whom he has heard about with the ear, but now is finding out to be the bitter enemy of his soul. And although behemoth is the mightiest animal in the earth, God can "make his sword to approach unto him" (Job 40:19). Although leviathan is the most frightful animal in the ocean, not even leviathan "is able to stand before me," the Lord assures Job (41:10). Satan can do his worst against Job, but God knows Job will emerge the victor, for God will give him strength and faith and salvation to the uttermost!

After his trials were over, Job lived another 140 years (Job 42:16), and he must have been at least 50 or 60 when they began (he had ten grown children and was considered the venerable leader of his community), so he obviously must have lived in the early centuries after the flood, when men were still living about 200 years.

The whole story of Job is extremely fascinating and illuminating and encouraging, but our purpose here is merely to note those portions of his book which give further confirmation and understanding of the world as it was from Adam to Abraham. As we have seen, this is the actual setting of Job's book, and it does indeed have many such illuminating references and insights.

Now, as we continue this odyssey through the Bible, entering Joshua and the later historical books, we are getting further away in time from these great events of the past. Nevertheless, we still encounter their memory, quite frequently, as we go.

6

Creation Memories in Israel

Joshua and the Judges

After the death of Moses, the chosen nation of Israel embarked on its long and turbulent history, from the conquest of the land of Canaan to its worldwide dispersion fifteen centuries later. Perpetually torn between monotheism and polytheism, between pure worship and pagan idolatry—which really is to say between creationism and evolutionism—Israel at least always had a remnant of its people who maintained and practiced the revealed faith of the true Creator, Jehovah, the Holy One of Israel. As essentially the only monotheistic—that is creationist—nation in the world, it is not surprising that its people and leaders were perpetually under pressure to compromise with their pagan neighbors. This is the same kind of pressure that besets creationist Christians today, and we also are all too ready to compromise our faith with the pantheistic or atheistic evolutionism that is all around us today, even in "Christian" nations.

We can be thankful that there have always been a few God-fearing leaders like Joshua and David and Nehemiah who have continued to stand for the truth regardless, and through whom the truth of creation, as well as God's full revelation, has been transmitted to us today. Even though these leaders were fully occupied with pressing conflicts of the moment, these were all really symptomatic of the basic, age-long conflict between the two world views—God-centered faith versus man-centered faith, or Creator worship versus creature worship.

There are relatively few specific references in the Bible's historical books to this fundamental philosophical issue as such, but these are well worth noting. As they prepared to enter the promised land, Joshua and the Israelites first had to conquer Jericho. They received strategic assistance from Rahab, who lived in its wall, because she had already come to believe that the God of Israel was the true Creator God. Here is her testimony: "The LORD your God, he is God in heaven above, and in earth beneath" (Josh. 2:11). She had heard how Jehovah had miraculously enabled them to triumph over the mighty Egyptian empire, as well as the Amorite kings in Canaan, and had come to believe that Jehovah was the only real and true God.

Once again, great miracles accompanied Israel as the people entered Canaan. The Jordan River was caused to "stand upon an heap" (Josh. 3:13), and the people crossed over Jordan on dry ground, though it was at flood stage at the time and returned to flood stage immediately afterward (Josh. 3:15; 4:18). In exhorting his people to step into the river in faith, Joshua acknowledged Jehovah to be "the living God" and "the Lord of all the earth" (Josh. 3:10, 13), and Jehovah demonstrated that he was, indeed, just that. Only the Creator could control his creation in such a way.

The other miracles described in the Book of Joshua likewise required creative power that resides only in God. The strong walls of Jericho "fell down flat" (Josh. 6:20) when the trumpet sounded and the people shouted.

One of the greatest miracles imaginable occurred soon afterwards when, in answer to Joshua's prayer of faith, "the sun stood still in the midst of heaven, and hasted not to go down about a whole day. And there was no day like that before it or after it . . ." (Josh. 10:13, 14). Men have devised various quasi-naturalistic explanations for "the long day of Joshua," but this begs the question. If God is really the Creator, he created both the sun and the earth, and he can as easily stop their motions relative to each other as he could start them up in the first place.

After the conquest of the land was largely completed, and Joshua's death was imminent, he reminded the Israelites again of their unique position among the nations, especially their responsibility to retain and transmit the knowledge of the true God of creation. "That ye come not among these nations, these that remain among you; neither make mention of the name of their gods, nor cause to swear by them, neither serve them, nor bow yourselves unto them" (Josh. 23:7). He reminded them that their ancestors had yielded to this very temptation, and that they had been called out of paganism to serve the true God. God had said: "Your fathers dwelt on the other side of the flood [that is the great Euphrates River] in old time, even Terah, the father of Abraham, and the father of Nachor: and they served other gods. And I took your father Abraham from the other side of the flood, and led him throughout all the land of Canaan, and multiplied his seed, and gave him Isaac. . . . And I have given you a land for which ye did not labour, and cities which ye built not, and ye dwell in them . . ." (Josh. 24:2–3, 13). Joshua then gave them this great challenge: "Now therefore fear the LORD, and serve him in sincerity and in truth: and put away the gods which your fathers served on the other side of the flood, and in Egypt; and serve ye the LORD. And if it seem evil unto you to serve the LORD, choose you this day whom ye will serve; whether the gods which your fathers served that were on the other side of the flood, or the gods of the Amorites, in whose land ye dwell: but as for me and my house, we will serve the LORD" (Josh. 24:14, 15).

All the people agreed and covenanted with Joshua and the Lord that they would, indeed, put away all the other gods—the various nature gods of the Chaldeans, the Egyptians, the Amorites, and all the Canaanites—and serve only the true God who had created heaven and earth and all men. But they quickly forgot, as soon as Joshua and the other elders died.

The familiar cycle that characterized the Book of Judges—the cycle of apostasy, punishment, repentance and revival—was punctuated with a few creative miracles, and with occasional acknowledgment of the Creator. The song of Deborah and Barak, after a great victory over Jabin king of the Canaanites and his general Sisera, included the following testimony: "They fought from heaven: the stars in their courses fought against Sisera. The river of Kishon swept them away, that ancient river, the river Kishon" (Judg. 5:20, 21).

This is in a "song," of course, and the entire song is poetic and figurative. As we have noted before, "stars" in the Bible often are identified with the angels. Thus, "stars in their courses" evidently is intended to mean "angels in their ministries," acting on behalf of the people of God in answer to their repentance and prayers. "That ancient river, the river Kishon," was the meandering river ("Kishon" means "tortuous") where Sisera's army had been routed by the armies of Barak, aided by the invisible host of heaven. The river is not mentioned in earlier books of the Bible but must have been formed in very ancient times, probably as part of the drainage pattern established when the waters drained off after the flood. The Kishon is not a long river but can become torrential in its swampy lower reaches during the rainy season, and this also must have contributed to the defeat of Sisera's chariots. In any case, Deborah's song recognized that the victory really came from God.

In addition to the above, the most notable miracles recorded in the Book of Judges are those performed on Gideon's fleece (Judg. 6:37–40) and Samson's strength (Judg. 16:28–30). In answer to Gideon's prayer for a sign, God caused the fleece to be wet with the dew one night, while the ground was dry. The next night, the ground was wet and the fleece dry. In answer to Samson's last prayer, the Lord gave him supernatural strength to destroy three thousand Philistines reveling in their pagan temple when he pulled it down upon them all. In general, however, the period of the judges was a humanistic time when "every man did that which was right in his own eyes" (Judg. 21:25).

The First Kings of Israel

By the time of Samuel, the last of the judges, it had been at least twelve centuries since the flood, and the memory of the great events of the past had faded into semi-legendary tales in the various pagan nations of the world. Even in Israel, where the true record had been preserved in the books of Moses, Joshua, and Job, the people apparently were very poorly instructed in these Scriptures and were easily led into compromise with the beliefs and practices of their pagan neighbors.

But then God called Samuel, and a new era began. Samuel's mother, Hannah, praying for a son, began her prayer by calling on the "LORD of hosts" (1 Sam. 1:11). Her husband, Elkanah, was also a godly man, who "went up out of his city yearly to worship and to sacrifice unto the LORD of hosts in Shiloh" (1 Sam. 1:3). These are the first occurrences (out of almost three hundred) in the Bible of this majestic title or its equivalent, recognizing that God has an innumerable host of angels at his command. It is, in effect, a way of acknowledging the omnipotence of God as Creator and Sustainer of all things.

In her prayer after her son was born, Hannah went on to pray to him in that vein: "The pillars of the earth are the LORD's, and he hath set the world upon them. . . . the LORD shall judge the ends of the earth; and he shall give strength unto his king, and exalt the horn of his anointed" (1 Sam. 2:8, 10).

This is the first occurrence in the Bible of the word "anointed," or *Messiah*, equivalent to *Christ* in Greek. Furthermore, Hannah here prayed concerning the coming "king" of Israel long before Israel ever had a king, or even started asking for one. It surely seems that she must somehow have been thinking of God's Edenic promise of a coming seed of woman who would destroy all sin (Gen. 3:15). She was also acknowledging that God was Creator, having set the earth upon pillars, or foundations, no doubt recalling God's revelation concerning the work of the third day of creation week. Small wonder that the child Samuel turned out to be a great man of God, playing such a key role in the history of Israel and of the world.

Years later, after Saul had become king, and David had been anointed by Samuel as future king because of Saul's presumptuous acts contrary to God's Word, an intriguing event took place. "The Spirit of the LORD came upon David from that day forward" (1 Sam. 16:13). This, of course, was the same Spirit of God who energized the formless earth following its creation (Gen. 1:2).

"But the Spirit of the LORD departed from Saul, and an evil spirit from the LORD troubled him" (1 Sam. 16:14). How could there be an *evil* spirit from God? Actually, all spirits are from God, for he created them. Furthermore, this is the Bible's first explicit reference to an "evil spirit" as a distinct entity, a person, as it were. Such a concept is common in pagan religions, for their practitioners believe in spirits and often seek to communicate with them, but God's people were forbidden to deal with such, or with the idols with which they are associated.

Nevertheless, evil spirits were all originally created by God, and we should remember that they were called "sons of God" in Genesis 6:2, 4. Even though they are in perpetual rebellion against God, they are still subject to his control. Thus, the "evil spirit from the LORD" that came upon Saul may well have been sent by Satan, either to destroy God's current king or to use him to destroy David, the future king. If so, God allowed it (just as he allowed Satan to attack Job), in order to accomplish his own greater purposes. In any case, the evil spirit was from the Lord, either in the sense that he was originally created by God or else in the sense that God allowed Satan to send him.

David's encounter with the giant Goliath, who was over nine feet tall, reminds us of the pre-flood demon invasion and of the note that "there were giants in the earth in those days; and also after that" (Gen. 6:4). There were giants in the land of Canaan when Moses sent the spies into the land (Num. 13:33), and Og, the Amorite king of Bashan was "of the remnant of giants" (Deut. 3:11). The giants that were among the Anakim and other tribes (Deut. 2:20, 21) were driven out by Caleb (Josh. 14:12, 14). Yet, some four hundred years later, there was still at least one family of demon-controlled giants in the land, for Goliath had a brother who was also a giant, and there were still other giants remaining (1 Chron. 20:5–8). These were all eventually slain by David and his men—at least, there are no further references to giants in the Scriptures. David's testimony to Goliath just before their battle is noteworthy: "I come to thee in the name of the LORD of hosts, the God of the armies of Israel, whom thou hast defied" (1 Sam. 17:45). Soon, Goliath lay dead on the ground and, not too long after that, so did all the other giants that remained.

There also remained in Israel a remnant of demon-controlled occultists, even though Saul, in obeying the commands of God's law, had attempted to "put away those that had familiar spirits, and the wizards, out of the land" (1 Sam. 28:3). After Samuel's death, when his own circumstances became desperate, Saul went to a woman with a "familiar spirit" and requested that she "bring up" Samuel from the place of departed spirits (*sheol* in Hebrew, *hades* in Greek) to consult with him. Although this was beyond her powers, the LORD himself sent Samuel's spirit back up from its resting place in the heart of the earth to inform Saul that this had been his final sin; he and his sons would be joining him in death and Hades the following day (1 Sam. 28:7–19).

God's ancient promise to Abraham was renewed to David (2 Sam. 7:16). The coming King would not only somehow be the seed of the woman, but also the seed of David. "I will set up thy seed after thee," said God in a night vision to David, "and I will stablish the throne of his kingdom for ever" (2 Sam. 7:12, 13).

In addition to David's physical and spiritual strengths, he was also a gifted writer, under the inspiration of the Holy Spirit, writing most of the psalms in the Book of Psalms. One of these is also included in 2 Samuel as part of the history of his times (2 Samuel 22, essentially the same as Ps. 18). In this psalm are a number of poetic references to God as Creator. David speaks of God as one who "rode upon a cherub, and did fly" (2 Sam. 22:11). The cherubim, of course, were the angelic beings who had been seen at the entrance to the Garden of Eden (Gen. 3:24), and whose likenesses had been placed over the ark of the covenant in the tabernacle (Exod. 37:7–9), in both cases representing access to the divine presence. David's song also speaks of "the channels of the sea" and "the foundations of the world" (v. 16). The uniqueness of Jehovah as the only true God is especially emphasized: "As for God, his way is perfect; the word of the LORD is tried: he is a buckler to all them that trust in him. For who is God, save the LORD?" (2 Sam. 22:31, 32).

Another of David's psalms (Ps. 105) is incorporated in part in the parallel history of 1 Chronicles. This song, included in 1 Chronicles 16:1–36, also acknowledges the unique greatness of the true God. "He is the LORD our God; his judgments are in all the earth. . . . Declare his glory among the heathen; his marvellous works among all nations. . . . he also is to be feared above all gods. For all the gods of the people are idols; but the LORD made the heavens. . . . Let the heavens be glad, and let the earth rejoice: and let men say among the nations, The LORD reigneth. Let the sea roar, and the fulness thereof: let the fields rejoice, and all that is therein. Then shall the trees of the wood sing out at the presence of the LORD, because he cometh to judge the earth" (1 Chron. 16:14, 24–5, 26, 31–33).

There is another explicit reference to Satan by name, in the account of David's sin in taking a census of his people to ascertain a human measure of his potential military might (1 Chron. 21:1). Except for the unique references in the book of Job, as already noted, this is the first mention of Satan by name in the Bible, and it shows clearly that the old serpent of Eden was still actively working behind the scenes, in the hearts of men, to thwart God's purposes. In David's case, Satan apparently could not trust the work of an inferior demon, but took it directly upon himself to cause David to bring God's heavy judgment upon his nation.

David's last great work was to make all the preparations for his son Solomon to build the temple in Jerusalem. His prayer of thanksgiving, as he turned the throne over to Solomon, contains this significant ascription: "Thine, O LORD, is the greatness, and the power, and the glory, and the victory, and the majesty: for all that is in the heaven and in the earth is thine: thine is the kingdom, O LORD, and thou art exalted as head above all" (1 Chron. 29:11).

Then, when Solomon had built the temple, he placed the ark of the covenant, with the overspreading cherubim, in the "most holy place" (1 Kings 8:6). Then a most solemn event occurred, symbolizing the greatness and significance of the occasion. "There was nothing in the ark save the two tables of stone, which Moses put there at Horeb [these contained the divinely handwritten listing of the Ten Commandments, including the statement of the primeval six-day creation of all things]. . . . And it came to pass, when the priests were come out of the holy place, that the cloud filled the house of the LORD. . . . for the glory of the LORD had filled the house of the LORD" (1 Kings 8:9–11; see also 1 Chron. 5:7, 10, 14).

In Solomon's great prayer of dedication of the temple, he again acknowledged God as Creator. "LORD God of Israel, there is no God like thee, in heaven above, or on earth beneath. . . . But will God indeed dwell on the earth? behold, the heaven and heaven of heavens cannot contain thee; how much less this house that I have builded?" (1 Kings 8:23, 27). The conclusion of his prayer confirmed that his goal was "that all the people of the earth may know that the LORD is God, and that there is none else" (1 Kings 8:60). Note also the parallel account of Solomon's prayer in 2 Chronicles 6 (especially verses 14 and 18), where the same ascriptions are recorded.

The Divided Kingdom

The great kingdom of David and Solomon, extending for a very brief time over the geographical range originally promised by God to Abraham, soon broke up into two kingdoms after Solomon died. Again we see cycles of apostasy and revival in the kingdom of Judah and Benjamin, ruled by descendants of David. In the northern ten-tribe kingdom of Israel, however, there is almost unbroken apostasy. Nevertheless, there are occasional glimpses of true faith, even in the northern kingdom.

In Judah, Solomon's heart had been partially turned to paganism by his many pagan wives; then under Rehoboam his son, the land descended into full-blown apostasy. "[Judah] built them high places, and images, and groves, on every high hill, and under every green tree. And there were also sodomites in the land: and they did according to all the abominations of the nations which the LORD cast out before the children of Israel" (1 Kings 14:23, 24). These were the trappings of the same old nature gods and evolutionary occultism which had radiated from Babel with the dispersion over thirteen centuries earlier, and these practices repeatedly plagued the children of Israel until the Lord finally sent them into captivity.

The deep apostasy in the northern kingdom was lightened only by the prophetic ministry of Elijah and Elisha, and the Lord did perform many miracles of true creation accompanying their ministries. Among those were the continual creation of meal and oil in the home of the widow of Zarephath where Elijah was staying (1 Kings 17:16), the restoration of the widow's son to life (1 Kings 17:22), the fire from heaven at the confrontation of Elijah with priests of Baal (1 Kings 18:38), the creation of a large amount of oil for the widow who called on Elisha (2 Kings 4:6), the restoration of the Shunammite woman's son (2 Kings 4:35), the healing of Naaman's leprosy (1 Kings 5:14), and the miraculous floating of the iron axehead (2 Kings 6:6).

Especially significant was the translation of Elijah into heaven in a chariot of fire (2 Kings 2:11). Long before, the great antediluvian prophet Enoch had also been translated into heaven without dying (Gen. 5:24). He and Elijah evidently remain in heaven to this very day, still in their natural flesh, supernaturally preserved from decay and death, awaiting a future ministry.

Another prophet in Israel, Micaiah, was given a special vision of heaven, while giving a prophecy against wicked King Ahab. "I saw the LORD sitting on his throne, and all the host of heaven standing by him on his right hand and on his left . . . And there came forth a spirit. . . . And he said, I will go forth, and I will be a lying spirit in the mouth of all [Ahab's] prophets. . . . Now therefore, behold, the LORD hath put a lying spirit in the mouth of all these thy prophets, and the LORD hath spoken evil concerning thee" (1 Kings 22:19, 21–23).

This vision provides an amazing insight into the heavenly counsels, supplementing that received in the Book of Job. "My spirit shall not always strive with man," God had said, back in the days of violence and corruption before the flood (Gen. 6:3).

Concerning the wicked Pharaoh in the days of the Exodus, God said, "I will harden his heart" (Exod. 4:21). Now here we see God sending a spirit to mislead the false prophets of Ahab, in order to lead that wicked king (with whom God would strive no longer, just as with Pharaoh) to his doom. The same story is repeated in 2 Chronicles 18:4–27.

As we know from the account in Job, Satan and the rebellious angels still have access to God's presence on occasion, and God on occasion allows them to test his own people on earth, as in the case of Job. Satan also desires that unbelievers die while still in unbelief, in order to avoid their possible repentance and salvation. We learn here that, when such a person goes too far in his rebellion against God, the Lord may allow one of Satan's demonic spirits to lead him into a situation which will bring about his death. This is a very sobering passage.

Eventually the entire nation of Israel went so deeply into idolatrous evolutionary occultism that the Lord gave them up into captivity in Assyria, probably the most wicked and cruel nation in all the world at that time. God had repeatedly sent prophets to call the Israelites back to the truth, but they refused. "They would not hear, but hardened their necks. . . . And they left all the commandments of the LORD their God, and made them molten images, . . . and worshipped all the host of heaven, and served Baal. And they caused their sons and their daughters to pass through the fire, and used divination and enchantments, and sold themselves to do evil in the sight of the LORD, to provoke him in anger. . . . the LORD removed Israel out of his sight, as he had said by all his servants the prophets. So was Israel carried away out of their own land to Assyria unto this day" (2 Kings 17:14, 16, 17, 23).

In the nation of Judah, the history was more favorable, for there were several periods of revival and true worship. Good King Asa was a godly man in most ways, but did compromise with the pagan Syrians. The prophet Hanani rebuked him with words that remind us of God's omnipresence and omniscience. "For the eyes of the LORD run to and fro throughout the whole earth, to shew himself strong in the behalf of them whose heart is perfect toward him" (2 Chron. 16:9).

Another good king, Jehoshaphat, openly prayed before his people to the God of creation, saying: "O LORD God of our fathers, art not thou God in heaven? and rulest not thou over all the kingdoms of the heathen? and in thine hand is there not power and might, so that none is able to withstand thee?" (2 Chron. 20:6).

Hezekiah, certainly one of the best of all the kings of Judah after David, was reigning when the ten tribes of the northern kingdom were carried captive into Assyria. At that time, the Assyrian armies thought to capture Judah as well, and besieged Jerusalem. The Assyrians argued that Judah's God could not save them, since the gods of the other nations had all been helpless before the invading Assyrian host. But Hezekiah knew that his God was the true God, so he prayed thus: "O LORD God of Israel, which dwellest between the cherubims, thou art the God, even thou alone, of all the kingdoms of the earth; thou hast made heaven and earth. LORD, bow down thine ear . . . and hear the words of Sennacherib, which hath sent him to reproach the living God. Of a truth, LORD, the kings of Assyria have destroyed the nations and their lands, and have cast their gods into the fire: for they were no gods, but the work of men's hands. . . . . Now therefore, O LORD our God, I beseech thee, save thou us out of his hand, that all the kingdoms of the earth may know that thou art the LORD God, even thou only"(2 Kings 19:15–19).

God did, indeed, answer Hezekiah's prayer in a most spectacular way. "The angel of the LORD went out, and smote in the camp of the Assyrians an hundred fourscore and five thousand: and when they arose early in the morning, behold, they were all dead corpses" (2 Kings 19:35). If God can create heaven and earth, he can certainly take care of the army of a pagan, God-rejecting king.

Another great miracle of creation occurred in Hezekiah's reign. In answer to his prayer for healing, God did heal him and then gave him a remarkable sign. "Isaiah the prophet cried unto the LORD: and he brought the shadow [that is, on the sun dial] ten degrees backward, by which it had gone down in the dial of Ahaz" (2 Kings 20:11). Whether the Lord actually reversed the earth's rotation for a time, or whether He somehow miraculously just reversed the direction of the shadow, we are not told. Either would require a miracle of creation, and only the Creator could accomplish it in any case.

The kings following Hezekiah—Manasseh and Amon—were vile kings, and the fifty-seven years under their reigns saw the whole nation degenerate into flagrant apostasy and wickedness, so that God would eventually have to send Judah into exile, too. However, there was one more good king, Josiah, and he led in a great revival, mainly resulting from the discovery in the temple of a copy of the long-forgotten Scriptures. After reading the Word to all the people, King Josiah embarked on a thorough cleansing of the land. "He brake down the houses of the sodomites." "Moreover the workers with familiar spirits, and the wizards, and the images, and the idols, and all the abominations that were spied in the land of Judah and in Jerusalem, did Josiah put away, that he might perform the words of the law which were written in the book that Hilkiah the priest found in the house of the LORD" (2 Kings 23:7, 24).

After Josiah, however, the nation again went into such apostasy that the Lord finally had to send them also into captivity—this time to Babylon, under King Nebuchadnezzar. "They mocked the messengers of God, and despised his words, and misused his prophets, until the wrath of the LORD arose against his people, till there was no remedy" (2 Chron. 36:16), and God sent them far away from their promised land.

There is one other important confirmation of the primeval records here in these historical books. The first nine chapters of the Book of 1 Chronicles consist of extensive lists of genealogical records, extending all the way from the first man, Adam, down to Zedekiah, the last king of Judah before the captivity.

The significant aspect of these genealogies for our purposes in this book is that the genealogy from Adam to Abraham (1 Chron. 1:1–27) is exactly the same as in Genesis 5 and 11. Furthermore, the names in the Table of Nations (Gen. 10)—the posterity of Japheth, Ham, and Shem—are the same here in the Chronicles lists.

Whoever the scribe may have been that originally penned these chapters in Chronicles, it is obvious that he had absolute confidence in the historical accuracy of the Genesis record. At the very least, this scribe (perhaps Ezra, as many surmise) was a careful and meticulous scholar, as is evident from the detailed compilations of old records he searched out and assembled into the two books of Chronicles.

Furthermore, for those who believe in the divine inspiration of the Scriptures, the fact that the same list appears twice, by divine intent, is strong confirmation that the genealogy is both correct and complete. Thus, there is no real *biblical* justification for trying to find gaps therein to accommodate a greater longevity for the human race. The genealogies should be taken and believed just as they are.

7

Creation in the Works of David and Solomon

Reflections of the Creation in the Psalms

There are many references to creation and the other events of primeval history, often in poetic terminology, in the Book of Psalms. The first of the creation psalms deals with man's creation and his dominion mandate, as recorded in Genesis 1:26–28. This is the majestic 8th psalm.

"O LORD our Lord, how excellent is thy name in all the earth! who hast set thy glory above the heavens" (Ps. 8:1). The infinite space of the heavens was created by God (Gen. 1:1): therefore, his glory is even greater. With respect to the earth and man, the psalm reveals a remarkable understanding of the tremendous extent of space. "When I consider thy heavens, the work of thy fingers, the moon and the stars, which thou hast ordained; What is man, that thou art mindful of him" (Ps. 8:3, 4). But then comes a reference to the dominion mandate. "Thou madest him to have dominion over the works of thy hands; thou hast put all things under his feet: all sheep and oxen, yea, and the beasts of the field; the fowl of the air, and the fish of the sea, and whatsoever passeth through the paths of the seas" (Ps. 8:6–8).

It is significant that this first great commandment of God is still in effect. The choosing of Israel did not remove this primeval commandment from the responsibility of all mankind. In fact, the mention of

91

"paths of the seas" inspired the "father of oceanography," Matthew Maury, to develop his epochal charts of submarine hydrography, in a remarkable example of carrying out the dominion mandate by a godly Christian creationist.

Next, the 19th psalm (Ps. 18 has already been discussed) is one of the most familiar songs of creation in the Bible. Its first verse is a commentary, in a sense, on the creating of the sun, moon and stars as "signs" (Gen. 1:14). "The heavens declare the glory of God." Even though "there is no speech nor language," nevertheless "their line [that is, their measuring line] is gone out through all the earth" (vv. 3–4). The testimony of creation, the Creator, and his purpose in the creation can be seen everywhere, in all ages, both revealing God and condemning those who refuse his witness.

The greatest of the "signs" in the heavens is the glorious sun itself, which provides light and life (in the physical sense) to the world. All of earth's processes derive their energy from the sun, directly or indirectly. It "going forth"—that is, the radiations going forth from its surface to provide life-sustaining energy to the earth and all its inhabitants—proceeds without ceasing everywhere the sun travels. And its itinerary is literally "from the end of the heaven, and his circuit unto the ends of it," as it traverses the enormous circuit around the center of the great Milky Way galaxy. Thus, "there is nothing hid from the heat thereof" (vv. 4–6).

Some may object and say that the sun doesn't move at all, it merely *seems* to move as the earth rotates on its axis daily and orbits the sun annually. But it *does* move, amidst the other stars, in a gigantic orbit through the Milky Way. Furthermore, it is perfectly legitimate to speak of the *relative* daily motion of the sun with respect to the earth. No one knows where the fixed center of the cosmos may be; therefore, all motions really should be stated as *relative* motions, with the reference point of zero motion being located at such a point that the equations describing its motions are simplest. It is thus not only legitimate, but scientifically preferable, to assume the sun moves around the earth each day, and among the zodiacal constellations each year. The sun was created to "give light upon the earth" (Gen. 1:15), and this it does, day after day and year after year—not only visible light, but all the earth-sustaining energies of the electromagnetic spectrum of forces.

Another great creation psalm is Psalm 24. "The earth is the LORD's, and the fulness thereof; the world, and they that dwell therein. For he hath founded it upon the seas, and established it upon the floods" (vv. 1, 2). God reminds us that, although he has given man dominion over the earth, it still belongs to him. Man is God's steward, not his replacement. God has created it and established it forever. The phrases "upon the seas" and "upon the floods" could be read more properly as "above the seas" and "above the floods." Although there is enough water in the earth to overwhelm it, God has permanently established it *above* the seas and *above* the flooding rivers. This was his promise to Noah, later repeated to Job (Gen. 9:11; Job 38:8, 11), and here confirmed again through David.

Next comes Psalm 33, with the strongest, most unequivocal statement of fiat creation in the Bible. "By the word of the LORD were the heavens made; and all the host of them by the breath of his mouth. . . . For he spake, and it was done; he commanded, and it stood fast" (vv. 6, 9). If anyone should try to distort the Genesis creation account into a record of slow processes over long ages, this clear affirmation of instantaneous creation would decisively refute any such notion. All the hosts of the heavens were simply called into being, fully functioning in their intended ministries, by the omnipotent word of the Creator.

There is also a reference to other events of creation week. "For the word of the LORD is right; and all his works are done in truth. . . . the earth is full of the goodness of the LORD. . . . He gathereth the waters of the sea together as an heap: he layeth up the depth [same word as "deep"] in storehouses" (vv. 33:4, 5, 7).

Then the psalm gives us a fascinating insight into God's concern with the men and women he created. Although he gave them the marvelous ability to produce children of their own, it is still God who forms each soul. "The LORD looketh from heaven; he beholdeth all the sons of men. From the place of his habitation he looketh upon all the inhabitants of the earth. He fashioneth their hearts alike; he considereth all their works" (vv. 13–15).

The fact that the Lord still rules the world, despite the opposition of Satan and despite the stewardship the Lord has given to man, is further indicated in Psalm 50:10–12. "For every beast of the forest is mine, and the cattle upon a thousand hills. I know all the fowls of the mountains: and the wild beasts of the field are mine. If I were hungry, I would not tell thee: for the world is mine, and the fulness thereof." The fact that God is greater than all his creation, rather than being identified with it (as pantheists, both ancient and modern, believe), is stressed twice in the 57th psalm. "Be thou exalted, O God, above the heavens; let thy glory be above all the earth" (vv. 5, 11).

In one of the psalms of Asaph, there is an intriguing reference to the work of creation. "The day is thine, the night also is thine: thou has prepared the light and the sun. Thou hast set all the borders of the earth: thou hast made summer and winter" (Ps. 74:16, 17). God prepared "light" and the sun independently of each other, with light coming first, just as outlined in Genesis 1. The "borders of the earth"—that is, the interfaces between land and sea—were also established by God, both during creation week and then again at new boundaries after the flood. The earth was also set at an angle on its axis, so that regular seasons would ensue.

"The heavens are thine, the earth also is thine: as for the world and the fulness thereof, thou hast founded them. The north and the south thou hast created them" (Ps. 89:11, 12). The above testimony to creation is in a psalm attributed to Ethan the Ezrahite, who also indicated that the sun and moon were created to last forever (Ps. 89:36, 37).

The great psalm of Moses is the next in order to contain a reference to creation. "LORD, thou hast been our dwelling place in all generations. Before the mountains were brought forth, or ever thou hadst formed the earth and the world, even from everlasting to everlasting, thou art God" (Ps. 90:1, 2). Only God—not the universe, as evolutionists believe—is eternal!

In the next psalm, possibly also written by Moses, there is a wonderful reference to the angels of God, in their ministry to those created in God's image. "For he shall give his angels charge over thee, to keep thee in all thy ways. They shall bear thee up in their hands, lest thou dash thy foot against a stone" (Ps. 91:11, 12).

Each of the seven psalms beginning with Psalm 94 contains one or more references to some aspect of God's creation. These testimonies are simply listed below.

He that planted the ear, shall he not hear? He that formed the eye, shall he not see? . . . He that teacheth man knowledge, shall not he know? (Ps. 94:9, 10).

For the LORD is a great God, and a great King above all gods. In his hand are the deep places of the earth: the strength of the hills is his also. The sea is his, and he made it: and his hands formed the dry land. O come, let us worship and bow down: let us kneel before the LORD our maker.

For he is our God; and we are the people of his pasture, and the sheep of his hand (Ps. 95:3–7).

For the LORD is great, and greatly to be praised: he is to be feared above all gods. For all the gods of the nations are idols: but the LORD made the heavens (Ps. 96:4–5).

For thou, LORD, art high above all the earth: thou art exalted far above all gods (Ps. 97:9).

Make a joyful noise unto the LORD, all the earth: make a loud noise, and rejoice, and sing praise. . . . Let the sea roar, and the fulness thereof; the world, and they that dwell therein. Let the floods clap their hands: let the hills be joyful together (Ps. 98:4, 7, 8).

The LORD reigneth; let the people tremble: he sitteth between the cherubims; let the earth be moved (Ps. 99:1).

Know ye that the LORD he is God: it is he that hath made us, and not we ourselves (Ps. 100:3).

One of the greatest psalms of creation—many would say the greatest—is the beautiful 104th psalm. Most of this psalm deals with the flood and the post-flood world, but the opening verses provide marvelous glimpses of creation from the perspective of heaven itself. "O LORD my God, thou art very great; thou art clothed with honour and majesty. Who coverest thyself with light as with a garment: who stretchest out the heavens like a curtain" (vv. 1–2).

Before creating the heavens (i.e., space), and then "stretching it out" (perhaps referring to the expanding universe which astronomers postulate), God first clothed himself, as it were, with "light," in effect entering his newly created universe in a garment of pure energy, as well as honor and majesty. Then, time began with the stretching out of space and the permeating of space and time with divine light.

The next event was the creation of his own heavenly throne room, as it were. "[God] layeth the beams of His chambers in the waters: who maketh the clouds his chariot: who walketh upon the wings of the wind" (Ps. 104:3). A portion of the divine energy was transmuted by its Creator into great waters surrounding his throne and radiating out into space, both liquid water and great banks of clouds. The "wings of the wind" is probably a reference to the vibrating movements of the Spirit in the pervasive presence of the waters. The words for "wind" and "Spirit" are the same in Hebrew, and the word "moved" in Genesis 1:2 is used to describe the fluttering motion of a bird's wings. Thus, Genesis 1:2, 3 effectively says the following: "And the earth material had no form as yet, nor any inhabitants, and there was pervasive darkness in the presence of the deep. And the Spirit of God began vibrating, sending out mighty waves of creating energy, in the presence of the waters. And God said, Let there be light: and there was light."

This also is the message of the psalm. In the mighty waters and clouds, God was moving in the Spirit, beginning his great work of creating and making all things. First, he created an innumerable company of angelic messengers, soon to be dwelling in fiery stars of the heavenly spaces. "[God] maketh his angels spirits; his ministers a flaming fire" (Ps. 104:4). It was in such a pervasive watery and fiery cosmos, therefore, that the angels had their first conscious existence. Small wonder that those angels that later rebelled against God, following Satan, would seek to describe the beginning of the universe as either an eternally existing watery chaos or fiery cosmos, out of which all things had evolved—even including God!

Then—after the initial creation, followed by that of the angels, along with the energizing of the universe with God's light and the structuring of the waters—God "laid the foundations of the earth, that it should not be removed for ever" (Ps. 104:5). This corresponds to the first work of Day Three of creation week, when solid lands congealed out of the pervasive waters, ready to receive a lush and verdant blanket of grass and trees and shrubs.

The remainder of this remarkable psalm deals with the flood and its after-effects. This will be discussed in the next section.

The absolute preeminence of God over all creation is stressed in the following passages:

> The LORD is high above all nations, and his glory above the heavens. Who is like unto the LORD our God, who dwelleth on high, who humbleth himself to behold the things that are in heaven, and in the earth! (Ps. 113:4–6).

> Wherefore should the heathen say, Where is now their God? But our God is in the heavens: he hath done whatsoever he hath pleased. Their idols are silver and gold, the work of men's hands (Ps. 115:2–4).

Ye are blessed of the LORD which made heaven and earth. The heaven, even the heavens, are the LORD's: but the earth hath he given to the children of men (Ps. 115:15, 16).

The last verse is of special significance. It confirms explicitly the revelation in Genesis that it is only the earth that has human inhabitants. The sun and moon and stars (including the planets) were made to give light on the earth and to be for signs and seasons and days and years—not to support various races of "aliens." The only "extraterrestrial" life is that of the angels.

The 119th psalm is the Bible's longest chapter, and almost every verse is a testimony to the Scriptures. Several of these include the remarkable revelation that God's Word actually preceded God's world. Note the following assertions: "For ever, O LORD, thy word is settled in heaven"(Ps. 119:89). "Concerning thy testimonies, I have known of old that thou hast founded them for ever" (v. 152). "Thy word is true from the beginning: and every one of thy righteous judgments endureth for ever" (v. 160).

There are also testimonies to the permanence of the created earth. "Thy faithfulness is unto all generations: thou hast established the earth, and it abideth. They continue this day according to thine ordinances: for all are thy servants" (Ps. 119:90–91).

Consider also the unique revelation that we were fashioned by God specifically to learn His Word. "Thy hands have made me and fashioned me: give me understanding, that I may learn thy commandments" (Ps. 119:73).

The fifteen psalms from 120 through 134 are called "the songs of degrees." These contain three reminders that the Lord made heaven and earth. "My help cometh from the LORD, which made heaven and earth" (Ps. 121:2). "Our help is in the name of the LORD, who made heaven and earth" (Ps. 124:8). "The LORD that made heaven and earth bless thee out of Zion" (Ps. 134:3).

Both the omnipotence of God as Creator and his providential control of his creation are noted in Psalm 135. "For I know that the LORD is great, and that our Lord is above all gods. Whatsoever the LORD pleased, that did he in heaven, and in earth, in the seas, and all deep places. He causeth the vapours to ascend from the ends of the earth; he maketh lightnings for the rain; he bringeth the wind out of his treasuries" (vv. 5–7).

The 136th psalm is a psalm of thanksgiving for the great works of God, beginning in particular with the successive works of creation, and with each of the twenty-six verses ending with the refrain "for his mercy endureth for ever." The verses dealing with the creation are as follows: "O give thanks to the LORD of lords: for his mercy endureth for ever. To him who alone doeth great wonders . . . To him that by wisdom made the heavens . . . To him that stretched out the earth above the waters . . . To him that made great lights . . . the sun to rule by day . . . the moon and stars to rule by night: for his mercy endureth for ever" (vv. 3–9). Note that the psalmist accepted the straightforward account of the creation events in Genesis.

There is tremendous insight into the amazing process of creation of each human being in the 139th psalm. "I will praise thee; for I am fearfully and wonderfully made: marvellous are thy works; and that my soul knoweth right well. My substance was not hid from thee, when I was made in secret, and curiously wrought in the lowest parts of the earth. Thine eyes did see my substance, yet being unperfect; and in thy book all my members were written, which in continuance were fashioned, when as yet there was none of them" (vv. 14–16). Not only did God create the first man and woman; he also created each one of their billions of descendants through the fantastically complex mechanism of human reproduction which he provided.

Finally we come to the grand epilogue of the Book of Psalms, the last five psalms, the Hallelujah psalms, each of which both begins and ends with the great exhortation, "Hallelujah"—"Praise ye the LORD." In the first of these is an assurance that the Creator is the God of absolute truth. "Happy is he that hath the God of Jacob for his help, whose hope is in the LORD his God: which made heaven, and earth, the sea, and all that therein is: which keepeth truth for ever" (Ps. 146:5–6).

The second speaks of his omnipotence and omniscience, as well as his providential care of his creation.

> He telleth the number of the stars; he calleth them all by their names. Great is our LORD, and of great power: his understanding is infinite. . . . who covereth the heaven with clouds, who prepareth rain for the earth, who maketh grass to grow upon the mountains. He giveth to the beast his food, and to the young ravens which cry. . . . He giveth snow like wool: he scattereth the hoarfrost like ashes. He casteth forth his ice like morsels: who can stand before his cold? He sendeth out his word, and

melteth them: he causeth his wind to blow, and the waters flow (Ps. 147:4–5, 8–9, 16–18).

Then, in the 148th psalm, which is the central psalm of the five Hallelujah psalms, there is the uniquely majestic exhortation to the whole creation to praise the Creator.

> Praise ye the LORD. Praise ye the LORD from the heavens: praise him in the heights. Praise ye Him, all His angels: praise ye him, all his hosts. Praise ye him, sun and moon: praise him, all ye stars of light. Praise him, ye heavens of heavens, and ye waters that be above the heavens. Let them praise the LORD: for he commanded, and they were created. He hath also stablished them for ever and ever: he hath made a decree which shall not pass (Ps. 148:1–6).

In these exhortations directed heavenward, there are several key bits of revelation. Although angels are often called stars, and both are called the host of heaven, the two are not identical. Both are exhorted in this psalm, but separately. Note also that the stars are called "stars of light," for their function is to "give light upon the earth" (Gen. 1:15). There is a specific reference to the "waters above the heavens," which seem to be the same as the "waters above the firmament" in the primeval creation (Gen. 1:7). These were evidently precipitated on the earth at the time of the flood, but here they are said to be—along with all the heavenly bodies—"stablished for ever and ever."

Great changes have taken place in the creation, and still more are to come in the prophesied period of judgment, but eventually all must be perfected and restored, for God cannot fail, and he has established the stars and the waters to last for eternity.

And, most significantly, here is another reference to his instantaneous, fiat creation of all things. "He commanded, and they were created." This confirms the assurance of Psalm 33:9 ("He spake, and it was done") and leaves no room whatever for any imaginary age-long "process" of creation.

Then the psalm continues with an exhortation to the earth and to God's living creatures.

> Praise the LORD from the earth, ye dragons [read dinosaurs?], and all deeps: fire, and hail; snow and vapour; stormy wind [perhaps read Spirit?] fulfilling his word: Mountains, and all hills; fruitful trees, and

all cedars: beasts, and all cattle: creeping things, and flying fowl: kings of the earth, and all people; . . . Let them praise the name of the LORD: for his name alone is excellent; his glory is above the earth and heaven (Ps. 148:7–11, 13).

The 149th psalm exhorts "the congregation of saints" to praise the Lord (Ps. 149:1). This probably refers to all the holy angels in the heavenly sanctuary, but may also be a prophetic assembly of all the redeemed people of God gathered with them at God's throne in the end-times.

The final psalm also begins with praise in the heavenly sanctuary, finally spreading out through the whole creation "Praise ye the LORD. Praise God in his sanctuary: praise him in the firmament [read spreading-out expanse] of his power. Praise him for his mighty acts: praise him according to his excellent greatness. . . . Let every thing that hath breath [or the Spirit] praise the LORD" (Ps. 150:1, 2, 6).

The Fall, the Curse, and the Flood

There are, as we have seen, many references in the Book of Psalms to the creation and its implications. In addition, there are also many reflections of the other events of primeval history, especially the introduction and effects of sin and the curse, as well as the great flood.

The 18th psalm describes a scene of terrible judgment and destruction in the earth. It is not explicit in the context whether the judgment is past or future, but the words used, whether intentionally or unintentionally, could surely reflect the thoughts and observations of the ancient patriarch Noah, as the flood was breaking on the earth. Therefore, try reading these passages in that sense.

> The sorrows of death compassed me, and the floods of ungodly men made me afraid. . . . Then the earth shook and trembled: the foundations also of the hills moved and were shaken, because he was wroth. There went up a smoke out of his nostrils, and fire out of his mouth devoured: coals were kindled by it. He bowed the heavens also, and came down: and darkness was under his feet. And he rode upon a cherub, and did fly: yea, he did fly upon the wings of the wind. He made darkness his secret place; his pavilion round about him were dark waters and thick clouds of the skies. . . . The LORD also thundered in the heavens, and the Highest gave his voice, . . . Then the channels of waters were seen, and the foundations of the world were discovered at thy rebuke,

O LORD. . . . He sent from above, he took me, he drew me out of many waters. . . . He brought me forth also into a large place; he delivered me, because he delighted in me (Ps. 18:4, 7–11, 13, 15, 16, 19).

This psalm was written by David, during the time of his persecution by Saul, but the Lord seems to have given David assurance of his own deliverance by means of a vision which translated him back in time to "experience," as it were, the far more dangerous time of Noah and the Lord's mighty intervention on behalf of his people then.

This is still more evident in the 29th psalm, in which the scene depicted is specifically said to be at the time when "the LORD sitteth upon the flood" (Ps. 29:10). Here, "flood" is the Hebrew *mabbul*, a word used exclusively for the great flood, as mentioned repeatedly in Genesis 6–9, but never used elsewhere in the Bible except right here. This psalm also was written by David, perhaps while viewing a great storm blowing in from the Mediterranean, but then somehow translated in vision back to the vastly greater storm experienced by Noah. Thus, this psalm, featuring "the voice of the LORD"—a phrase occurring seven times—should be read in that light, as a description of the phenomena associated with the flood. A verse-by-verse exposition is available in a commentary by the writer,[1] but note some of the high points here.

First, the angelic hosts in the beautiful heavenly sanctuary are exhorted to ascribe unto the Lord all glory and strength, probably in view of the lawless activity of the rebellious "sons of God" (Genesis 6:2, 4) on earth. "Give unto the LORD, O ye mighty [here the Hebrew is actually *bene el*, or sons of God], . . . the glory due unto his name; worship the LORD in the beauty of holiness [that is, the beautiful sanctuary]" (Ps. 29:1, 2).

Next, "the voice of the LORD is upon . . . many waters" (v. 3). The psalm goes on to describe, after this onset of the flood waters, the uprooting of mighty forests, like the great cedar forests of Lebanon with which David was familiar, then the eroding and dissolution of the mighty hills themselves, interspersed with erupting volcanic fires and floods from the great deep (vv. 4–7).

Then the emergence of the barren wilderness of the post-flood world is noted in verses 8-9, under the figure of a woman giving birth. "The voice of the LORD shaketh [the word here is that for a woman shaking with travail pains] the wilderness." Then, the same mighty "voice" makes the emerging animals to begin to "calve" (same word), so the lands will again be stocked with animal life, and "discovereth [that is, brings out] the forests." Thus the devastated world will gradually come to maintain plant and animal life once more, though not in the lush abundance of the antediluvian creation.

Thereupon, "in his temple doth every one speak of his glory," because "the LORD sitteth upon the flood; yea, the LORD sitteth King for ever" (vv. 9, 10).

A somewhat similar scene is encountered in Psalm 46, with the terminology, at least, reflecting the events of the great flood, and possibly also foreseeing a future judgment as well. "God is our refuge and strength, a very present help in trouble. Therefore will not we fear, though the earth be removed, and though the mountains be carried into the midst of the sea; though the waters thereof roar and be troubled, though the mountains shake with the swelling thereof. Selah" (Ps. 46:1–3).

Then there is the 74th psalm, which also has a section applicable to the great flood and its later retreat. "For God is my king of old, working salvation in the midst of the earth. Thou didst divide the sea by thy strength. . . . Thou brakest the heads of leviathan in pieces, and gavest him to be meat to the people inhabiting the wilderness. Thou didst cleave the fountain and the flood: thou driedst up mighty rivers" (Ps. 74:12–15). As noted before, the terms "dragon" and "leviathan" are used synonymously and probably refer to marine dinosaurs.

Similar intimations of the flood can be spotted also in Psalm 89.

> And the heavens shall praise thy wonders, O LORD: thy faithfulness also in the congregation of the saints [or holy ones]. For who in the heaven can be compared unto the LORD? who among the sons of the mighty [here, again, is the Hebrew phrase *bene el,* or sons of God, reminding us of the rebellious "sons of God" in Genesis 6:2, 4] can be likened unto the LORD? [Satan thought *he* could!] God is greatly to be feared in the assembly of the saints . . . . Thou rulest the raging of the sea: when the waters thereof arise, thou stillest them (Ps. 89:5–7, 9).

In Psalm 90, the great psalm of Moses, there is a reference to the great curse on the earth because of man's sin, then to the antediluvian longevity, then to the flood. "Thou turnest man to destruction [or dust]; and sayest, Return, ye children of men. For a thousand years [that is, the approximate life span of men before the flood] are but as yesterday when it is past, and as a watch in the night. Thou carriest them away as with a flood" (Ps. 90:3–5).

Psalm 91, perhaps also written by Moses, contains an allusion to the protevangelic promise of the ultimate destruction of Satan by the promised Redeemer. "Thou shalt tread upon the lion and adder: the young lion and the dragon shalt thou trample under feet" (Ps. 91:13).

The 102nd psalm refers both to the primeval creation and then to the decay principle (now recognized as the universal scientific law of increasing entropy, or decay). "My days are like a shadow that declineth; and I am withered like grass. But thou, O LORD, shalt endure for ever. . . . Of old hast thou laid the foundation of the earth: and the heavens are the work of thy hands. They shall perish, but thou shalt endure: yea, all of them shall wax old like a garment; as a vesture shalt thou change them, and they shall be changed: but thou art the same, and thy years shall have no end" (Ps. 102:11–12; 25–27).

The curse and the decay law are also mentioned in the next psalm. "For he knoweth our frame; he remembereth that we are dust. As for man, his days are as grass: as a flower of the field, so he flourisheth. For the wind passeth over it, and it is gone; and the place thereof shall know it no more. But the mercy of the LORD is from everlasting to everlasting upon them that fear him" (Ps. 103:14–17). In this psalm also is an important testimony to the service of the holy angels. "The LORD hath prepared his throne in the heavens; and his kingdom ruleth over all. Bless the LORD, ye his angels, that excel in strength, that do his commandments, hearkening unto the voice of his word. Bless ye the LORD, all ye his hosts; ye ministers of his, that do his pleasure" (Ps. 103:19–21).

Now we come back again to Psalm 104. We have already noted the significance of this psalm in our understanding of creation; now we find it is equally important in its information about the flood. Speaking of the earth at the flood's climax, the psalmist (unknown in identity, but somehow reflecting what must originally have been revealed to Noah or Shem or another ancient patriarch) says:

> Thou coveredst [the earth] with the deep as with a garment: the waters stood above the mountains. At thy rebuke they fled; at the voice of thy thunder they hasted away. They go up by the mountains; they go down by the valleys [or, better, they go up with the mountains; they go down with the valleys] unto the place which thou hast founded for them. Thou hast set a bound that they may not pass over; that they turn not again to cover the earth (Ps. 104:6–9).

The awesome picture is one of worldwide orogeny, with mountains rising up out of the flood waters, and corresponding basins opening up to receive the waters off the mountain slopes, with the waters eventually coming to rest in permanent ocean basins that will hold them within their boundaries as long as the earth remains, as God promised Noah (Gen. 8:21–22; 9:11–17). Whether this tremendous readjustment of the earth's surface was accomplished by purely miraculous forces or by providentially controlled geophysical forces in the earth's crust, we are not told. But this passage does answer the frequent question as to what happened to the waters of the earth-covering flood.

The rest of Psalm 104 is a beautiful outline of God's provision for the inhabitants of the post-flood world, both man and beast. The waters were eventually cleansed by filtration through the recently deposited sediments, because we are told that God "sendeth the springs into the valleys, which run among the hills. They give drink to every beast of the field" (vv. 10, 11). A new hydrologic cycle was established: "He watereth the hills from his chambers" (v. 13). Grass and trees soon were growing on the lands (vv. 14, 16) and all the marine animals were fed as well (vv. 27, 28). Volcanic and tectonic activity continued after the flood (v. 32), though with decreasing intensity, and the whole world gradually assumed its post-flood structure and activity. The psalm closes with an imprecation reminiscent of God's purpose in sending the flood. "Let the sinners be consumed out of the earth, and let the wicked be no more. Bless thou the LORD, O my soul. Praise ye the LORD" (v. 35).

There seems also to be a glimpse back at the aftermath of the flood in Psalm 65.

> [God] by his strength setteth fast the mountains . . . which stilleth the noise of the seas, the noise of their waves, and the tumult of the people. . . . thou makest the outgoings of the morning and evening to rejoice. Thou visitest the earth, and waterest it: thou greatly enrichest it with the river of God, which is full of water: thou preparest them corn. . . . Thou waterest the ridges thereof abundantly . . . thou blesseth the springing thereof. Thou crownest the year with thy goodness; and thy paths drop fatness. They drop upon the pastures of the wilderness: and the little hills rejoice on every side (Ps. 65:6–12).

We have now reviewed briefly some of the more explicit commentaries on creation and the flood that are found in the beautiful Book of Psalms. In a more pervasive sense, the entire book is a testimony of man as sinner by both birth and practice and of God as omnipotent Creator, loving Redeemer, and fearful Judge.

Creation in the Books of Wisdom

Solomon, the son and successor of David, "passed all the kings of the earth in riches and wisdom" (2 Chron. 9:22), and he was responsible, under God, for three Bible books that focus especially on true wisdom—Proverbs, Ecclesiastes, and Song of Solomon. There are certain key references to creation in these books, and we shall examine these in this section.

The first is Proverbs 3:18–20. Speaking of the divine wisdom, Solomon says: "She is a tree of life to them that lay hold upon her: and happy is every one that retaineth her. The LORD by wisdom hath founded the earth; by understanding hath he established the heavens. By his knowledge the depths are broken up, and the clouds drop down the dew." True wisdom, like the tree of life in Eden's garden, yields eternal life to those who partake of it, for this Wisdom is the very Creator himself!

There are three other symbolic references to the tree of life and its (his!) virtues in Proverbs. These are as follows: "The fruit of the righteous is a tree of life: and he that winneth souls is wise" (Prov. 11:30). "Hope deferred maketh the heart sick: but when the desire cometh, it is a tree of life" (Prov. 13:12). "A wholesome tongue is a tree of life: but perverseness therein is a breach in the spirit" (Prov. 15:4).

The most extensive exposition of creation in the writings of Solomon is in the remarkable eighth chapter of Proverbs, where Wisdom is again personified as the divine agent of creation. Here, Wisdom possesses all the attributes of God—notably that of eternal preexistence—yet is somehow distinct in its (his) own right. Just as in the creation record of Genesis, there is the intimation that God is somehow one God, yet more than one in manifestation.

The LORD possessed me in the beginning of his way, before his works of old. I was set up from everlasting, from the beginning, or ever the earth was. When there were no depths, I was brought forth; when there were no fountains abounding with water. Before the mountains were settled, before the hills was I brought forth. While as yet he had not made the earth, nor the fields, nor the highest part of the dust of the world. When he prepared the heavens, I was there: when he set a compass upon the face of the depth: when he established the clouds above: when he strengthened the fountains of the deep: When he gave to the sea his decree, that the waters should not pass his commandment: when he appointed the foundations of the earth: Then I was by him, as one brought up with him: and I was daily his delight, rejoicing always before him; Rejoicing in the habitable part of his earth: and my delights were with the sons of men (vv. 22–31).

This amazing passage follows the same order of the events of creation as in Genesis 1, yet yields many new insights to that foundational chapter. Note that the speaker, Wisdom, was "from everlasting, from the beginning" an attribute which can only be true of God. Yet in some mysterious way, Wisdom was "brought forth," and this divine "birth" was before anything was ever created. Wisdom is thus both God and also the eternally "begotten" Son of God!

The word "depth" is the same as "deep," both referring to the primeval deep (Gen. 1:2), which comprised the original matrix of all matter. Then God "prepared the heavens," "made the earth" and even "the highest part of the dust of the world," a reservoir of matter consisting of the same elements as the earth matter, but spreading out infinitely high above earth to fill all the prepared heavens with stars and other bodies in the heavens.

God then "set a compass upon the face of the depth," where the Hebrew word for "compass" means, simply, "sphericity." That is, gravitational forces were activated, and the waters of the earth came together as a great sphere. Presumably, this command also brought together "the highest part of the dust [or elements] of the world" to coalesce into innumerable stars and galaxies throughout space. The Hebrew word for "highest part" is *rosh*, a word meaning "chief" or "greatest." Then he "established the clouds above" (that is, the "waters above the firmament," where the Hebrew word for "clouds" actually favors the concept of vapors, or very small particles of water), and "strengthened the fountains of the deep" (that is, the "waters below the firmament," to be controlled by reservoirs leading through conduits to fountains, through which water could be provided for the land surfaces). These would become "fountains abounding with water," providing abundantly for the needs of the plants, animals, and people on earth's surface.

Next, God "appointed the foundations of the earth" and caused land surfaces to emerge out of the waters to rest upon these foundations, establishing fixed "seas" for the waters to settle in. The strengthened "fountains of the deep" would, much later, be cleaved open through these foundations of the lands to pour out the great flood upon the earth.

Finally, after the creation of human beings, God testifies that he was "rejoicing in the habitable part of his earth" and that his delights were with the "sons of men." The word "men" here is actually *Adam*. His creation was "very good," and he could rejoice in prospect with all the future "sons of Adam," to whom he had given instructions to "multiply, and replenish the earth" (Gen. 1:28), thereby expanding the "habitable part of [the] earth" as they were to carry out the great dominion mandate.

Then, however, this divine Wisdom, the eternal Son of God, must warn those in whom He delighted. Paralleling the account of the divine warning in Genesis 2:16, 17, the chapter concludes as follows: "Now therefore hearken unto me, O ye children: for blessed are they that keep my ways. Hear instruction, and be wise, and refuse it not. Blessed is the man that heareth me, watching daily at my gates, waiting at the posts of my doors. For whoso findeth me findeth life, and shall obtain favour of the LORD. But he that sinneth against me wrongeth his own soul: all they that hate me love death" (vv. 32–36).

This divine warning and choice, given first in substance to God's first two "children," is essentially the same choice and warning given to all his subsequent children. In the true Wisdom, the Son of God, is life and favor; to all who refuse his Word, sinning against God, there is death and a lost soul.

An even more explicit reference to the Son of God is given in Proverbs 30:4: "Who hath ascended up into heaven, or descended? who hath gathered the wind in his fists? who hath bound the waters in a garment? who hath established all the ends of the earth? what is his name, and what is his son's name, if thou canst tell?" The answer to these rhetorical questions about the creation can only be God and his Word, the divine Wisdom whose delights are with the children of Adam.

It is significant that one of the strongest testimonies to the inerrant and complete authority of the Word of God is given in the two succeeding verses. "Every word of God is pure: he is a shield unto them that put their trust in him. Add thou not unto his words, lest he reprove thee, and thou be found a liar" (Prov. 30:5, 6). When Satan added to God's words as he tempted Eve, he became the father of all liars, and this also becomes the real root of every human sin. It is a mortal danger to delete, supplement, or destroy any part of the pure Word of God.

Solomon's Book of Ecclesiastes opens with the observation that "one generation passeth away, and another generation cometh: but the earth abideth for ever" (Eccles. 1:4). This seems to reflect the chronicle of the successive generations of patriarchs in Genesis 5 and 11, while noting that God does not fail and, therefore, his created earth "abide for ever." This assurance is further expounded in Ecclesiastes 3:14: "I know that, whatsoever God doeth, it shall be for ever: nothing can be put to it, nor any thing taken from it: and God doeth it, that men should fear before him." This striking verse actually anticipates the great principle of energy conservation, which states that "energy" (which actually comprises every system of matter and every process of operation in the physical universe) can be neither created nor destroyed. The only way of accounting for the infinite reservoirs of energy in the universe is that "God doeth it."

A dominant theme in Ecclesiastes is that all human wisdom and self-directed effort are "vanity and vexation of spirit" (Eccles. 1:14). Many individual passages, as well as the book as a whole, reflect the primeval curse on man and his dominion because of sin (Gen. 3:17–19). A typical example is the following: "For what hath man of all his labour, and of the vexation of his heart, wherein he hath laboured under the sun? For all his days are sorrows, and his travail grief" (Eccles. 2:22, 23). The decay principle enunciated in the curse is noted in Ecclesiastes 3:20: "All go unto one place; all are of the dust, and all turn to dust again." This clearly reflects God's words to Adam: "In the sweat of thy face shalt thou eat bread, till thou return unto the ground; for out of it wast thou taken: for dust thou art, and unto dust shalt thou return" (Gen. 3:19). "God hath made man upright; but they have sought out many inventions" (Eccles. 7:29).

The last chapter of Ecclesiastes begins with the wise admonition to the young, needed now as never before: "Remember now thy Creator in the days of thy youth" (Eccles. 12:1). For everyone, living under the curse of sin and death, must eventually decline in strength and finally die, and return to the dust, just as God had told Adam. "Then shall the dust return to the earth as it was: and the spirit shall return unto God who gave it" (Eccles. 12:7). Thus "the whole duty of man" is to "fear God, and keep his commandments" (Eccles. 12:13).

The Song of Solomon, or Canticles, stresses love rather than wisdom, in a setting of human marital love, no doubt typifying the redemptive love of God and his redeemed ones. Solomon must have sensed, if he did not know by revelation, that no man could really keep all God's commandments, though that was, indeed, man's whole duty. Therefore the love of God (who *is* Love, as well as Wisdom) must seek and find and restore his lost children. This is the underlying theme of Solomon's Song.

There seems, symbolically, to be first a recollection of the primal delights of Eden: "As the apple tree among the trees of the wood, so is my beloved among the sons. I sat down under his shadow with great delight, and his fruit was sweet to my taste" (Song of Sol. 2:3). But then the fellowship was broken, and the bridegroom had to prepare a way to restore his lost bride, while she, in turn, tried futilely to find him on her own. "My soul failed when he spake: I sought him, but I could not find him" (Song of Sol. 5:6). Adam and Eve hid when they, in their sin, heard the voice of God, and God was no longer their delight, but their judge.

When they recognized that they had been deceived by the forbidden fruit of worldly wisdom and human pleasure, they turned again to God, who was waiting for them with garments of righteousness, provided by him. Similarly, when the bride turned only to him, acknowledging her bridegroom as the "chiefest among ten thousand" and "altogether lovely" (Song of Sol. 5:10, 16), then their loving fellowship was restored.

8

Creation and the Major Prophets

The Witness of Isaiah

In chapter 6 we noted the references to creation and other ancient events of earth history that had been included in the books of Israel's history, from the times of Joshua until the Assyrian and Babylonian captivities. During the period of the kings, in particular, God raised up many prophets, who tried to call the people back to God during times of apostasy and also to prophesy concerning things to come. Although their main concern was the present and the future, they did occasionally insert important references to the primeval world, obviously assuming the reality of the one God of creation and the historical reality of the events described in the early chapters of Genesis.

This is particularly true of the first of the major prophets, Isaiah, who wrote during the reigns of four kings of Judah—Uzziah, Jotham, Ahaz, and Hezekiah. In his sixth chapter, we are introduced to a remarkable scene at God's throne room in the heavens, as seen by Isaiah in a great vision. "In the year that king Uzziah died I saw also the LORD sitting upon a throne, high and lifted up, and his train filled the temple. Above it stood the seraphims: each one had six wings; with twain he covered his face, and with twain he covered his feet, and with twain he did fly.

And one cried unto another, and said, Holy, holy, holy, is the LORD of hosts: the whole earth is full of his glory" (Isa. 6:1–3).

This is the only reference in the Bible to the angelic beings called seraphim. On the other hand, cherubim are mentioned at the Garden of Eden and in a number of other Scriptures. Both cherubim and seraphim have ministries particularly associated with the immediate presence of the thrice-holy Creator.

Then, in the next chapter occurs the remarkable prophecy of the coming virgin birth of the promised Savior. "Behold, a virgin shall conceive, and bear a son, and shall call his name Immanuel" (Isa. 7:14). The sense in the original conveys that of a definite article—*the* virgin—a particular virgin of whom God had previously spoken. Almost certainly, this refers back to the protevangelic promise of the unique "seed" of the woman who would come some day to destroy the old serpent and his rebellion against God (Gen. 3:15). This is further indicated by the name, Immanuel, meaning "God with us." No one but God could accomplish such a work, yet he would also be part of the human family—"with us." Such a divine incarnation could only be accomplished through a specially created seed in a virgin's womb, not a male seed implanted therein.

The promise is shortly confirmed and amplified still further. "For unto us a child is born, unto us a son is given: and the government shall be upon his shoulder: and his name shall be called Wonderful, Counseller, The mighty God, The everlasting Father, The Prince of Peace. Of the increase of his government and peace there shall be no end. . . . The zeal of the LORD of hosts will perform this" (Isa. 9:6, 7).

If there were still any question that the promised "seed" of the woman, the virgin-born son, would really be both human and divine, this prophecy should settle it. He is to be a "child" and a "son," but also the mighty God and everlasting Father. When He finally puts down all rebellion, his government of peace will last eternally. God's plan in creation, though interrupted by sin for a season, cannot fail.

But then there is further insight into the nature of the Satanic rebellion, also given through Isaiah. In a prophecy of the coming judgment on the evil king of Babylon (given long before the ascendancy of Babylon's greatest era under Nebuchadnezzar), the prophecy suddenly shifts for a time from the human king to the evil spirit possessing and controlling him. The prophet addresses this spirit as Lucifer (never the name of any human king of Babylon, but long recognized as a title of Satan), meaning "day-star." Here is the amazing revelation:

> How art thou fallen from heaven, O Lucifer, son of the morning! how art thou cut down to the ground, which didst weaken the nations! For thou hast said in thine heart, I will ascend into heaven, I will exalt my throne above the stars of God: I will sit also upon the mount of the congregation, in the sides of the north: I will ascend above the heights of the clouds; I will be like the most High. Yet thou shalt be brought down to hell, to the sides of the pit (Isa. 14:12–15).

This primeval rebellion of Lucifer, or Satan, in heaven has been implied in earlier Scriptures but is made quite explicit here. Lucifer desired to dethrone God and to usurp his place as king of the universe. Such an irrational ambition on the part of a being created by God— even though he was perhaps the highest of all the angelic hierarchy— can only be understood on the assumption that he refused to believe that God *was* his Creator!

After all, he only had God's Word to go on. At his first moment of awareness, he was there with God in the primeval deep, and he must have reasoned that God was the same order of being as himself, both having somehow "evolved" out of the eternal waters. This concept possibly explains why so many ancient mythological cosmogonies (e.g., Sumeria, Egypt) begin with the unexplained presence of two divine beings in an eternal watery chaos. It also possibly accounts for Satan's arrogant, age-long efforts to usurp the throne of God. He not only has deceived Eve—and countless others—with his own lying promise to become like God, but he deceived himself most of all. He was, therefore, both the first evolutionist and the first liar. He aspired to ascend above God's throne in heaven, but he was "cut down to the ground" and will ultimately be "brought down to hell" (Hebrew *sheol*, the great pit in the heart of the earth).

There is another symbolical representation of Satan and his defeat in Isaiah 27:1—this time not as a star falling down from heaven, but as the great dragon (leviathan, as in Job 41, or the great marine dinosaur) slain in the sea. "In that day, the LORD with his sore and great and strong sword shall punish leviathan the piercing serpent, even leviathan that crooked serpent; and he shall slay the dragon that is in the sea."

The second division of the great prophecy of Isaiah begins with chapter 40, and this mountain-peak chapter contains many notations of the creation. First, however, there is a reference which speaks of God's curse on the earth. "All flesh is grass, and all the goodliness thereof is as the flower of the field . . . The grass withereth, the flower fadeth: but the word of our God shall stand for ever" (Isa. 40:6, 8).

Next comes a series of rhetorical questions, all pointing up the omnipotence and omniscience of the Creator. "Who hath measured the waters in the hollow of his hand, and meted out heaven with the span, and comprehended the dust of the earth in a measure, and weighed the mountains in scales, and the hills in a balance? Who hath directed the Spirit of the LORD, or being his counseller hath taught him?" (Isa. 40:12–13).

Modern ecologists and earth scientists are concerned lest man upset the precise balances in nature—in the hydrosphere, the atmosphere, the lithosphere, and the geosphere. All components of earth's preparation for life were carefully planned and designed by their Creator. "Have ye not known? have ye not heard? hath it not been told you from the beginning? have ye not understood from the foundations of the earth? It is he that sitteth upon the circle of the earth, and the inhabitants thereof are as grasshoppers; that stretcheth out the heavens as a curtain, and spreadeth them out as a tent to dwell in" (Isa. 40:21–22).

All of this has, indeed, been told us from the beginning, in Genesis 1! Only God could lay the foundation of the earth, then shape it into a "circle" (Hebrew khug, meaning "sphericity"—same word as that which is translated "compass" in Proverbs 8:27; thus, both the earth and the deep are components of the great terrestrial sphere), while also stretching out the heavens—possibly an allusion to the expanding universe—like a great canopy around the world, making it habitable for all his living creatures.

Then comes a magnificent exhortation to comprehend the magnitude and majesty of his creation: "To whom then will ye liken me, or shall I be equal? saith the Holy One. Lift up your eyes on high, and behold who hath created these things, that bringeth out their host by number: he calleth them all by names by the greatness of his might, for that he is strong in power; not one faileth" (Isa. 40:25, 26). This passage suggests God's omnipresence (great "numbers" of the heavenly host throughout the universe), his omniscience (able instantly to name trillions of stars in trillions of galaxies), and his omnipotence (not one failing in its appointed purpose).

Then, in the chapter's glorious final challenge, Isaiah says: "Hast thou not known? hast thou not heard, that the everlasting God, the

LORD, the Creator of the ends of the earth, fainteth not, neither is weary? there is no searching of His understanding" (Isa. 40:28).

God also speaks of the great salvation which he, as Creator, will be able and willing to provide for his people. "Thus saith God the LORD, he that created the heavens, and stretched them out; he that spread forth the earth, and that which cometh out of it; he that giveth breath unto the people upon it, and spirit to them that walk therein: I the LORD have called thee in righteousness, and will hold thine hand, and will keep thee, and give thee for a covenant of the people, for a light of the Gentiles" (Isa. 42:5, 6).

There is an unusual act of creation stated in Isaiah 43:1: "But now thus saith the LORD that created thee, O Jacob, and he that formed thee, O Israel, Fear not: for I have redeemed thee, I have called thee by thy name; thou art mine." The verb "create" (Hebrew *bara*) always has God for its subject, for it invariably describes a supernatural creation, which can be performed only by the Creator. There were so many miracles of creation involved in the call of the nation Israel (or Jacob) that it was proper to speak of the very formation of this nation as a special *creation!* Remember, for example, the water from the rock sustaining them for forty years, and many others. Note also Isaiah 43:7. "Even every one that is called by my name: for I have created him for my glory, I have formed him; yea, I have made him." This verse answers, at least in part, as to just *why* God created, not only Israel, but us as well! We should, therefore, by every means, seek to bring glory to him, for this is our very cause for living. "This people have I formed for myself; they shall shew forth my praise" (Isa. 43:21).

Note also the comprehensive testimony of Isaiah 44:24. "Thus saith the LORD, thy redeemer, and he that formed thee from the womb, I am the LORD that maketh all things; that stretcheth forth the heavens alone; that spreadeth abroad the earth by myself." The same God who made the whole universe also formed each of us in our mother's womb, and has also become our redeemer!

An unexpected insight occurs in Isaiah 45:7. "I form the light, and create darkness: I make peace, and create evil: I the LORD do all these things." Nowhere do the Scriptures say that God *created* light; rather he had to "create darkness" for there to be a division between day and night. God *is* light, and he merely had to "let" the light "be" (Gen. 1:3), then "form" it in locations and periods according to his will. As far as evil is concerned, God could not create wickedness, for whatever *he* does is *right,* by definition. But he has created physical "evils" (e.g., storms, pestilence) when moral conditions or human discipline have needed such.

Similarly, "Let the earth open, and let them [i.e., the heavens] bring forth salvation, and let righteousness spring up together; I the LORD have created it. Woe unto him that striveth with his Maker! . . . I have made the earth, and created man upon it: I, even my hands, have stretched out the heavens, and all their host have I commanded" (Isa. 45:8, 9, 12).

One of the most frequently cited "proof texts" for the so-called gap theory is found in this chapter: "For thus saith the LORD that created the heavens; God himself that formed the earth and made it; he hath established it, he created it not in vain, he formed it to be inhabited: I am the LORD; and there is none else" (Isa. 45:18).

First, note that everything about the earth is due to God alone. He "created it," he "formed it," he "made it," he "established it." God is not capricious; he did not do all this "in vain." He formed the earth to be *inhabited!*

The argument of those who promote the gap theory, however, is that the Hebrew word for "in vain" is *tohu,* the same word as that used in Genesis 1:2, where it says that, initially, "the earth was *tohu* [i.e., without form]." They maintain, then, that since God did not create the earth *tohu,* it must later have "become" *tohu,* after the supposed pre-Adamic cataclysm.

It should be realized, however, that *tohu* has many different meanings, depending upon context. It is best translated "unformed" in the context of Genesis 1:2, but is better rendered "in vain" in Isaiah 45:18. The point of the latter verse is that God does nothing that is pointless or capricious—all of this in the broader context of assurance of his purposes for his people Israel. He did not create the earth to no purpose; it was formed to be inhabited, and it *was* inhabited, just a few days afterward when it had been fully prepared for its inhabitants. The earth was called into existence—*created*—in basic elemental character, with no particular form, but this was not the result of some imaginary cataclysm. It was created perfect for its immediate purpose, but it was not complete, until God *said* it was "finished" at the end of the six days, by which time it was "inhabited." It only remained very briefly in the *tohu* state, unformed, and this certainly does not contradict Isaiah when he says it was not created (to be) *tohu,* "in vain." The very next verse, Isaiah 45:19, uses the same word: "I said not unto the seed of Jacob, Seek ye me in vain [i.e., *tohu*]." There is no possibility of translating the word by "waste" or "desolation" or something of the sort here, as the gap theory promoters want to do with Genesis 1:2. The context determines the meaning, and there is certainly nothing in the context, either here or in Genesis 1:2, to justify the notion of long ages after creation followed by a global cataclysm that left the earth *tohu*. Yet this is the strongest "proof text" for the gap theory, which ought therefore to be abandoned by all serious expositors of the text.

Isaiah does, indeed, insert many reminders of the creation in his prophecies of things to come. Here is yet another. "Mine hand also hath laid the foundation of the earth, and my right hand hath spanned the heavens: when I call unto them they stand up together" (Isa. 48:13). This verse stresses the *fiat*, simultaneous creation of both heaven and earth.

There is also a remembrance of the curse and the imposed principle of decay. "Lift up your eyes to the heavens, and look upon the earth beneath: for the heavens shall vanish away like smoke, and the earth shall wax old like a garment, and they that dwell therein shall die in like manner: but my salvation shall be for ever, and my righteousness shall not be abolished" (Isa. 51:6).

A striking confirmation of the historicity of Noah and the flood is also recorded in Isaiah. "For this is as the waters of Noah unto me: for as I have sworn that the waters of Noah should no more go over the earth; so have I sworn that I would not be wroth with thee, nor rebuke thee" (Isa. 54:9).

Then, there is a remarkable scientific insight into the vastness of the created universe. "For as the heavens are higher than the earth, so are my ways than your ways, and my thoughts than your thoughts" (Isa. 55:9). God is called "the high and lofty One that inhabiteth eternity" (Isa. 57:15).

Lastly, the Lord promises to "create new heavens and a new earth: and the former shall not be remembered, nor come into mind" (Isa. 65:17). In addition, God promises to *create*(!) a new city of Jerusalem, in this new earth. "Be ye glad and rejoice for ever in that which I create: for, behold, I create Jerusalem a rejoicing, and her people a joy" (Isa. 65:18). These new heavens, and new earth, and new Jerusalem, being perfected and newly re-created, will last forever. "The new heavens and the new earth, which I will make, shall remain before me, saith the LORD" (Isa. 66:22).

Jeremiah and the Creator

The prince of prophets, Isaiah, contains more references to creation than all the other major prophets together. However, the subject is by no means neglected in these, either. Let us look next at the "weeping prophet," Jeremiah, who prophesied in the closing days of the kings of Judah, just before the Babylonian captivity.

First of all we encounter, not a testimony to creation, but an indictment of evolution, the religion of the pagan idolatry which so traumatized the people of Judah. "As the thief is ashamed when he is found, so is the house of Israel ashamed; they, . . . saying to a stock, Thou art my father; and to a stone, Thou hast brought me forth" (Jer. 2:26, 27).

The ancient idolaters who thought they had evolved from sticks and stones were no more foolish than modern idolaters who attribute our evolutionary ancestry to hydrogen gas! "Truly in vain is salvation hoped for from the hills, and from the multitude of mountains: truly in the LORD our God is the salvation of Israel" (Jer. 3:23). Nature, as personified in sticks and stones, cannot provide life. Neither can nature, as personified in mountains and hills, provide salvation. Evolutionary pantheism, personified in Mother Nature, or Mother Earth, is no substitute for the true God of creation.

There is a passage in Jeremiah (4:23–28) which has language similar to Genesis 1:2 and has been used (actually misused) in an attempt to support the gap theory. The whole passage is quoted below:

> I beheld the earth, and, lo, it was without form, and void; and the heavens, and they had no light. I beheld the mountains, and, lo, they trembled, and all the hills moved lightly. I beheld, and, lo, there was no man, and all the birds of the heavens were fled. I beheld, and, lo, the fruitful place was a wilderness, and all the cities thereof were broken down at the presence of the LORD, and by his fierce anger. For thus hath the LORD said, The whole land shall be desolation; yet will I not make a full end. For this shall the earth mourn, and the heavens above be black: because I have spoken it, I have purposed it, and will not repent, neither will I turn back from it.

This was obviously a vision given to Jeremiah (four times he says, "I beheld") concerning a coming judgment on the land of Israel, nothing else. The fact that verse 23 speaks of "the earth" as "without form, and void" (same words as in Genesis 1:2) must be taken in context, which has nothing to do with an imaginary pre-Adamic cataclysm, as the gap theory suggests.

The gap theory interpretation, if applied to this passage, would mean, not only that the pre-gap world contained mountains and hills, but also that it had fruitful fields and birds and people and cities, and that all of these were destroyed by an angry God who left the earth without form and void! That is, it was a world altogether like the one which he then created over again after the cataclysm.

There is not the slightest suggestion of anything like this, either in Genesis or here in Jeremiah. Verse 23 could as well be translated: "The land [same Hebrew word as "earth"] was unformed and empty." All the cities and other structures were seen in Jeremiah's vision as broken down, and their inhabitants all removed, after God's judgment on the nation's wickedness. Evidently a great earthquake would contribute to this, and then an enemy invasion (v. 29).

The judgment was against God's people in Israel, not some hypothetical pre-Adamic population of whom the Scriptures know nothing. This is made plain by the preceding verse: "For my people is foolish, they have not known me . . . they are wise to do evil, but to do good they have no knowledge" (Jer. 4:22). It is also confirmed by the final verse of the chapter, which specifically notes that "the voice of the daughter of Zion" will be wailing, "Woe is me now!" (Jer. 4:31). Surely the people to whom Jeremiah was writing could only have understood it in this way; they would never have dreamed it was describing some unknown race in a hypothetical world before Adam and Eve!

There is a brief reference instead to the divine promise to Noah never to submerge the world by the sea again. "Fear ye not me? saith the LORD: will ye not tremble at my presence, which have placed the sand for the bound of the sea by a perpetual decree, that it cannot pass it: and though the waves thereof toss themselves, yet can they not prevail; though they roar, yet can they not pass over it?" (Jer. 5:22).

In chapter 10 of Jeremiah's prophecy occurs a ringing affirmation of Jehovah as the one true God and Creator in contrast to all the nature gods of the nations that had corrupted their worship.

But the LORD is the true God, he is the living God, and an everlasting king: at his wrath the earth shall tremble, and the nations shall not be able to abide his indignation. Thus shall ye say unto them, The gods that have not made the heavens and the earth, even they shall perish from the earth, and from under these heavens. He hath made the earth by his power, he hath established the world by his wisdom, and hath stretched out the heavens by his discretion. When he uttereth his voice, there is a multitude of waters in the heavens, and he causeth the vapours to ascend from the ends of the earth; he maketh lightnings with rain, and bringeth forth the wind out of his treasures (Jer. 10:10–13).

This passage assures that the false gods (idols in fact, but energized by the demonic spirits following Satan) will eventually be banished from the heavens and the earth. The last verse may be a reference to the waters prepared for the great flood or, more likely, a note on the providential ordering of the post-flood hydrologic cycle, which sustains life in the present world. The last two verses are repeated almost verbatim in Jeremiah 51:15, 16.

A brief reference to God's omnipresence is found in Jeremiah 23:24. "Can any hide himself in secret places that I shall not see him? saith the LORD. Do not I fill heaven and earth? saith the LORD."

We have noted in several places the revelation that the sun, moon, and stars were created to last forever. Jeremiah now uses this fact to assure the nation of Israel that, despite their imminent captivity, God will never forsake them.

Thus saith the LORD, which giveth the sun for a light by day, and the ordinances of the moon and of the stars for a light by night, which divideth the sea when the waves thereof roar; The LORD of hosts is His name: if those ordinances depart from before me, saith the LORD, then the seed of Israel also shall cease from being a nation before me for ever. Thus saith the LORD; If heaven above can be measured, and the foundations of the earth searched out beneath, I will also cast off all the seed of Israel for all that they have done, saith the LORD (Jer. 31:35–37).

This passage also notes the impossibility of measuring the infinite heavens or of ever penetrating the deep core of the earth, as far as human technology is concerned.

One of my own favorite verses in all the Scriptures is the marvelous affirmation of Jeremiah 32:17: "Ah Lord GOD! behold, thou hast made the heaven and the earth by thy great power and stretched out arm, and there is nothing too hard for thee." If a person believes—really *believes*—the very first verse in the Bible, he should have no trouble with anything else revealed therein. God shortly thereafter responds to Jeremiah's prayer of faith with these echoing words: "Behold, I am the LORD, the God of all flesh: is there any thing too hard for me?" (Jer. 32:27).

Jeremiah was also the author of the Book of Lamentations, of course, lamenting the sins of Israel and the destruction of Jerusalem. There is almost nothing in this five-chapter book except sorrow for sin and mourning over the judgment, as well as prayer for forgiveness and restoration. However, just before the final chapter ends, Jeremiah does remember that, after all, their God of judgment is also the eternal Creator and can restore his people. Here is his prayer: "Thou, O LORD, remainest for ever; thy throne from generation to generation. . . . Turn thou us unto thee, O LORD, and we shall be turned; renew our days as of old" (Lam. 5:19, 21).

Ezekiel and Daniel are usually associated with the major prophets, Isaiah and Jeremiah. For our purposes here, however, it is more appropriate to explore their prophecies in connection with the post-exile histories and prophecies. We are trying to think in terms of God's chronologically progressing revelation. Therefore, before thinking of creation in the context of the Babylonian exile, and then the return from exile, we need to hear the testimony of those minor prophets whose ministries paralleled those of Isaiah and Jeremiah, in the years before the captivity.

9

The Minor Prophets
Before the Captivity

Testimonies of Creation in Israel

There is nothing "minor" about the minor prophets except the length of their prophecies. None of them compare in length with Isaiah or Jeremiah, but their messages are all rich and vital.

After the glory days of David and Solomon, the great kingdom established under David was divided into two kingdoms. The northern kingdom, still called Israel, consisted of ten tribes, the most prominent being Ephraim. It survived about 250 years, before being conquered and taken into captivity by the Assyrian empire. The southern kingdom, called Judah, included also the tribe of Benjamin. It lasted for some 375 years, before going into the Babylonian exile.

In this section, therefore, we shall consider the prophets in the northern kingdom, Israel. The greatest of Israel's prophets were Elijah and Elisha, but they left no written prophecies. Israel's writing prophets included Hosea, Amos, Jonah, and possibly Obadiah.

The prophets of Judah included Joel, Micah, Nahum, Habakkuk, and Zephaniah. Some of the prophets of Israel (e.g., Hosea) also prophesied concerning Judah. Amos was a native of Judah, but his prophecies were directed toward Israel. Although all the minor prophets were writing of future judgment, they did continue to recognize the truth of creation and to honor the one true God of creation.

Looking first at the prophet Hosea, we find first a passing reference to the terminology of the classification system for animals used in Genesis. "And in that day will I make a covenant for them with the beasts of the field, and with the fowls of heaven, and with the creeping things of the ground" (Hos. 2:18; compare Gen. 1:30). There is also a reference to "the beasts of the field, and . . . the fowls of heaven; yea, the fishes of the sea also" in Hosea 4:3. There is no direct reference to creation in these verses, but it is significant that the prophet is still using the animal taxonomic scheme of Genesis at least 3,200 years after Adam. Hosea specifically calls God their "Maker" at least once (Hos. 8:14) and "the most High" at least once (Hos. 11:7).

There is a more explicit reference to God as Creator in the Book of Amos. "For, lo, he that formeth the mountains, and createth the wind, and declareth unto man what is his thought, that maketh the morning darkness, and treadeth upon the high places of the earth, The LORD, The God of hosts, is his name" (Amos 4:13).

A little later, Amos reminds the apostate nation of both the creation and the flood, urging them to return to their God. "Seek him that maketh the seven stars and Orion, and turneth the shadow of death into the morning, and maketh the day dark with night: that calleth for the waters of the sea, and poureth them out upon the face of the earth: The LORD is his name" (Amos 5:8). Note that Amos, like Job, attributes the formation of specific constellations of stars (the "seven stars," or Pleiades, and "Orion") to God, as well as the stars individually.

A similar reminder is added in the final chapter of the prophecy of Amos. "It is he that buildeth his stories in the heaven, and hath founded his troop in the earth; he that calleth for the waters of the sea, and poureth them out upon the face of the earth: The LORD is his name" (Amos 9:6).

The one-chapter Book of Obadiah is the shortest book in the Old Testament, with only twenty-one verses. The sole theme is coming judgment on the nation of Edom, descendants of Esau, the brother of Israel. There is possibly an allusion to the primeval fall of Satan, however, in these verses: "The pride of thine heart hath deceived thee, thou that dwellest in the clefts of the rock, whose habitation is high; that saith in his heart, Who shall bring me down to the ground? Though thou exalt thyself as the eagle, and though thou set thy nest among the stars, thence will I bring thee down, saith the LORD" (Obad. 3, 4).

This passage is quite similar to Isaiah's much later prophecy against Lucifer, or Satan (Isa. 14:12–15). Perhaps it served as a model for the construction of Isaiah's prophecy. The latter was ostensibly addressed to the wicked king of Babylon, just as Obadiah's was addressed to Edom and its king. In both cases, however, the language goes beyond what could appropriately be applied to an earthly king, and evidently is addressed in each case to the wicked spirit possessing the king's body and controlling his actions.

The story of Jonah is the most familiar among the minor prophets, because of his unique experience with the great fish. The inability of liberal scholars to believe in this miracle has led them to deny Jonah's existence, even though he is specifically mentioned in the books of history (2 Kings 14:25).

The omnipotence of God as Creator is manifest throughout the brief book. First, "the LORD sent out a great wind into the sea" (Jon. 1:4). In answering the questions of the pagan mariners whose ship was about to be broken in the storm, Jonah bravely testified: "I am an Hebrew; and I fear the LORD, the God of heaven, which hath made the sea and the dry land" (Jon. 1:9). They cast him overboard, and the Lord calmed the sea.

Next, "the LORD had prepared a great fish to swallow up Jonah" (Jon. 1:17). This fish (not necessarily a whale) was a special creation of the Creator, just for this occasion. After Jonah's prayer of repentance, "the LORD spake unto the fish, and it vomited out Jonah upon the dry land" (Jon. 2:10).

When Jonah then preached to the wicked and cruel Assyrians in their capital city of Nineveh, the king and the entire city "believed God, . . . from the greatest of them even to the least of them," and "God repented of the evil, that he had said he would do unto them" (Jon. 3:5, 10).

Then, when Jonah was displeased at this revival, wanting to die, preferring that God destroy the city as he had been prophesying, "the LORD God prepared a gourd, and made it to come up over Jonah, that it might be a shadow over his head" (Jon. 4:6). But then, the next day, "God prepared a worm . . . , and it smote the gourd that it withered" (Jon. 4:7).

Both the gourd and the worm, like the wind and the great fish, were apparently special creations of God, for only the Creator could have done such things, and Jonah —who believed in the God of heaven— surely could recognize this.

Finally, God (as he had to Adam and Job, David and others) indicated again that he cared about his animal creation, as well as those created in his own image. In the closing verse of the Book of Jonah, he said, "And should not I spare Nineveh, that great city, wherein are more than sixscore thousand persons that cannot discern between their right hand and their left hand; and also much cattle?" (Jon. 4:11).

Probably this suggests 120,000 small children, so that the total population of Nineveh (maybe including other parts of Assyria, since Nineveh was the capital) must have been over a million people, plus herds of animals adequate to support such a population. God cares for all his creatures and is long-suffering, always wanting sinners to repent and return to him. There will, as a result of these miracles and the preaching of Jonah, be many Assyrians in heaven!

The Witness in the Land of Judah

As noted before, there were five writing prophets in the kingdom of Judah before the captivity, in addition to the major prophets, Isaiah and Jeremiah. These were Joel, Micah, Nahum, Habakkuk, and Zephaniah. Each book has just three chapters, except for Micah, which contains seven. They probably are placed in the canon of Scripture in approximate chronological order.

The first is Joel, whose prophecy centers on the coming "day of the LORD," the future time of judgment—precursively on the nations of his own day, ultimately on the whole world in the last days. The omnipotence of God, "the Almighty" (Joel 1:15), is recognized throughout.

There is a passing reference to the Garden of Eden, which Joel certainly regarded as historical. In describing the coming devastation of the land, he said, "A fire devoureth before them; and behind them a flame burneth: the land is as the Garden of Eden before them; and behind them a desolate wilderness: yea, and nothing shall escape them" (Joel 2:3).

God's power over the whole creation is indicated by the prophecies of changes he will produce therein:

The earth shall quake before them; the heavens shall tremble: the sun and the moon shall be dark, and the stars shall withdraw their shining (Joel 2:10).

And I will shew wonders in the heavens and in the earth, blood, and fire, and pillars of smoke. The sun shall be turned into darkness, and the moon into blood (Joel 2:30, 31).

The sun and the moon shall be darkened, and the stars shall withdraw their shining (Joel 3:15).

And it shall come to pass in that day, that the mountains shall drop down new wine, and the hills shall flow with milk, and all the rivers of Judah shall flow with waters (Joel 3:18).

Clearly Joel—like all the prophets—regarded the God of Israel as the God of all the universe, the Creator.

Micah was a contemporary of Isaiah in Judah and was later mentioned by Jeremiah as a great prophet in the days of King Hezekiah (Jer. 26:18). It was Micah who delivered the great prophecy of the coming birth of the Messiah in Bethlehem. In this prophecy is the promise that this promised "ruler in Israel" is also one "whose goings forth have been from of old, from everlasting" (Mic. 5:2). He can, therefore, be none other than the Creator himself. We recall Isaiah's prophecy that this coming "child" will be "The mighty God, The everlasting Father" (Isa. 9:7). Isaiah also says that the child will be born of "a virgin" (Isa. 7:14), reflecting the primeval promise of the seed of the woman, who will crush the old serpent (Gen. 3:15). This same protevangelic prophecy seems implied in Micah's next verse, which notes that "the time that she which travaileth hath brought forth" will be the time when Israel will be restored and when this ruler shall "be great unto the ends of the earth" (Mic. 5:3, 4).

Following this great assurance, it is noted that he will conquer "the land of Assyria . . . and the land of Nimrod" (Mic. 5:6). Nimrod—who, according to Genesis 10:11, was the founder of Nineveh, as well as Babylon—was still regarded in that day (at least thirteen centuries after the scattering of the nations at Babel) as a historical person, the leader of the great post-flood rebellion and the founder of the two greatest nations that were enemies of God's people.

Nahum then later wrote his whole book of three chapters specifically against Nineveh and the Assyrians. There had been a great turning to God there under the preaching of Jonah, perhaps 150 years earlier, but by this time the inhabitants had reverted to their old ways of pagan cruelty and licentiousness, and God would not give them another chance. Nahum warns unequivocally of coming doom.

In addition to Nineveh, there are several references in Nahum to other lands and cities listed in the ancient Table of Nations (Gen. 10), among which Assyria (Asshur) and Babylonia (Babel), both founded by Nimrod, as well as Egypt, founded by Ham and Mizraim (Nimrod's grandfather and uncle), became leaders in the great spread of evolutionary pantheistic idolatry and immorality around the world following the dispersion.

Those ancient nations and cities so impacted by Nineveh included Ethiopia (i.e., Cush), Egypt (or Mizraim) Put, and Lubim (Nah. 3:9; compare Gen. 10:6, 13; there Lubim is called Lehabim). Nineveh is said to be "the mistress of witchcrafts, that selleth nations through her whoredoms, and families through her witchcrafts" (Nah. 3:4). Put and Lubim were evidently neighbors of Egypt, Put possibly is the region now known as Somalia (although often also associated with Libya) and Lubim (meaning "people of Lubia") probably etymologically related also to Libya. These were merely examples of ancient nations influenced for evil by Assyria/Babylonia, beginning with Nimrod.

The prophet Habbakuk is believed to have prophesied during or soon after the reign of King Josiah. He foresaw the coming invasion of the cruel Babylonians and then prayed to God, "Art thou not from everlasting, O LORD my God, mine Holy One? . . . Thou art of purer eyes than to behold evil, and canst not look on iniquity" (Hab. 1:12, 13).

He sharply rebuked the belief that wood and stone could produce life. "Woe unto him that saith to the wood, Awake: to the dumb stone, Arise, it shall teach! Behold, it is laid over with gold and silver, and there is no breath at all in the midst of it. But the LORD is in his holy temple: let all the earth keep silence before him" (Hab. 2:19, 20).

Then, as Habakkuk was praying, he received a glorious vision of the God of creation. Habakkuk wrote of God as follows:

His glory covered the heavens, and the earth was full of his praise. And his brightness was as the light; he had horns coming out of his hand: and there was the hiding of his power. . . . He stood, and measured the earth: he beheld, and drove asunder the nations; and the everlasting mountains

were scattered, the perpetual hills did bow: his ways are everlasting. . . .
The mountains saw thee, and they trembled: the overflowing of the water
passed by: the deep uttered his voice, and lifted up his hands on high.
The sun and moon stood still in their habitation: at the light of thine
arrows they went, and at the shining of thy glittering spear. . . . Thou
wentest forth for the salvation of thy people, even for salvation with thine
anointed [i.e., Messiah]; thou woundedst the head out of the house of
the wicked, by discovering the foundation unto the neck. Selah (Hab.
3:3–4, 6, 10–11, 13).

There may be in this passage poetic allusions to the great flood and
the long day of Joshua, the two greatest world-shaking events of the
past. There is also a possible allusion to the protevangelic promise of
the coming Redeemer in verse 13. The Messiah, bringing salvation, will
wound "the head [i.e., probably, the founder] . . . of the house of the
wicked," perhaps referring to the future crushing of the serpent's head
by the seed of the woman (Gen. 3:15).

The last of the preexilic minor prophets to be considered is Zephaniah, who prophesied during and after the reign of Josiah. Like Joel,
Zephaniah prophesied with special emphasis on the coming day of the
Lord. At that time, "the LORD will be terrible unto them: for he will
famish all the gods of the earth: and men shall worship him, every one
from his place" (Zeph. 2:11). All the nature gods of the pantheistic religions and all the naturalistic gods of the pseudo-intellectuals, with all
the evolutionary scenarios supporting them, will come to nought, and
all will recognize and worship the true Creator/Redeemer of the world.

A fascinating prophecy is given in Zephaniah 3:9. "For then will I
turn [i.e., return] to the people a pure language, that they may all call
upon the name of the LORD, to serve him with one consent."

This is clearly in reference to the original language of all people (very
likely Hebrew) before the confusion of tongues and the dispersion of
the nations at the tower of Babel. Instead of wanting to make a name
for themselves, as did the followers of Nimrod, all people will rejoice
in the name of the Lord, serving him with joy instead of rebelling against
him. There will be no more language barriers in that great day, when
God restores all things and makes all things right, as they were in the
beginning.

10

Memories of Creation in Exile

Ezekiel, Daniel, and the God of Israel

Ezekiel and Daniel are considered two of the major prophets but, unlike Isaiah and Jeremiah, they prophesied out of the land, after the Jews had been carried into captivity in Babylon. Nevertheless, they still believed in the true God of creation, the Holy One of Israel, and maintained a strong witness for him in a pagan land. Ezekiel was of the priestly tribe of Zadok, preparing for service in the temple, but was taken to Babylon while still a young man. There, however, God used him greatly as his prophet.

Much of his book consists of visions, including several of the mighty cherubim surrounding the throne of God (Ezek. 1:4–28; 3:10–14; 8:2–4; 10:1–22; 11:22–24). These cherubim were first encountered at the gate to Eden (Gen. 3:24) and were symbolically represented over the ark of the covenant in the tabernacle (Exod. 25:18–22) and in Solomon's temple (1 Kings 6:23–29). They are often mentioned in the Psalms and elsewhere (e.g., Ps. 80:1; 99:1; Isa. 37:16), always as associated with the immediate presence of God. Nowhere are they described in more detail than by Ezekiel.

He first calls them "four living creatures," each having "the likeness of a man" (Ezek. 1:5). Yet "every one had four faces, and every one had four wings" (Ezek. 1:6). "As for the likeness of their faces, they four had the face of a man, and the face of a lion, on the right side: and they four had the face of an ox on the left side; they four also had the face of an eagle" (Ezek. 1:10). Perhaps the animal faces suggest God's created "living creatures" as named by Adam, the first man—"all cattle [the ox] . . . the fowl of the air [the eagle] . . . every beast of the field [the lion]" (Gen. 2:19, 20).

The description goes into more detail, but the most important aspect was their ministry Godward. "And above the firmament that was over their heads was the likeness of a throne . . . and upon the likeness of the throne was the likeness as the appearance of a man above upon it. . . . As the appearance of the bow that is in the cloud in the day of rain, so was the appearance of the brightness round about. This was the appearance of the likeness of the glory of the LORD. And when I saw it, I fell upon my face, and I heard a voice of one that spake" (Ezek. 1:26, 28).

As with Moses (Exod. 33:18–23), Ezekiel could not have survived the sight of the ineffable glory of God, so God only revealed "the appearance of the likeness of the glory," as he prepared to Ezekiel his call as his prophet. The "firmament" (Hebrew *raqia*—"stretched-out expanse" or simply "space") suggests the primeval firmament (Gen. 1:7), stretched out between the waters below and the waters above. The firmament here in Ezekiel's vision was stretched out between the cherubim below and the divine throne above.

The mention of a rainbow around the throne is the only mention of a rainbow in the Old Testament except when the rainbow was placed in the sky as a sign of God's unconditional covenant with Noah and with "all flesh" after the flood that God would never again send the worldwide flood on the earth (Gen. 9:11–15). Even in wrath, God remembers mercy, and the perpetual rainbow around his throne indicates that he is always "seeing" the rainbow and, therefore, repeatedly tempers judgment with salvation.

These four "living creatures" are not actually called "cherubim" (note that "cherubim" is the plural of "cherub") until Ezekiel's last encounter with them. "Then the glory of the LORD went up from the cherub, and stood over the threshold of the house; and the house was filled with the cloud, and the court was full of the brightness of the LORD's glory. . . . And the cherubims were lifted up. This is the living creature that I saw by the river of Chebar. . . . Then the glory of the LORD departed from off the threshold of the house, and stood over the cherubims" (Ezek. 10:4, 15, 18).

This, of course, showed Ezekiel that the Shekinah glory of God, which had filled the holy place in Solomon's temple when it was dedicated (2 Chron. 7:1, 2), was now permanently leaving it, because of the gross sins of the people of Judah and their leaders. Very soon afterward, Nebuchadnezzar again invaded Jerusalem and destroyed the temple altogether, along with these events come the second deportation of its people (2 Chron. 36:5–7; 17–20).

In the course of these visions of the cherubim, Ezekiel left a significant acknowledgment of the historicity of the ancient patriarchs Noah and Job. "Though these three men, Noah, Daniel, and Job, were in it, they should deliver but their own souls by their righteousness, saith the Lord GOD. . . . Though Noah, Daniel, and Job, were in it, as I live, saith the Lord GOD, they shall deliver neither son nor daughter; they shall but deliver their own souls by their righteousness" (Ezek. 14:14, 20).

Ezekiel also confirms the real existence of the prophet Daniel, who was his contemporary in Babylon. He further affirms the high degree of righteousness in God's sight demonstrated by each.

In the 28th chapter of Ezekiel occurs a most remarkable prophecy against the proud and wicked king of Tyre and the Satanic spirit possessing his body and controlling his decisions and actions. It is similar to the prophecy against the king of Babylon and Lucifer, the possessing spirit, as discussed in connection with Isaiah 14. Here the prophecy is in the context of a warning to the earthly king, but it goes far beyond anything appropriate for a mortal tyrant. It can apply ultimately only to Satan.

> Thus saith the Lord GOD; Thou sealest up the sum, full of wisdom, and perfect in beauty. Thou hast been in Eden the garden of God: every precious stone was thy covering . . . .: the workmanship of thy tabrets and of thy pipes was prepared in thee in the day that thou wast created. Thou art the anointed cherub that covereth; and I have set thee so: thou wast upon the holy mountain of God; thou hast walked up and down in the midst of the stones of fire. Thou wast perfect in thy ways from the day that thou wast created, till iniquity was found in thee. . . . therefore I will cast thee as profane out of the mountain of God: and I will destroy thee, O covering cherub, from the midst of the stones of fire. Thine heart was lifted up because of thy beauty, thou hast corrupted thy wisdom by rea-

son of thy brightness: I will cast thee to the ground, I will lay thee before kings, that they may behold thee (Ezek. 28:12–17).

Satan was in the Garden of Eden, as described in Genesis 2 and 3, possessing and speaking through the body of the serpent. However, *that* garden was a park-like garden of beautiful trees and plants. *This* garden, where Satan first was appointed as the highest of all the angelic creation, the preeminent cherub, was a garden in the heavenly temple, of which the earthly garden was merely a type, or model. This exalted cherub—unlike the other cherubim, below the divine throne—was the *anointed* cherub, *covering* the holy mountain of God. He was arrayed in "every precious stone," "full of wisdom, and perfect in beauty," walking "in the midst of the stones of fire." He "sealest up the sum," the highest of all the heavenly host.

But he was not God! Twice, God reminded him that he, like all the others, had been "created" by himself (vv. 13, 15). Yet, evidently, he chose not to believe God, thinking he could dethrone God and take his place. Satan's "heart was lifted up." Therefore, God had to cast him down, all the way to the ground (or earth). "Iniquity was found in [him]," God said, and eventually "never shalt [he] be any more" (Ezek. 28:19).

After being cast to the earth, he first tempted Adam and Eve to follow him in his rebellion against God and his ambition to become God, still doubting that God was his Creator and thus could never be overcome. Since then, multitudes of men and women have been taken in by this same lie, but God has promised his eventual defeat and eternal banishment.

In spite of the great judgments upon Israel because she had followed the pagan beliefs and practices of the God-rejecting nations around her, God did promise ultimate restoration of her land, even comparing it to the primeval paradise. "And they shall say, This land that was desolate is become like the garden of Eden" (Ezek. 36:35).

Finally, Ezekiel describes the future temple and its worship, with the presence of the glory of God restored therein. As in the original Garden of Eden, where a river emerged, parting into four heads to water the ground, so a great river will issue out of the temple "toward the east country, and go into the desert, and go into the sea" (Ezek. 47:8). The name of the city whence the river flows "from that day shall be, The LORD is there" (Ezek. 48:35).

Daniel and the God of Heaven

Although Daniel, in his long ministry, was a mere captive in exile from Judah, his strong faith in the one true God enabled him to bear an uncompromising testimony before four great pagan kings—Nebuchadnezzar and Belshazzar of Babylon, Darius and Cyrus of Persia.

When Nebuchadnezzar, the greatest monarch in the world at that time, asked Daniel to interpret his dream, after his own wise men had failed, Daniel responded with a testimony of praise to God: "Then Daniel blessed the God of heaven. Daniel answered and said, Blessed be the name of God for ever and ever: for wisdom and might are his: and he changeth the times and the seasons: he removeth kings, and setteth up kings: he giveth wisdom unto the wise, and knowledge to them that know understanding: he revealeth the deep and secret things: he knoweth what is in the darkness, and the light dwelleth with him" (Dan. 2:19–22).

Much later, when Belshazzar had become king and wanted Daniel to read and interpret the strange handwriting on the wall, Daniel replied boldly: "Thou, O Belshazzar, . . . hast lifted up thyself against the Lord of heaven . . . and thou hast praised the gods of silver, and gold, of brass, iron, wood, and stone, which see not, nor hear, nor know: and the God in whose hand thy breath is, and whose are all thy ways, hast thou not glorified" (Dan. 5:22, 23).

Soon after this condemnation, Babylon was conquered by the Medes and Persians, and Darius became king. When a conspiracy forced Darius to place Daniel in a den of lions, God delivered Daniel and Darius gave this testimony: "I make a decree, That in every dominion of my kingdom men tremble and fear before the God of Daniel; for he is the living God, and stedfast for ever, and his kingdom that which shall not be destroyed, and his dominion shall be even unto the end. He delivereth and rescueth, and he worketh signs and wonders in heaven and in earth" (Dan. 6:26, 27).

King Nebuchadnezzar, like Darius, acknowledged Daniel's God as a great God after Daniel interpreted his dream, saying "Of a truth it is, that your God is a God of gods, and a Lord of kings" (Dan. 2:47). Nevertheless, he still exalted himself as deserving of worship, and God severely humbled him with a seven-year period of madness. He was told that he must learn that "the most High ruleth in the kingdom of men, and giveth it to whomsoever He will, and setteth up over it the basest of men" (Dan. 4:17, 25, 32).

Nebuchadnezzar did learn this lesson and, after his restoration, gave this testimony: "Nebuchadnezzar the king, unto all people, nations, and languages, that dwell in all the earth; Peace be multiplied unto you. I thought it good to shew the signs and wonders that the high God hath wrought toward me. How great are his signs! and how mighty are his wonders! his kingdom is an everlasting kingdom, and his dominion is from generation to generation" (Dan. 4:1–3).

After recounting the entire experience, King Nebuchadnezzar concluded his testimony with these words. "And at the end of the days I Nebuchadnezzar lifted up mine eyes unto heaven, and mine understanding returned unto me, and I blessed the most High, and I praised and honoured him that liveth for ever. . . . he doeth according to his will in the army of heaven, and among the inhabitants of the earth . . . Now I Nebuchadnezzar praise and extol and honour the King of heaven, all whose works are truth, and his ways judgment: and those that walk in pride he is able to abase" (Dan. 4:34, 35, 37).

All these testimonies, both those of Daniel and those extracted from heathen kings, affirm that God alone is Creator and Sustainer and Judge of all things. He knows all things, and controls all things, because he created all things!

Later chapters of Daniel are mostly prophetic visions and revelations of the last days, but there are occasional references to the creation and God's purposes for his creation. In the vision recorded in the seventh chapter, God on his throne in heaven is three times called "the Ancient of days" (Dan. 7:9, 13, 22) and five times "the most High" (Dan. 7:18, 22, 25, 27). The kingdom, given to "the Son of man" (Dan. 7:13), is also said four times to be given to "the saints of the most High" (Dan. 7:18, 22, 25, 27). That kingdom is "an everlasting dominion" and "an everlasting kingdom" (Dan. 7:14, 27).

Two high angels of God are featured in Daniel—Gabriel (Dan. 8:16; 9:21) and Michael (Dan. 10:13, 21; 12:1)—in addition to other unnamed angels. We learn from these encounters that angels "fly swiftly" (Dan. 9:21) and sometimes engage in battle with Satanic angels on behalf of God's people (Dan. 10:12, 13).

The Satanic rebellion will be represented on earth in the last days by a great man who, like Satan, "shall exalt himself, and magnify himself above every god, and shall speak marvellous things against the God of gods. . . . Neither shall he . . . regard any god. . . . But in his estate shall he honour the god of forces" (Dan. 11:36–38). He will also be "a king of fierce countenance, and understanding dark sentences" (Dan. 8:23). In modern terminology, he will be an evolutionary pantheistic humanist. However, "he shall also stand up against the Prince of princes; but he shall be broken without hand" (Dan. 8:25).

The permanence of God's physical universe is finally noted in Daniel's last chapter. "They that be wise shall shine as the brightness of the firmament; and they that turn many to righteousness as the stars for ever and ever" (Dan. 12:3). The wise, and the firmament, and the stars will last forever!

Esther and the God of Heaven

It is well known that the Book of Esther is unique among books of the Bible, in that it contains no mention at all of God. Yet both Jews and Christians have always regarded it as belonging in the canonical Scriptures because of its strong evidence of the providential hand of God ordering these great events described in Esther, behind the scenes, as it were.

As Ezekiel and Daniel were among the Jewish exiles in Babylon, Esther and her older cousin, Mordecai, were in Shushan (also known as Susa), the great capital city of the vast Persian empire, which, by this time, had displaced Babylonia as the world's most powerful kingdom. Ahasuerus (probably a title; most scholars believe this was Xerxes) was king and Vashti was queen.

Had it not been for an almost incredibly unlikely chain of circumstances described in this book, the Jews throughout the empire would have been massacred in the genocidal program of a high official named Haman, and the whole history of the world would have been altogether different. God would not allow the disruption of his creative purposes for the world, however, and these involved his unconditional covenant with Abraham and Jacob on behalf of the people and land of Israel, not to mention his primeval promise of a Redeemer (Gen. 3:15), who was later promised to come through David.

Only the sovereign Creator God could bring so many events together (yet all involving freely made decisions of men and women) to assure the promised end result.

In the story of Esther, consider the significance of each of these events, in order:

(1) The calling of a great assembly of officials to Shushan from throughout the Persian empire;

(2) The drunken command of the king to display Queen Vashti's beauty to the reveling crowd;

(3) The unwise disobedience of Queen Vashti—honorable though her reasons may have been—with her resulting loss of position;

(4) The unlikely selection of an unknown Jewish maiden to become Queen of Persia;

(5) The care and counsel of Mordecai, who had raised Esther after her parents died and who advised her not to reveal her nationality;

(6) Mordecai's opportunity to thwart an assassination of the king, through reporting to Esther a conversation he chanced to hear ;

(7) Mordecai's refusal to bow down to Haman, considering such an act contrary to Jewish law;

(8) Haman's resultant vengeful determination to kill all the Jews, on the excuse that they followed their own laws rather than those of Persia, and thus were dangerous to the king;

(9) A time of fasting and mourning among all the Jews (and, no doubt, of repentant prayer and cleansing);

(10) Mordecai's plea to Esther to intercede with the king on behalf of the Jews;

(11) Esther's courage in risking her life to approach the king without an invitation;

(12) Esther's invitation to Haman and the king to come to her banquet;

(13) Haman's preparation of a gallows on which to hang Mordecai;

(14) The king's sleepless night, during which he accidentally happened on the record of how Mordecai saved his life;

(15) The ironical choice of Haman to give honor to Mordecai throughout the city;

(16) Esther's exposure of Haman's plot to destroy her people, along with Mordecai and herself;

(17) The king's anger at the plot, aggravated by what appeared to be a rape attempt by Haman on Esther;

(18) The hanging of Haman on the gallows he had constructed for Mordecai;

(19) The granting to the Jews the right of self-defense against the ordered genocide throughout the kingdom;

(20) The slaying of those who attempted to kill the Jews on the legally unalterable day of intended genocide;
(21) The elevation of Mordecai to high position in the kingdom and the conversion of many people of the land to the Jewish faith.

The naturalistic probability of all these events coming together by chance—not only keeping the nation from destruction but also uniting them in fasting and prayer and preparing them and the Persians for a future repatriation—must be almost nil. But God's promises are sure and His wisdom and power are infinite. The essence of His providential guidance is distilled in the oft-quoted words of Mordecai to Esther; "For if thou altogether holdest thy peace at this time, then shall there enlargement and deliverance arise to the Jews from another place; but thou and thy father's house shall be destroyed: and who knoweth whether thou art come to the kingdom for such a time as this?" (Esther 4:14).

Mordecai knew that God's promises could not fail; therefore the Jews could not be destroyed. Esther had been providentially placed in the role of deliverer, but if she should fail, God could not fail, and would bring other arrangements to pass to save the Jews.

Thus, although there is no *specific* mention of God or his creation in this book, it is everywhere implicit that he is present working out his plans, all prepared before the foundation of the world.

11

Returning to the Land

Creation References in Ezra and Nehemiah

The Jewish people began their return from exile under the reign of King Cyrus of Persia, who had come into power during the late years of Daniel's life. Somehow Cyrus, apparently on his own initiative (possibly influenced by the remarkable prophecy of Isaiah 44:28–45:4, where Cyrus was called by name almost two hundred years in advance and assigned to rebuild Jerusalem), made the following proclamation, acknowledging the God of Israel as the one true God of all creation.

> Thus saith Cyrus king of Persia, The LORD God of heaven hath given me all the kingdoms of the earth; and he hath charged me to build him an house at Jerusalem, which is in Judah. Who is there among you of all his people? his God be with him, and let him go up to Jerusalem, which is in Judah, and build the house of the LORD God of Israel, (he is the God,) which is in Jerusalem (Ezra 1:2, 3).

The first contingent of Jews returned under the leadership of Zerubbabel (Ezra 2:1, 2). Ezra, a scribe, well instructed in the laws of Moses, followed many decades later. In the meantime, adversaries arose in the land, attempting to stop the restoration. The Jews appealed, however, in the name of the one God of heaven, again acknowledging the Creator: "And thus they returned us answer, saying, We are the servants of the God of heaven and earth, and build the house that was builded these many years ago, which a great king of Israel builded and set up" (Ezra 5:11).

The decree was renewed by Darius as a result, and eventually Ezra came, under a new decree by Artaxerxes. There seem to be no other references to creation in Ezra's book, but it is worth noting that the Jews never again—after their captivity—fell into the temptations of evolutionary pantheism, even though all the peoples around them, even down to the time of Roman rule, continued in the accompanying idolatry.

Nehemiah followed a decade or so after Ezra, this time with another decree from Artaxerxes, authorizing the building of a wall around Jerusalem and its temple. He had first prayed to the "LORD God of heaven, the great and terrible God, that keepeth covenant and mercy for them that love him and observe his commandments" (Neh. 1:5), and *that* God answered his prayer for the decree he requested of Artaxerxes.

When the work was finished, all the people gathered together to hear Ezra read from the books of Moses (Neh. 8:1). Presumably he started at the beginning, with the creation record in Genesis. On the first day, he read from morning until midday (Neh. 8:3), with all the people standing at attention. "They read in the book in the law of God distinctly, and gave the sense, and caused them to understand the reading" (Neh. 8:8).

They continued reading on the second day, and continued for seven more days, while observing the feast of tabernacles.

On the last day of the feast, after reading for a fourth part of the day, the priests and Levites led all the people in a great prayer of confession and dedication. Appropriately, following their reading of the Pentateuch in particular, beginning with Genesis, their prayer likewise rehearsed their history, beginning with a great testimony of their faith in creation as foundational to all the rest. Here is how they began: "Stand up and bless the LORD your God for ever and ever: and blessed be thy glorious name, which is exalted above all blessing and praise. Thou, even thou, art LORD alone; thou hast made heaven, the heaven of heavens, with all their host, the earth, and all things that are therein, the seas, and all that is therein, and thou preservest them all; and the host of heaven worshippeth thee" (Neh. 9:5, 6).

Their eternal God had created everything in heaven and earth and was sustaining them all (as now confirmed scientifically in the laws of conservation); furthermore, all his created angels worshipped him (i.e., bowed down to do his will in all things), except, of course, for those that had been banned from "the host of heaven."

It is significant that here, at the end of the Old Testament histories (except for the few bits of history in the last three books of prophecy, as discussed in the next section), the Jews still were able to express a clear understanding and strong conviction of the special creation of all things by the eternal, transcendent God.

Testimony of the Last Three Prophets

Three of the so-called minor prophets lived and ministered with the returning exiles. Among the first to return, under Zerubbabel, were the prophets Haggai and Zechariah. Malachi came much later, perhaps with Nehemiah, and his prophecy is the final book of the Old Testament. All three were much aware of the doctrine of creation of all things by their God and referred to it in their writings.

From this perspective, Haggai prophesied of future changes in the creation, for example: "For thus saith the LORD of hosts; Yet once, it is a little while, and I will shake the heavens, and the earth, and the sea, and the dry land; and I will shake all nations, and the desire of all nations shall come . . . The silver is mine, and the gold is mine, saith the LORD of hosts" (Hag. 2:6–8).

The coming king in the last days will be not merely the Jewish Messiah, but "the desire of all nations," probably reflecting the Edenic promise of the conquering seed of the woman (Gen. 3:15). Further, since God created the world, he owns all its resources and can do with them as he pleases.

Zechariah's prophecy begins with ten symbolic visions. The seventh of these is particularly interesting for our study. He saw a golden candlestick, with seven lamps and with a bowl on its top to receive oil from two olive trees flanking it. The angel who was explaining the symbols to Zechariah said that the seven lamps represented "the eyes of the LORD, which run to and fro through the whole earth" (Zech. 4:10). The fact that the LORD has *seven* eyes no doubt indicates completeness of vision, seeing everything that happens at once throughout the earth. God is omnipresent and what was happening in Jerusalem, where Zerubbabel under great difficulties was essaying to build the temple, was of great significance to the whole creation. God reminded Zerubbabel through this vision that it was "not by might, nor by power, but by my spirit, saith the LORD of hosts. . . . For who hath despised the day of small things?" (Zech. 4:6, 10).

The angel also informed Zechariah that the two olive trees emptying the oil into the lamps represented "the two anointed ones, that stand by the Lord of the whole earth" (Zech. 4:14). Although this is not completely explained, it is probable that these "anointed ones" are two specially chosen men, rather than two angels (angels are all "messengers" of God, but none are ever said to be "anointed"; the Messiah is, of course, the "Anointed One," but here there are two, not one). If so, they could only be men who have been taken into heaven without dying; all others, at this stage in history, were still confined in *sheol*, the pit in the heart of the earth where the spirits of men were taken at death.

We have already noted the unique cases of Enoch (whose prophecy to the Gentiles was left unfinished by his bodily translation into heaven) and Elijah (whose ministry to the Jews was similarly left incomplete). They are in heaven, yet today in their specially preserved natural bodies, just "standing by the Lord," intensely concerned with developments on earth and awaiting a special future ministry of their own.

The eighth vision was a "flying roll" (or "scroll"), representing the Word of God. The Scriptures condemn all sin, as represented by stealing and swearing, breaking the two tables of the law, respectively. "Then said he unto me, This is the curse that goeth forth over the face of the whole earth" (Zech. 5:3). This may refer merely to the "curse" of the Mosaic laws, which required perfect obedience (Deut. 27:26). However, the universality of the curse carried by the flying roll suggests that it may more likely refer to the primeval curse on the very ground itself because of man's sin (Gen. 3:17–19).

The ninth vision is quite significant, showing an evil woman being transported in a sealed ephah (i.e., a measuring container, symbolizing commerce), "to build it an house in the land of Shinar: and it shall be established, and set there upon her own base" (Zech. 5:11). Shinar is the ancient name for Babylonia, to which the vessels of the temple had been carried by Nebuchadnezzar (Dan. 1:2), to be placed in the idol temples instead of the house of the true God. At this point in history, Babylonia had been conquered and displaced by the Persian empire, but just as the true religion had been taken captive into Babylon, so, in the last days, would the center of world commerce—as well as immorality—be set again in Babylon.

Shinar is the ancient equivalent of Sumer, which is the name assigned by the world's secular archaeologists to the world's first civilization, there at Babylon. It was there in "a plain in the land of Shinar" (Gen. 11:2) that Nimrod built the great tower of Babel, centering the primeval post-flood rebellion against God. And it was from that "base" in the "land of Shinar" that God did "scatter them abroad upon the face of all the earth" (Gen. 11:9).

According to this vision, however, the world center of covetous commerce, apostate religion, and "wickedness" (Zech. 5:8) will again return to Babel where Satan started it. Presumably this will be in the last days. True religion in that day, however, will return to be centered at Jerusalem. "Thus saith the LORD; I am returned unto Zion, and will dwell in the midst of Jerusalem: and Jerusalem shall be called a city of truth; and the mountain of the LORD of hosts the holy mountain" (Zech. 8:3).

The last three chapters of Zechariah deal with the final divine judgments on the nations and the restoration of Israel and Jerusalem. Appropriately this climactic revelation begins with the foundation of God's right, as Creator, to accomplish all this. "The burden of the word of the LORD for Israel, saith the LORD, which stretcheth forth the heavens, and layeth the foundation of the earth, and formeth the spirit of man within him" (Zech. 12:1).

The end result of the judgments described in these chapters will be great changes in the physical creation as well as the spiritual. "It shall come to pass in that day, that the light shall not be clear, nor dark: But it shall be one day which shall be known to the LORD, not day, nor night, but it shall come to pass, that at evening time it shall be light. And it shall be in that day, that living waters shall go out from Jerusalem; half of them toward the former sea, and half of them toward the hinder sea: in summer and in winter shall it be. And the LORD shall be king over all the earth: in that day shall there be one LORD, and his name one" (Zech. 14:6–9). The God of creation, who divided the day and night at the beginning (Gen. 1:3–5), will forever banish darkness from restored Jerusalem, where (as he did in Eden) he will dwell with his people. As in Eden, where living waters emerged from the garden to water the garden (Gen. 2:10), so will living waters go out from Jerusalem. And, as at the beginning, God will once again reign over his whole creation.

Finally, we come to the last Old Testament prophet and his prophecy, the Book of Malachi. At the very end of the Old Testament, after the marvelous providences of God in reestablishing their land and city and temple worship, the people of Israel were again rebelling—this time not in overt pagan idolatry, but in greed and covetousness, a more subtle form of idolatry.

As Malachi rebuked the religious leaders, the priests, for this state of affairs, he did so on the basis of their origin by divine creation. "Have we not all one father? hath not one God created us? why do we deal treacherously every man against his brother, by profaning the covenant of our fathers?" (Mal. 2:10).

In promising blessing for faithfulness in their stewardship of material possessions granted by the Lord, Malachi used the striking terminology associated with the coming of the great flood in the ancient days of Noah. "Prove me now herewith, saith the LORD of hosts, if I will not open the windows of heaven, and pour you out a blessing, that there · shall not be room enough to receive it" (Mal. 3:10). As torrents of judgment waters from the windows of heaven destroyed a wicked people, so torrents of living waters shall bless a faithful people!

A reminder of the protevangel is given in Malachi's last chapter. "Unto you that fear my name shall the Sun of righteousness arise with healing in his wings. . . . And ye shall tread down the wicked; for they shall be ashes under the soles of your feet in the day that I shall do this, saith the LORD of hosts" (Mal. 4:2, 3; compare Gen. 3:15).

Lastly, there is a promise of the return of Elijah, now waiting in heaven, still in his natural body. "Behold, I will send you Elijah the prophet before the coming of the great and dreadful day of the LORD: and he shall turn the heart of the fathers to the children, and the heart of the children to their fathers, lest I come and smite the earth with a curse" (Mal. 4:5, 6). These are the final words of the Old Testament, calling us back to the faith of our fathers. As we have seen, Elijah will yet come back to finish his prophetic ministry to the Jews (to whom this passage was specifically addressed) and Enoch likewise to the Gentile world.

In the meantime, we now turn to the rich teaching in the New Testament regarding the creation, the flood, and all God's great purposes for his creation.

12

Creation in the Synoptic Gospels

Genesis in the New Testament

Many Christians all but ignore the Old Testament, especially the Book of Genesis, on the assumption that, with the coming of Christ, the Old Testament has been superseded and we are now in the Christian dispensation. This is a serious mistake for many reasons, not least among which is the fact that Jesus Christ and the writers of the New Testament did not ignore it. In fact, it is impossible really to understand the New Testament without at least a general knowledge of the Old Testament.

As far as the foundational Book of Genesis is concerned, it is the most important of all. The New Testament contains at least two hundred quotations or clear allusions to Genesis, and these are scattered throughout the writings of each of the eight or nine writers of the New Testament. All such references indicate that each New Testament writer took the narratives of Genesis literally and seriously.

When the Lord Jesus talked with the two confused disciples on the road to Emmaus after his resurrection, he rebuked them gently for not understanding their Old Testament Scriptures which had revealed prophetically the events which had come to pass. Then, "beginning at

Moses and all the prophets, he expounded unto them in all the scriptures the things concerning himself" (Luke 24:27).

Thus, if we really want to learn about Christ, we ought to begin our Bible study where the greatest Teacher of all did—with "Moses"! And this, of course, means beginning first of all with Genesis, which was compiled and edited into its present form, as the first book of the Pentateuch, by Moses.

In fact, the Lord Jesus has sharply rebuked all who would reject or ignore these writings of Moses (obviously including Genesis). "For had ye believed Moses," he said, "ye would have believed me: for he wrote of me. But if ye believe not his writings, how shall ye believe my words?" (John 5:46, 47).

Further discussion of this Christologic evaluation of Genesis is found in my book, *The Genesis Record,* which also includes a tabulation of all two hundred of the New Testament references to Genesis (pp. 676–82).

It is still more significant that at least one hundred such references are to the first eleven chapters of Genesis. These are the chapters we have been concerned with in this book, the ones dealing with creation, the fall, the flood, and the other events of primeval earth history.

As we shall see, the Lord Jesus Christ himself quoted from—or referred to—events in each of the first seven chapters of Genesis in his teachings as reported in the four Gospels. There can be no question that Jesus Christ, the Son of God, *the Creator himself(!)* believed in the literal historical accuracy and fundamental importance to all Christian doctrine and practice of these great events of primeval history.

The Witness of Matthew

In this chapter, we want to look at the relevant passages in the three synoptic Gospels—Matthew, Mark, and Luke. Since John wrote his Gospel much later than the other three, the early church did not receive his revelations concerning these events until near the end of the apostolic period. Although a few of the Epistles (e.g., 1 Thessalonians, James) may have been written earlier than the Gospels, it will be better to discuss them later, with the other Epistles.

The witness of Matthew is very important, beginning with his very first verse. "The book of the generation of Jesus Christ, the son of David, the son of Abraham" (Matt. 1:1). The comparison with Genesis 5:1 is obvious: "This is the book of the generations of Adam."

As noted earlier, Adam himself probably wrote the early chapters of Genesis, then signed his name when he finished, in the manner cited. The Hebrew for "generations" is *toledoth*, and the repeated *toledoth* formula in Genesis marks the terminus of the contributions of each of the successive original authors.

This parallel use of the phrase here in Matthew, however, is the *only* time the word is used in the New Testament. In a way, the Old and New Testaments are summarized in these two verses. The first is "the book of the generations of Adam"; the second is "the book of the generation of Jesus Christ," the second Adam, the Lord from heaven.

It is significant that the Greek word for "generation" in Matthew 1:1 is *geneseos,* the very word from which we get our English word "genesis." Thus, the title of the first book of the Bible is derived from this key word "generations" (*toledoth* in Genesis, *geneseos* in Matthew).

The verses following this first, key verse of the New Testament then give the genealogy of the ancestors of Jesus Christ, beginning with Abraham, bypassing the links from Adam to Abraham (these, however, are given by Luke, as we shall note shortly).

Matthew frequently refers to Old Testament messianic prophecies, and it is significant that the first reference harks back to the very first prophecy. "Now all this was done, that it might be fulfilled which was spoken of the Lord by the prophet, saying, Behold, a virgin [actually, *the* virgin] shall be with child, and shall bring forth a son, and they shall call his name Emmanuel, which being interpreted is, God with us" (Matt. 1:22, 23).

Matthew here is quoting from Isaiah 7:14, which in turn, as we have already noted, is clearly referring back to the primeval protevangelic promise concerning the coming "seed" of the woman (Gen. 3:15), given by God to Adam and Eve in the Garden of Eden. The divine Son, born of the Virgin Mary, is the long-awaited "seed" of a chosen woman.

Matthew also introduces John the Baptist in his ministry as forerunner of the Messiah. John stressed the nature of God as Creator when he preached to the Pharisees and Sadducees that "God is able of these stones to raise up children unto Abraham" (Matt. 3:9; see also Luke 3:8). Satan, in tempting Jesus in the wilderness, also acknowledged—in a backhanded, perhaps doubting, way—that Jesus claimed to be the Creator. Satan mocked: "If thou be the Son of God, command that these stones be made bread" (Matt. 4:3; see also Luke 4:3, for Luke's report of the same challenge).

In the Sermon on the Mount, Jesus made a number of passing references to God's unique creative power. "He maketh his sun to rise on the evil and on the good, and sendeth rain on the just and on the unjust" (Matt. 5:45). "Behold the fowls of the air: . . . your heavenly Father feedeth them" (Matt. 6:26). The permanence of the created kinds is suggested in Matthew 7:16, 18: "Ye shall know them by their fruits. Do men gather grapes of thorns, or figs of thistles? . . . A good tree cannot bring forth evil fruit, neither can a corrupt tree bring forth good fruit." Note also Luke 6:43.

Many of the miracles of Jesus were clearly miracles of creation, requiring control of nature in ways that only nature's Creator could exercise. For example: "Then he arose, and rebuked the winds and the sea; and there was a great calm. But the men marvelled, saying, What manner of man is this, that even the winds and the sea obey him!" (Matt. 8:26, 27; also see Mark 4:39–41). When he rebuked a group of demons and cast them out of the man whose body they had possessed, they recognized him, crying out: "What have we to do with thee, Jesus, thou Son of God? art thou come hither to torment us before the time?" (Matt. 8:29). Note also Mark 1:24 and Luke 4:41 and 8:28.

Jesus acknowledged the Father as "Lord of heaven and earth" (Matt. 11:25). In teaching his disciples how to pray, he told them to acknowledge that God's will is done in heaven and to conclude with the affirmation "Thine is the kingdom, and the power, and the glory, for ever" (Matt. 6:10, 13).

Two other striking examples of Christ's miracles of creation were his multiplication of the loaves and fishes to feed the multitude (creating bread and meat) and then walking on water (creating an anti-gravity force), as described in Matthew 14:19–33 and Mark 6:37–52.

An especially significant confirmation of Genesis by Christ is found in his answer to the question of the Pharisees about the number of reasons justifying divorce. "Have ye not read," he said, "that He which made them at the beginning made them male and female, and said, For this cause shall a man leave father and mother, and shall cleave to his wife: and they twain shall be one flesh? Wherefore they are no more twain, but one flesh. What therefore God hath joined together, let not man put asunder" (Matt. 19:4–6).

The Lord Jesus Christ clearly taught that marriage—the most basic and important human institution—should be the permanent union of one man and one woman, and his authority for this was the creation record in Genesis! It is obvious that Christ (who was himself the Creator before he became man) regarded the Genesis record as literal, historical, and authoritative. If he did, so should we!

Note also that he was quoting from *both* accounts of creation (Gen. 1:27 and Gen. 2:24) in the same context. He did not regard them as contradictory accounts (as do many modern skeptics), and, therefore, neither should we. If there were no other reasons for doing so (and there are many), this one quotation from the Lord Jesus *should* settle forever the question of the accuracy, clarity, and reliability of the Genesis record of creation.

In a further rebuke to the scribes and Pharisees concerning their rejection of him even as their fathers had rejected their earlier prophets, he even confirmed that Abel, the son of Adam and Eve, was one of these ancient prophets, referring to "the blood of righteous Abel" which had been shed soon after the creation (Matt. 23:35).

In his great prophetic discourse on the Mount of Olives, Jesus not only made reference to "the beginning of the world" (Matt. 24:21), but claimed authority to "send his angels . . . from one end of heaven to the other" (Matt. 24:31) and even to assure that the present "heaven and earth shall pass away" (Matt. 24:35; see also Mark 13:31 and Luke 21:33). None but the Creator of heaven and earth could control their future demise.

In the same discourse, he also confirmed the historicity of Noah, the ark, and the worldwide flood. "But as the days of Noe were, so shall also the coming of the Son of man be. For as in the days that were before the flood they were eating and drinking, marrying and giving in marriage, until the day that Noe entered into the ark, and knew not until the flood came, and took them all away; so shall also the coming of the Son of man be" (Matt. 24:37–39). Thus, if the flood was only a local flood, as many modern evangelicals choose to believe, then the second coming of Christ would only apply to a small region of the world. The flood and its worldwide cataclysmic effects may be an embarrassment to compromising Christian intellectuals, but Jesus Christ confirmed that it happened nonetheless!

In concluding the Olivet discourse, Christ confirmed that he would "come in his glory, and all the holy angels with him" and sit as Judge of all nations "upon the throne of his glory" (Matt. 25:31). None but the Creator could make such a claim and prediction. He also confirmed that the lost would be cast "into everlasting fire, prepared for the devil and his angels" (Matt. 25:41). All rebels against God as Creator/Redeemer, through Christ, must share the eternal destiny of the greatest rebel, Satan, and all the fallen angels.

The greatest of all evidences that Jesus Christ was actually God the Creator, in human flesh, was his bodily resurrection from the dead. Only the Creator of life could conquer death! Thus, after his resurrection, when he died for our sins and rose again, he could claim: "All power is given unto me in heaven and in earth" (Matt. 28:18).

The Confirming Witness of Mark

The Gospel of Mark contains a number of sections that are almost identical with certain sections in Matthew. It may be that one of them drew information from the other, but it has never been firmly settled as to which was the earlier. Since Matthew is almost twice as long as Mark, it may be that Matthew took Mark as a base, then expanded it with further information. It doesn't really matter, since both are divinely inspired and fully consistent, and both contain significant material not found in the other.

One passage in Mark is especially significant in relation to the doctrine of creation. In Mark's account of Christ's response to the Pharisees concerning marriage and divorce, he reports Christ's words as follows: "But from the beginning of the creation God made them male and female" (Mark 10:6; see Matt. 19:4–6 for the parallel account).

This is a reference to the creation of Adam and Eve—in fact, it includes an actual quote from Genesis 1:27—on the sixth day of the primeval week of creation. The important point is that "God made them male and female" *from the beginning of the creation*—not 4.6 billion years after the creation began! Modern evolutionists believe that the "creation" (if that is what one could call it) started with the "big bang" perhaps 15 billion years ago, and human life about a million years ago—long, long *after* the beginning of the creation! Jesus Christ, however, who was *there* at the beginning of the creation, said that man and woman were there, too! "Christian evolution" is a contradiction in terms; there is no such thing. The Lord Jesus Christ was no evolutionist. As God, he was the Creator; as man, he was a creationist. Furthermore, he was a "young-earth creationist"; the very idea of billions of years of meaningless history before man appeared on earth is directly contradicted by this straightforward statement of his. Then, in Mark's account of the Olivet discourse, speaking of the coming time of God's judgment on wicked man, Christ said: "In those days shall be affliction, such as was not from the beginning of the creation which God created unto this time, neither shall be" (Mark 13:19).

At his trial a few days later, his claim of deity was the justification needed by the Sanhedrin to condemn him to death. Here was his claim when they asked him if he was "the Christ, the Son of the Blessed." "I am," he said "and ye shall see the Son of man sitting on the right hand of power, and coming in the clouds of heaven" (Mark 14:62). The centurion in charge of his crucifixion testified: "Truly this man was the Son of God" (Mark 15:39).

After his resurrection, recognizing that all men and women had been *created* by God, Jesus gave his Great Commission: "Preach the gospel to every creature" (Mark 16:15).

The Further Testimony of Luke

The third Gospel may take some material from both Matthew and Mark, but at least half of Luke's material is unique to his book alone, including a number of interesting and significant allusions to the early chapters of Genesis.

At the birth of John the Baptist, his father Zacharias offered praise to God because of the imminent fulfillment of all God's ancient messianic promises given "by the mouth of his holy prophets, which have been since the world began" (Luke 1:70). Note his testimony that God's prophets had been prophesying "since the world began"— not beginning over 4 billion years later! The first of these prophecies had been the promise of the coming "seed" of the woman who would destroy the serpent and bring salvation (Gen. 3:15). Luke describes beautifully the coming of the angel Gabriel from "the presence of God" (Luke 1:19) to announce that the time had come. The forerunner had been prepared and the chosen virgin called. To Mary, he promised that her miraculously conceived child would "be called the Son of the Highest" and that "of his kingdom there [would] be no end" (Luke 1:32, 33). The miracle would be accomplished, said Gabriel, when "the Holy Ghost shall come upon thee, and the power of the Highest shall overshadow thee: therefore also that holy thing which shall be born of thee shall be called the Son of God" (Luke 1:35). In her song of thanksgiving, Mary "rejoiced in God my Saviour" (Luke 1:47), thus acknowledging that her child would also be her God and her Savior. The whole account clearly speaks of the Creator God now undertaking to fulfill his great protevangelic promise. That "holy thing" could be nothing less than a specially created body, just as the body of Adam had been specially created.

The message of the "angel of the Lord" (probably Gabriel) to the shepherds announcing the birth of Jesus further shows this. "I bring you good tidings [i.e., a gospel] of great joy, which shall be to all people" (Luke 2:9, 10). This was not a message only to Israel, but to all the people in God's world. The babe would be "a Saviour, which is Christ the Lord." Then the host of heaven (compare Gen. 2:1) sang: "Glory to God in the highest, and on earth peace, good will toward men" (Luke 2:13, 14).

The aged prophet Simeon, seeing the babe in the temple, likewise recognized that God's "salvation" had been prepared by God "before the face of all people; a light to lighten the Gentiles, and the glory of thy people Israel" (Luke 2:30–32). God was going to fulfill his promises—not only those to Abraham and David, but also the primeval promise to Adam and Eve.

The last half of Luke's third chapter is remarkable as the New Testament substantiation of the ancient genealogy from Adam to Abraham, then on to Mary, mother of Jesus. The listing is carried backward, however, beginning with Joseph, the son-in-law of Heli (who apparently was Mary's father), then continuing back to Nathan, the son of David (Luke 3:23, 31). The parallel genealogy in Matthew goes from David through Solomon—giving the royal lineage—down to Jacob, the father of Joseph, the husband of Mary (Matt. 1:6, 16).

It is interesting that Matthew lists twenty-eight generations from David to Jesus, whereas Luke lists forty-two, both corresponding roughly to one thousand years of actual history. However, it is possible to show that four generations are omitted by Matthew in his genealogy from Solomon to Jechoniah, so it could easily be that several more are omitted by him from Jechoniah down to Joseph. The purpose of such omissions is to be able (perhaps as a memory device) to highlight just fourteen generations each from Abraham to David, David to Jechoniah, and Jechoniah to Jesus (Matt. 1:17).

However, only a relatively small number of generations are omitted, so this structured genealogy in Matthew is certainly no justification for trying to insert many thousands of years of supposed missing generations in the patriarchal genealogies from Adam to Abraham (Gen. 5 and 11), as many have done, thereby hoping to harmonize Genesis with the evolutionary chronology of modern anthropologists. Furthermore, even if several names are omitted for some good reason from Matthew's genealogy, Luke's contains fourteen more names than Matthew, so it is highly probable that Luke's genealogy is complete.

Thus it is significant that Luke does include the genealogy all the way from Jesus back to "Adam, which was the son of God" (Luke 3:38). Luke's record is actually the same as already incorporated, not only in Genesis 5 and 11, but also in 1 Chronicles 1:1–4; 24–27. However, he does include one additional name—Cainan (Luke 3:36), evidently taken from the Septuagint translation of the Old Testament. The name Cainan is not included in any of the ancient Hebrew manuscripts, so its presence here is probably best explained as a copyist's error. Since Cainan had been the name of Adam's great-grandson (Luke 3:37), it may be, for example, that a scribe accidentally also inserted the same name as Noah's great-grandson. In any case, the important point is that Luke— in New Testament times—essentially corroborated the patriarchal genealogy before Abraham back to Adam, thus confirming the historicity of the Genesis genealogies.

Luke also, as does Matthew, mentions "the blood of Abel" as the first in a long line of martyred prophets, the blood of whom "was shed from the foundation of the world" (Luke 11:50, 51), not starting 4 billion years *after* the foundation of the world. He also reports the words of Christ concerning Noah. "And as it was in the days of Noe, so shall it be also in the days of the Son of man. They did eat, they drank, they married wives, they were given in marriage, until the day that Noe entered into the ark, and the flood came, and destroyed them all" (Luke 17:26, 27). Clearly, that flood that "destroyed them all" could have been nothing less than a global cataclysm!

"The things which are impossible with men are possible with God." Here, in Luke 18:27, is another unequivocal affirmation of God's omnipotence as Creator; he is even capable of making a camel pass through a needle's eye. "For he is not a God of the dead, but of the living: for all live unto him" (Luke 20:38). All life, that is, comes from God, for he is the eternally living one. His very words are more permanent than the physical universe, for Christ said: "Heaven and earth shall pass away: but my words shall not pass away" (Luke 21:33). None but the Creator of heaven and earth could make such a claim.

13

The Apostolic Witness and Creationism

The Creationist Approach to Missions

The Apostle Paul was the human writer of fourteen of the twenty-seven books of the New Testament (assuming the Pauline authorship of Hebrews), and he had much to say about creation. He is first encountered, however, in the Book of Acts, where his messages on creation provide a most important pattern for the use of creationism in missions.

Although all Christians were included in the command to go and preach the gospel, Paul was especially called to proclaim salvation to the Gentiles. His testimony to the Jews on his first missionary journey was this: "For so hath the Lord commanded us, saying, I have set thee to be a light of the Gentiles, that thou shouldest be for salvation unto the ends of the earth" (Acts 13:47). Not only was God the Creator of all men, but Christ had come to be the Savior of all men.

Paul, however, never forgetting that the gospel should go "to the Jew first" (Rom. 1:16), typically would go first to the synagogue in any new city he entered. The Jews in the congregation, of course, already knew and believed the Scriptures, including in particular the account of creation in Genesis. The burden of his message in the synagogue was to show from the prophetic Scriptures that Jesus was the Messiah and from his confirmed resurrection that Jesus was the Son of God. Paul did not have to begin with an exposition of the Creator and creation, because they already knew and believed these truths.

It was a different story, however, when he preached to pagans—people who neither knew nor believed the Bible and who did not believe in creation or in a personal God who had created all things. Such people were either atheists or pantheists, and all believed in some form of evolution of all things out of the primeval eternal chaos. This ancient pagan evolutionary system, like that of modern evolutionism, attributed the development of the world and its living creatures to the forces and systems of nature, even though these forces were often personified as various gods and goddesses, inhabiting the stars of the heavens (or even identified *as* the various stars—Venus, Mars, Mercury, etc.).

The first recorded encounter of Paul (accompanied by Barnabas) with followers of these religions was at Lystra, in Asia Minor. After the miraculous healing of a lifelong cripple, the pagan people sought to worship Paul and Barnabas as gods, saying: "The gods are come down to us in the likeness of men. And they called Barnabas, Jupiter; and Paul, Mercurius" (Acts 14:11, 12).

The apostles, however, were appalled at such a turn of events and would have none of their adulation. Instead they cried out, "Sirs, why do ye these things? We also are men of like passions with you, and preach unto you that ye should turn from these vanities [that is, idols] unto the living God, which made heaven, and earth, and the sea, and all things that are therein: who in times past suffered all nations to walk in their own ways. Nevertheless he left not himself without witness, in that he did good, and gave us rain from heaven, and fruitful seasons, filling our hearts with food and gladness" (Acts 14:15–17).

It would have been pointless to quote gospel Scriptures to such people, until they first of all would acknowledge God as Creator. Accordingly, Paul directed them to this great foundational truth—that the true Creator God, the "living God," was the Maker of *all* things, and that the creation itself was filled with evidences of his existence, his power, and his providential goodness.

Paul at Athens

Paul had a similar, but even more significant, encounter at Athens, the great world center of pagan culture and religion. As usual, he went first to the synagogues in the various cities of Greece. His method at

Thessalonica was typical. "Paul, as his manner was, went in unto them, and three sabbath days reasoned with them out of the scriptures, opening and alleging, that Christ must needs have suffered, and risen again from the dead; and that this Jesus, whom I preach unto you, is Christ" (Acts 17:2, 3). He did the same at Berea (Acts 17:10, 11) and at Athens (Acts 17:17). At Athens, however, with the emblems of pagan idolatry everywhere, "his spirit was stirred in him, when he saw the city wholly given to idolatry" (Acts 17:16), so he began to witness "in the market daily with them that met with him."

"Then certain philosophers of the Epicureans, and of the Stoicks, encountered him" (Acts 17:18) and began to dialogue with him. Both types of philosophies had been prevalent in Greece and in the Roman world generally for several centuries. The Epicureans were atheists, believing in the random evolutionary origins of all things (much like modern Darwinians and neo-Darwinians). The Stoicks were evolutionary pantheists (much like modern evolutionary punctuationists, occultists, and mystics, as well as followers of the various ethnic religions). Both, of course, believed in evolution and both encouraged their followers to worship the idols which personified the different forces of nature that had developed and sustained the world.

"Then Paul stood in the midst of Mars' hill, and said, Ye men of Athens, I perceive that in all things ye are too superstitious. For as I passed by, and beheld your devotions, I found an altar with this inscription, TO THE UNKNOWN GOD. Whom therefore ye ignorantly worship, him declare I unto you" (Acts 17:22, 23).

With all their multiplicity of gods and goddesses, the Greeks still retained a dim and all-but-forgotten memory of the "high God," who was above all their quasi-natural, quasi-human, divinities. Ethnologists have found this hazy remembrance of the Creator to be characteristic of most animistic tribes of today, as well as of the many ethnic religions of past and present, but such tribes have allowed their everyday affairs to be dominated by the wide-ranging pantheon of "spirits" of the natural systems surrounding them in their direct environments. They have all but forgotten their Creator in their worship of his creation, though they still subconsciously acknowledge his existence out there, somewhere.

Paul, therefore, knew he needed to bring these Greek philosophers back first of all to an awareness of the Creator's transcendent superiority to all other so-called gods. So he began preaching in this vein. "God that made the world and all things therein, seeing that he is Lord of heaven and earth, dwelleth not in temples made with hands; neither is worshipped with men's hands, as though he needed any thing, seeing he giveth to all life, and breath, and all things" (Acts 17:24, 25).

This is a pattern for us to follow also, whenever we have occasion to witness to such people today—whether they are outright atheists or (more commonly) some variety of pantheist. Both types of evolutionists need, first of all, to be confronted with the true God of creation, the one who made all things and sustains all things—even sustaining their very breath. This Almighty God is not confined to some man-made structure, whether that structure is an ornate temple or a stone image or the mental construct of a philosopher. Furthermore, he is not an "ethnic god" who directs a particular tribe or nation.

This God of the whole world "hath made of one blood all nations of men for to dwell on all the face of the earth, and hath determined the times before appointed, and the bounds of their habitation; that they should seek the Lord, if haply they might feel after him, and find him, though he be not far from every one of us: for in him we live, and move, and have our being; as certain also of your own poets have said, For we are also his offspring" (Acts 17:26–28).

Here is an implied reference by Paul to the primeval command to fill the earth, as given first to Adam, then to Noah (Gen. 1:28; 9:1). All nations are descendants of Adam and Noah and are thus of "one blood," negating all notions, ancient or modern, of long, separate evolutionary histories of different "races." The Bible never uses the term "race," which is purely an evolutionary concept. Darwin, Huxley, and other evolutionists of the post-Darwin century were racists, viewing the "races" as evolving "sub-species" and believing in an evolutionary hierarchy of the races of man, with Negroes at the bottom and Caucasians at the top. Paul here completely refutes all such notions. There is only *one* race—the *human* race! And all are of "one blood."

Furthermore, each tribe and nation has a specific purpose in the divine economy, with God assigning each both spatial and temporal boundaries. There may be in this a reminder of the primeval enforced dispersion of the nations at Babel (Gen. 11:1–9) in order to enable each to fulfill its purpose. Moses also alluded to this (Deut. 32:7–8), and the original divisions of the first wave of nations were outlined in the Table of Nations (Gen. 10).

Paul also reminded these Greek evolutionists that God their Creator was holding their very bodies together. They *could* ignore him, but they *shouldn't*, since they could not even exist without him. Paul, further-more, demonstrated his knowledge of their own literature by citing two of their own philosophers (probably the Stoic Cleanthes and the astronomer Aratus), who had argued for the unitary origin of all men.

Paul then continued to draw the legitimate inferences from these great truths. "Forasmuch then as we are the offspring of God, we ought not to think that the Godhead is like unto gold, or silver, or stone, graven by art and man's device" (Acts 17:29). If it was God who had made them, how could they presume to think they could make "gods" with their own hands—or even with their own philosophical concepts?

"And the times of this ignorance God winked at [that is, overlooked]; but now commandeth all men every where to repent" (Acts 17:30). For many centuries, God had to some extent allowed the people of each nation to go their own way, more and more leaving him out of their thinking, while he was dealing especially with just one nation, through which nation he would convey his written Word and into which he could finally become incarnate as Son of man, bringing his promised redemption to all nations. Now, however, he had finally come back into his world, and it was time for *all* nations to turn back to himself, acknowledging him as both Creator and Savior.

But how could *they* know this? The answer would be to note that one—and only one—man, in all human history, could defeat death. The universal experience of that greatest of all enemies—the inevitable death of every man, no matter how great—provided universal proof that something was dreadfully wrong in the world. In spite of all the good things in the world, giving their testimony to the goodness of God (as Paul had preached to the pagans at Lystra), death always even-tually triumphed. The only one who could ever conquer death must be the one who had pronounced the judgment of death in the first place, and *he* must be the one who had created *life!*

This was Paul's climactic conclusion. "[God] hath appointed a day, in the which he will judge the world in righteousness by that man whom he hath ordained; whereof he hath given assurance unto all men, in that he hath raised him from the dead" (Acts 17:31).

Presumably this was only a summary of the main points of Paul's evan-gelistic message to the Athenian philosophers, as it would take only a minute or two to recite the ten verses (Acts 17:22–31) as recorded here. But they *were* the main *points!* Note that he did not use the Scriptures (as he had with the Jews in their synagogues), for the Athenians neither believed nor even knew the Scriptures. What he *did* emphasize were the twin truths of creation and resurrection. Only the Creator could conquer death, yet death *must* be conquered somehow if this created world were ever to make sense. There *was* too much order and complexity and intelligence and beauty in it—too much *goodness*—for it to be explained by chance or by an evil origin, but its "good" creation would be belied by death if death were never to be conquered by life. The twin evidences of creation—the best proved fact of science—and the bodily resurrection of Christ—the best proved fact of history—constituted absolute assurance of eternal salvation to all who would receive the Creator and his mighty work of redemption by personal faith.

And as always, when such a message is preached, "some mocked," some said, "We will hear thee again," but "certain men clave unto him, and believed" (Acts 17:32, 34).

This was the example left for us by the apostle Paul, that greatest of all evangelists and missionaries. When seeking to lead those to Christ who already know and believe the Bible, then we should *use* the Bible, citing the biblical evidences of his deity and saving gospel. But when trying to reach those who do not know or believe the Scriptures, then we should stress the great evidences of creation and resurrection. Not all will believe—but *some* will!

The testimony of modern missionaries in pagan lands, as well as in the modern pagan enclaves in Christendom (e.g., the college and university campuses), provides abundant confirmation of the ongoing validity of this Pauline approach to missions.

Peter and James and Creation

The most important sections on creationism in the Book of Acts, by far, are the messages of the apostle Paul at Lystra and Athens. There are, however, certain inferences in the messages and testimonies of the other apostles, as recorded in this book, which should also be mentioned.

The experience on the first day of Pentecost after Christ's resurrection was most notable. "Suddenly there came a sound from heaven as of a rushing mighty wind. . . . And they were all filled with the Holy Ghost, and began to speak with other tongues, as the Spirit gave them utterance" (Acts 2:2, 4).

To those Jews who could only understand the Hebrew and Greek and perhaps the Aramaic languages, this must have sounded like Babel and the primeval confusion of tongues. In fact, certain scoffers who were present attributed it all to mere drunken babbling (Acts 2:13).

In a sense, however, it was the reverse of Babel. There, the different tongues were used to *prevent humanistic communication,* thus forcing all the people to scatter and build their own various nations. Here, the purpose of the different languages was to *implement communication of the gospel,* so that all could hear in their own tongues (at least fifteen are mentioned specifically by name, with the further implication that "every nation under heaven" was actually included—note Acts 2:5, 8–11) "the wonderful works of God," and thus unite them all as *one* holy nation under God. In his sermon following, Peter stressed that all this was in fulfillment of the Old Testament prophecy (Joel 2:28–32) when God said, "I will pour out of my Spirit upon all flesh" (Acts 2:17). No longer was God ignoring the Gentile nations that had been formed after the dispersion at Babel, for now "whosoever shall call on the name of the Lord shall be saved" (Acts 2:21). The promise, he said, was now "unto you, and to your children, and to all that are afar off, even as many as the Lord our God shall call" (Acts 2:39).

In his next sermon, Peter reminded the people of God's primeval promises, which were now in process of fulfillment. "And he shall send Jesus Christ, which before was preached unto you: whom the heaven must receive until the times of restitution [that is, restoration] of all things, which God hath spoken by the mouth of all his holy prophets since the world began" (Acts 3:20, 21).

Contrary to the opinions of the pagan philosophers, there had been a *beginning!* And from the beginning (not several billion years after the beginning!), God had been promising the coming Savior. In fact, the word here for "world" is the Greek *aion,* meaning "time" or "age" or even "space/time." Thus Peter was saying that the promise had been given through the prophets since the very beginning of time, or the beginning of the space/time universe. There is surely no room for any evolutionary ages before man in this context!

The global implications of the gospel were further emphasized by Peter in yet another message when he said, "Neither is there salvation in any other: for there is none other name under heaven given among men, whereby we must be saved" (Acts 4:12). The absolute omnipotence and foreordaining omniscience of the Creator were stressed by Peter when he with the other believers prayed, "Lord, thou art God, which hast made heaven, and earth, and the sea, and all that in them is

. . . For of a truth against thy holy child Jesus, whom thou hast anointed, both Herod, and Pontius Pilate, with the Gentiles, and the people of Israel, were gathered together, for to do whatsoever thy hand and thy counsel determined before to be done" (Acts 4:24, 27–28).

Another of the early preachers, Stephen, in his mighty address to his persecutors, reminded the Jews that they had often rejected the true God for the pantheistic religion of their enemies. Finally God "gave them up to worship the host of heaven" (Acts 7:42) and sent them into captivity. Even now, they were forgetting that "the most High dwelleth not in temples made with hands," and that God had said, "Heaven is my throne, and the earth is my footstool" (Acts 7:48, 49). The Jews, he said, "have received the law by the disposition of angels, and have not kept it" (Acts 7:53). As they stoned him to death, he said, "Behold, I see the heavens opened, and the Son of man standing on the right hand of God" (Acts 7:56).

As a result of the persecution against the church that followed Stephen's assassination, "they were all scattered abroad," and "they that were scattered abroad went every where preaching the word" (Acts 8:1, 4). The first Great Commission (the dominion mandate) had to be first implemented by an enforced scattering from Babel. Now the second Great Commission had to be first energized by an enforced scattering from Jerusalem.

Peter's remarkable vision of all God's created animals was what impelled him first to preach to the Gentiles. "He fell into a trance, and saw heaven opened, and a certain vessel descending unto him, as it had been a great sheet knit at the four corners, and let down to the earth: wherein were all manner of fourfooted beasts of the earth, and wild beasts, and creeping things, and fowls of the air. . . . And the voice spake unto him again the second time, What God hath cleansed, that call not thou common" (Acts 10:10–12, 15).

Thus God eliminated his ancient distinction between clean and unclean animals, first mentioned by Noah (Gen. 7:2; 8:20). Only the clean animals had been suitable for sacrifice, but now Christ's one great sacrifice had eliminated all need for further sacrifices, and the distinction was obsolete. Also, of course, the vision showed Peter that the gospel made no distinction between Jew and Gentile, so he proceeded to the house of the Gentile Cornelius to lead him to Christ.

Peter, of course, like Paul, has much to say about creation and the flood in his Epistles, but these references will be discussed in the following chapters. The same is true in the Epistle of James. James also makes one important appearance and an important reference to creation here in the Book of Acts.

At the council in Jerusalem, assembled to consider the question of Gentiles in the church, and their relation to the law of Moses, the apostle James was apparently the presiding elder. After hearing the testimony of Peter, as well as that of Paul and Barnabas, James issued his decision that the Gentiles, like the Jewish Christians, were saved by the grace of Christ alone and were not under bondage to the law.

In justification of his conclusion, James made the following important observation: "Known unto God are all his works from the beginning of the world" (Acts 15:18). James thus added his own testimony to that of many others—namely, that God is Creator of time (so that he knows all things before they happen) as well as space and matter and all things that happen in space and time, and secondly, that the world of space and time did, indeed, have a *beginning!* The universe has not been here from eternity, as evolutionary philosophy presupposes. Only God is eternal; he is, therefore, the Creator, Sustainer, Controller, and Judge of all things.

14

Creation and the Fall in Paul's Epistles

The Vital Word to the Romans

The thirteen Epistles of Paul (fourteen, if Hebrews is included) contain many key references to the events of Genesis 1–11, especially creation and the fall. There can be no question that Paul viewed these ancient records as literal, historically accurate, divinely inspired, completely inerrant, vital components in the saving gospel of Christ.

Probably the most important references, appropriately enough, are in the Epistle to the Romans, the longest of Paul's letters. Rome, of course, was the capital of the great Roman empire, which ruled the Mediterranean world (including the land of Israel and all the countries covered by Paul's missionary travels) during New Testament times. The Roman culture and religion had been inherited in large measure from Greece and Persia, Assyria and Egypt, and ultimately from Babylon. This was all, as previously emphasized, essentially a system built around a philosophy of evolutionary pantheistic humanism.

This, in fact, is the theme of the central portion of the very first chapter of Romans. All men once knew the true God of creation, and he was still very evident in his creation, but they rejected him, the Creator, to worship his creatures. Here is the terrible indictment, applicable to all the Gentile nations, from Nimrod and ancient Babel, down to the present day.

When they knew God, they glorified him not as God, neither were thankful; but became vain in their imaginations [or reasonings], and their foolish heart was darkened. Professing themselves to be wise, they became fools, and changed the glory of the uncorruptible God into an image made like to corruptible man, and to birds, and fourfooted beasts, and creeping things. Wherefore God also gave them up to uncleanness through the lusts of their own hearts, to dishonour their own bodies between themselves: who changed the truth of God into a lie, and worshipped and served the creature more than the Creator, who is blessed for ever. Amen (Rom. 1:21–25).

This classic passage looks far back to the immediate post-flood world, when Noah and his family all "knew God." It was not long, however, before Nimrod led most of his own generation into apostasy, with all of them finally worshiping various components of God's creation (men, birds, beasts, creeping things) instead of God. These natural systems and forces, personified by the idol images and astrological emblems representing various men and women and animals, became objects of worship and the true God was soon forgotten. They changed the truth of creation into the lie of evolution. Making a great profession of humanistic wisdom, they actually became vain fools, according to Paul.

And since godless philosophy begets godless behavior, they soon also abandoned any concern for God's moral standards, especially his primeval establishment of permanent, monogamous marriage and God-centered family and home life. "For this cause God gave them up unto vile affections: for even their women did change the natural use into that which is against nature: and likewise also the men, leaving the natural use of the woman, burned in their lust one toward another; men with men working that which is unseemly, and receiving in themselves that recompence of their error which was meet. And even as they did not like to retain God in their knowledge, God gave them over to a reprobate mind, to do those things which are not convenient" (Rom. 1:26–28).

One cannot help but note the striking similarity of this tragic descent of the ancient world into the gross darkness of evolutionary pantheism with that of the precipitous apostasy of modern "Christendom" into the same morass. The account in Romans 1:29–32 goes on to list the terrible agenda of evil practices resulting from this godless philosophy, so characteristic of both the ancient world and the modern world. Because men would not honor the true God who created them, preferring to attribute ultimate reality and meaning to the world itself, God "gave them up to uncleanness," then "gave them up unto vile affections," and finally "gave them over to a reprobate mind" (Rom. 1:24, 26, 28).

There was never—and is not now—any justification for this rejection of the Creator and acceptance of any form of evolutionism. "For the invisible things of him from the creation of the world are clearly seen, being understood by the things that are made, even his eternal power and Godhead; so that they are without excuse" (Rom. 1:20).

The "things that are made," rather than suggesting evolution, give an unequivocal witness to creation, in their complexity, their beauty, their utility, their interrelationships, and in many other ways. The basic laws controlling all the processes through which they interact (that is, the laws of energy and entropy) demonstrate the necessary *fact* of their primeval supernatural creation by God's "eternal power." The trinitarian structure of the universe in which they function similarly speaks analogously of the trinitarian nature of their Creator, the "Godhead." That is, the universe is a marvelous trinity of trinities, a *uni*-verse (not a multi-verse) of space, time, and the phenomena (matter and energy) which occupy all space and all time. Space is three-dimensional (length, width, height), with each dimension comprising the whole. Time is also tri-une (future, present, past), with each component of time comprising all of time. The events of matter/energy which perpetually occupy all space/time originate in omnipresent, unseen energy; then become seen and identified by their motions through space during time; and ultimately are experienced as distinct phenomena (light, heat, hardness, sound, etc.). These all are beautifully analogous to the Godhead—one God, yet three persons (Father, Son, Spirit).

All this is discussed more fully elsewhere,[1] but the vital fact is that there is such an abundance of clear evidence of the Creator in his creation that those who reject or ignore it are "without excuse." The word in the Greek here is *apologia*, or "defense." It is a legal term referring to the arguments put up by an attorney for the defense, trying to support a client who is under indictment. Thus, the evolutionist is said to be without an apologetic for his position, defenseless against the overwhelming evidence for creation!

The next important reference in Romans has to do with the fall of man and the resultant curse of death on man and his dominion.

Wherefore, as by one man sin entered into the world, and death by sin; and so death passed upon all men, for that all have sinned (. . . death reigned from Adam to Moses, even over them that had not sinned after the similitude of Adam's transgression, who is the figure of him that was to come. . . . For if through the offence of one many be dead, much more the grace of God, and the gift by grace, which is by one man, Jesus Christ, hath abounded unto many. And not as it was by one that sinned, so is the gift: for the judgment was by one to condemnation, but the free gift is of many offences unto justification. For if by one man's offence death reigned by one; much more they which receive abundance of grace and of the gift of righteousness shall reign in life by one, Jesus Christ.) Therefore as by the offence of one judgment came upon all men to condemnation; even so by the righteousness of one the free gift came upon all men unto justification of life. For as by one man's disobedience many were made sinners, so by the obedience of one shall many be made righteous (Rom. 5:12, 14–19).

This extended quotation emphasizes over and over again, in various ways, the first man, Adam, as a contrasting type of Christ. The sin of Adam, rebelling against the word of God, brought death into God's previously "very good" world (compare Gen. 1:31; 3:17–20). In contrast, the obedience of Christ brought the free gift of salvation into the lost world.

Adam, therefore, beyond doubt, is viewed by the apostle Paul as a real man, not some kind of allegory. If he is not real, then Christ is not real. If sin and death are not real, then salvation and eternal life are not real. The sin and death of the first man, passed through him to all men, thus provide the very foundation of Christian theology. The reason we need Christ as Savior is that in Adam (as well as in our own actions) we have sinned against our Maker. We are all "dead" in Adam "through the offence of one" (v. 15), but also we "all have sinned" (v. 12) as a result of our inherited sin-nature.

It is very important also to note that there was no death in the world until sin entered the world through Adam (v. 12). Modern evolutionary theory assumes that suffering and death reigned in the world for hundreds of millions of years before man appeared and brought sin into the world. By such a concept, death is part of nature itself, having no relation to sin at all. Thus God would become directly responsible for the supposed worldwide, billion-year-long monstrous system of suffering and death—and this cannot possibly be true of the omniscient, omnipotent, loving, gracious God revealed in the Bible. Evolution perhaps can be rationalized in terms of atheism or pantheism, but certainly not in monotheism.

Furthermore, if death reigned for a billion years and, therefore, is not really the divine penalty for sin, then the death of Christ can have no special significance, and we have no promise of salvation and eternal life after all. The whole scenario of evolution, however, is nothing but a humanistic nightmare, with no reality to it at all. Adam *did* bring sin and death into the world, and Christ *did* bring righteousness and life back into the world, and the free gift of God's grace is real!

There are still certain Christian compromisers, however, who argue that it was only human death that Adam brought into the world with his sin, and that animals (including human-like creatures before Adam) had, indeed, been suffering and dying for long ages prior to man. This unwarranted twisting of the plain meaning of the Scriptures is completely refuted by the tremendous testimony of Romans 8:19–23.

> For the earnest expectation of the creature [same as "creation"] waiteth for the manifestation of the sons of God. For the creature was made subject to vanity, not willingly, but by reason of him who hath subjected the same in hope, because the creature [same as "creation"] itself also shall be delivered from the bondage of corruption into the glorious liberty of the children of God. For we know that the whole creation groaneth and travaileth in pain together until now. And not only they, but ourselves also, which have the firstfruits of the Spirit, even we ourselves groan within ourselves, waiting for the adoption, to wit, the redemption of our body.

It is thus not just the human realm but the *whole creation* which is travailing in pain under the "bondage of corruption" brought on by man's sin. The "bondage of corruption," incidentally, suggests the second law of thermodynamics, for it can also be translated "bondage of decay." The creation will one day be delivered from this bondage under sin and death and we shall "be also glorified together" with Christ (Rom. 8:17) when he comes to complete his work of redemption and to accomplish all his purposes in creation.

In the great predestination chapter (Rom. 9), Paul speaks of God as the great Potter. "O man, who art thou that repliest against God. Shall the thing formed say to him that formed it, Why hast thou made me thus? Hath not the potter power over the clay, of the same lump to make one vessel unto honour, and another unto dishonour?" (Rom. 9:20, 21).

In the next chapter, he speaks of the witness in the heavens, quoting the 19th psalm. "But I say, Have they not heard? Yes verily, their sound went into all the earth, and their words unto the ends of the world" (Rom. 10:18).

Then, in the eleventh chapter, Paul utters a tremendous doxology to God's omniscience and omnipotence, as well as his eternal preexistence, before the creation. "O the depth of the riches both of the wisdom and knowledge of God! how unsearchable are his judgments, and his ways past finding out! For who hath known the mind of the Lord? or who hath been his counseller. . . . For of him, and through him, and to him, are all things: to whom be glory for ever. Amen" (Rom. 11:33, 34, 36).

There is also a confirmation of the divine institution of human government in all nations, as implied in the Noahic covenant, in particular confirming the prerogative of capital punishment (see Gen. 9:6). "Let every soul be subject unto the higher powers. For there is no power but of God: the powers that be are ordained of God. . . . For [the ruler] is the minister of God to thee for good. But if thou do that which is evil, be afraid; for he beareth not the sword in vain: for he is the minister of God, a revenger to execute wrath upon him that doeth evil" (Rom. 13:1, 4).

Finally, there is even an implied reference in Romans to the protevangel of Genesis 3:15, as tentatively fulfilled in each Christian believer. "And the God of peace shall bruise Satan under your feet shortly" (Rom. 16:20).

And one last passing reference to the beginning of the world is contained in Paul's closing word to the Romans. "Now to him that is of power to stablish you according to my gospel, and the preaching of Jesus Christ, according to the revelation of the mystery, which was kept secret since the world began . . . to God only wise, be glory through Jesus Christ for ever" (Rom. 16:25, 27).

The Creation Testimony from Corinth to Ephesus

As in the Epistle to the church at Rome, Paul's two letters to the Corinthian church contain several significant references to creation and the subsequent curse on the creation. These are highly significant events for Christian theology, according to the apostle Paul.

The first of these is a confirmation of the unique nature of the creation of the first woman. "For the man is not of the woman; but the woman of the man. Neither was the man created for the woman; but the woman for the man. . . . For as the woman is of the man, even so is the man also by the woman; but all things of God" (1 Cor. 11:8–9, 12).

This is obviously a reference to the unique formation of Eve from the side of Adam (Gen. 2:18, 21–23). In addition to the doctrinal significance of this event—indicating, as it does, the divinely intended roles for men and women in the home and family—this reference in the Corinthian letter is an important confirmation of the literal historicity of the Genesis account. The remarkable formation of the first woman from the man is the despair of the theistic evolutionist, who must try to interpret this in some esoteric way to correlate with his assumed premise of human evolution from hominid precursors, including both male and female members of an evolving population. This invariably proves an impossible task, so he usually must simply regard the Genesis record as some kind of imaginative allegory, perhaps depicting woman as near and dear to man's heart, or something.

The most important Corinthian references to Genesis, however, are in the great resurrection chapter, 1 Corinthians 15. It is fitting to note once again the vital relationship of these two greatest of all miracles—the creation of the world and the resurrection of its Creator. "For since by man came death, by man came also the resurrection of the dead. For as in Adam all die, even so in Christ shall all be made alive" (1 Cor. 15:21, 22).

Here again (as in Rom. 5), Paul not only confirms the true historicity of Adam, but also the truth that it was Adam who brought death into the world when he rejected God's word. In Adam *all* die, and now the whole creation is in bondage to the principle of decay and death. None but the Creator himself, who is the giver of life, and who imposed the judgment of death on man's dominion, can possibly reverse that judgment and bring it back to life again. Therefore, "in Christ shall all be made alive." His death for the sin of the world perfectly satisfied divine justice, and his resurrection from the dead—unique in all history—gives full assurance that the debt is forever paid.

We note again how completely this negates the evolutionary scenario, which visualizes death as reigning in the world for long ages before Adam. Or—if one prefers to believe in evolution—the meaning of the death of Christ is completely lost. One cannot have it both ways. But Christ *did* rise from the dead, as this great 15th chapter of 1

Corinthians so compellingly demonstrates, thereby defeating not death only but also the whole evolutionary lie of Satan.

But there is still more in this chapter. The creation record in Genesis notes ten times that each kind of animal and plant that God created was distinctively different, with each kind created only "after its kind." This is specifically confirmed in the following passage.

> And that which thou sowest, thou sowest not that body that shall be, but bare grain, it may chance of wheat, or of some other grain: but God giveth it a body as it hath pleased him, and to every seed his own body. All flesh is not the same flesh: but there is one kind of flesh of men, another flesh of beasts, another of fishes, and another of birds. There are also celestial bodies, and bodies terrestrial: but the glory of the celestial is one, and the glory of the terrestrial is another. There is one glory of the sun, and another glory of the moon, and another glory of the stars: for one star differeth from another star in glory (1 Cor. 15:37–41).

Note that every "seed"—whether of plant, or man, or beast, or fish, or bird—is distinctive. God has implanted within each type of seed its "own body," guaranteeing that it must produce only its own kind, not evolving into some other kind. This passage not only confirms the account of creation of the different kinds in Genesis but also is itself confirmed by all the actual *facts* (as opposed to evolutionary speculations) of genetics, physiology, and all other relevant sciences.

The principle applies also to other aspects of the created universe, even in the heavens. God is not capricious; every system was created with its own distinctive structure to accomplish its own divine purpose. Even though all stars look alike to human observers—either to the naked eye or through a telescope—as mere points of light, modern astronomy confirms that every star is uniquely different from every other star. Each will plot at a different point on the "H-R Diagram," a type of plot which relates temperature and luminosity. Each star does, indeed, differ from every other star "in glory."

There is still one further reference to Adam in this chapter, once again noting Adam as a contrasting type of Christ. "And so it is written, The first man Adam was made a living soul [quoting Gen. 2:7]; the last Adam was made a quickening [that is, life-giving] spirit. . . . The first man is of the earth, earthy: the second man is the Lord from heaven" (1 Cor. 15:45, 47).

Twice in this passage Adam is called "the first man." This explicitly refutes the oft-expressed notion that there may have been "pre-Adamite men" in the world, as represented by the various "hominid" fossils. This is not the place to discuss these fossils. They can all be shown, I believe, to be either descendants of Adam (in some cases, such as the Neanderthals) or extinct apes (such as the Australopithecines), but the Bible itself allows no such notion as men before Adam. Adam was made from "earth" and, because of sin, returned to earth, but the "second Adam" is the one who brings life out of death!

As we move on to the next book, we note that there are two key passages in Paul's second letter to the Corinthians. First, the entrance of the gospel into a sin-darkened life is likened to the primeval entrance of light into a world where there was initially nothing but darkness. "If our gospel be hid, it is hid to them that are lost: in whom the god of this world hath blinded the minds of them which believe not, lest the light of the glorious gospel of Christ, who is the image of God, should shine unto them. . . . For God, who commanded the light to shine out of darkness, hath shined in our hearts, to give the light of the knowledge of the glory of God in the face of Jesus Christ" (2 Cor. 4:3–4, 6).

Paul is referring here, of course, to the first day of creation week, when "darkness was upon the face of the deep," and then "God said, Let there be light" (Gen. 1:2, 3). "The god of this world" is Satan, who "hath blinded the minds" of both men and women ever since he succeeded in this with Adam and Eve. Only the saving gospel of Christ can bring salvation's light into a mind darkened with innate sin against the Creator.

The historicity of Eve's temptation is also confirmed. "I fear, lest by any means, as the serpent beguiled Eve through his subtilty, so your minds should be corrupted from the simplicity that is in Christ" (2 Cor. 11:3). This is an explicit reference to Satan's use of the serpent—which was more subtil than any beast of the field"—to tempt Eve to doubt God's word (Gen. 3:1–6). Satan is still using devious means to tempt the unwary. "And no marvel; for Satan himself is transformed into an angel of light. Therefore it is no great thing if his ministers also be transformed as the ministers of righteousness; whose end shall be according to their works" (2 Cor. 11:14, 15).

One other familiar verse could possibly be mentioned in this connection. "Therefore if any man be in Christ, he is a new creature [same as "creation"]: old things are passed away; behold, all things are become new" (2 Cor. 5:17). The transition from darkness to light, from death to life, when a person believes on the Lord Jesus Christ requires the same creative power that God exercised when he created man in his image in the beginning. Such a person is "a new creation," nothing less.

The same term occurs again in Paul's Epistle to the churches of Galatia. "For in Christ Jesus neither circumcision availeth any thing, nor uncircumcision, but a new creature" (Gal. 6:15). The Galatian letter contains only one other possible reference to the Genesis record, when Paul notes that "the Scripture hath concluded all under sin, that the promise by faith of Jesus Christ might be given to them that believe" (Gal. 3:22). The sin of Adam not only brought the penalty of death on himself but also, because of the curse on his entire dominion, on all his descendants as well. At the same time, the protevangelical promise of the eventual coming of Jesus Christ was given to Adam and Eve and all their progeny, faith in which would provide salvation from sin and death—first to Adam and Eve themselves, then for all others who would believe later. Note he was "made of a woman" (Gal. 4:4).

The Book of Ephesians, unlike Galatians, does contain a number of significant comments on the primeval world, beginning in its opening verses. "[God] hath chosen us in [Christ] before the foundation of the world" (Eph. 1:4). This is an amazing revelation, impossible to comprehend with the mind, but marvelous to believe with the heart! Somehow God knew us and chose us who believe even before he created the universe.

In the next chapter, the Scripture tells us *why* God chose us and then created us. "For we are his workmanship, created in Christ Jesus unto good works, which God hath before ordained that we should walk in them" (Eph. 2:10).

He *created* us in Christ just as he had *chosen* us in Christ. The Greek word for "workmanship" is *poema*, from which we get the English word "poem." Each person who has been newly created by Christ is like a divine poem being written by the Creator. The same word is used in Romans 1:20, where it is rendered by the phrase "the things that are made"—that is, the created cosmos. These are the only two occurrences of *poema*, indicating that the creation of the universe is quite comparable to the new creation of a redeemed soul—both are divine poetic masterpieces.

A similar attribution is found in Ephesians 4:23, 24. "Be renewed in the spirit of your mind; and . . . put on the new man, which after God is created in righteousness and true holiness." Our new special creation in Christ is a creation unto good works, righteousness, and true holiness, though it is conditioned only on faith in Christ and his saving work.

Another amazing purpose of our creation to new life in Christ "to make all men see what is the fellowship of the mystery, which from the beginning of the world hath been hid in God, who created all things by Jesus Christ: to the intent that now unto the principalities and powers in heavenly places might be known by the church the manifold wisdom of God, according to the eternal purpose which he purposed in Christ Jesus our Lord" (Eph. 3:9–11).

This remarkable passage reveals plainly that, at the beginning of the world, God created all things by Jesus Christ. The Lord Jesus Christ was our Creator as well as our Savior! Furthermore we are given the remarkable insight that we are being observed by the angels—"the principalities and powers in heavenly places"—probably both the holy angels and the fallen angels. Somehow even *this* was involved in God's eternal purpose to choose and save us. We have indeed a high calling, even teaching God's mighty angels something about his amazing grace!

Another important passage in Ephesians teaches the permanence of the marriage relationship, treating it as a type of Christ and the church and basing it on the Genesis record of the first marriage. "Husbands, love your wives, even as Christ also loved the church, and gave himself for it. . . . For we are members of his body, of his flesh, and of his bones. For this cause shall a man leave his father and mother, and shall be joined unto his wife, and they two shall be one flesh. This is a great mystery: but I speak concerning Christ and the church" (Eph. 5:25, 30–32).

This is a strong Pauline confirmation of the historical reality of the remarkable formation of the body of Eve from the flesh and bones of Adam. He is quoting specifically from the original account in Genesis 2:21–25. The Lord Jesus also referred to this passage in his own teaching on marriage in Matthew 19:3–6. However, this is the first and only place where the creation of Eve out of Adam, and for Adam, is taken also as a type of the relation between Christ and his church. Since every marriage subsequent to Adam and Eve also, by this unique passage, constitutes a type of Christ and the church, this becomes a great incentive to husbands and wives to keep their own marriages pure and permanent.

The sole reference in Philippians to the primeval world is the famous passage on the incarnation of the Creator. "Christ Jesus . . ., being in the form of God, thought it not robbery to be equal with God: but made himself of no reputation, and took upon him the form of a ser-

vant, and was made in the likeness of men" (Phil. 2:5–7). The Lord
Jesus, our Redeemer and Savior, was also our Creator.

Colossians and Thessalonians

Paul's Epistle "to the saints and faithful brethren in Christ which are
at Colosse" contains some of the most important references to creation
in the New Testament. Note the following tremendous passage in particular.

[Christ] is the image of the invisible God, the firstborn of every creature:
for by him were all things created, that are in heaven, and that are in
earth, visible and invisible, whether they be thrones, or dominions, or
principalities, or powers: all things were created by him, and for him: and
he is before all things, and by him all things consist. And he is the head
of the body, the church: who is the beginning, the firstborn from the
dead; that in all things he might have the preeminence. For it pleased
the Father that in him should all fulness dwell; and, having made peace
through the blood of his cross, by him to reconcile all things unto Himself; by Him, I say, whether they be things in earth, or things in heaven
(Col. 1:15–20).

This is perhaps the greatest of all Christological passages. Note the
repeated references to "by him" and "all things," recording the past,
present, and future works of Christ with reference to the whole creation, all things in earth and heaven.

By him were all things created.
By him all things consist [literally, are sustained].
By him [it pleased the Father] to reconcile all things

Again Paul stresses (as he does in Ephesians) that Jesus Christ was
the person in the Godhead by whom all things were created in the
beginning. It is noteworthy that here—as well as in all other passages
in the Bible which mention the creation of all things—creation is in the
past tense. All things *were created,* in the beginning; they are *not still
being created,* as evolutionism assumes. This confirms again the statement that "God rested" from all his work of creating and making all
things during creation week.

Christ is not only the Creator but also the Sustainer of the creation, by his infinite power keeping all its systems from collapsing into chaos. Finally he will ultimately reconcile all things to himself, having already paid the redemption price with the blood of his cross.

He is twice called "the firstborn." He is the eternally begotten (therefore the firstborn) Son, in the bosom of the Father. He is also "the first-born from the dead," having defeated the great enemy, death, and been raised from the dead. He has "the preeminence" in all things, both because he created life and all things in the beginning and also because he conquered death after dying for the world's sin.

Therefore, whenever anyone boasts that he does not preach about creation but only about the person and work of Christ, he is really preaching "another Jesus," not the real Jesus Christ. The real Jesus was Creator and created all things long before he became Savior and Redeemer. The very reason we need him as Savior is that we have all rebelled against him as our Creator.

In continuing the same discussion, Paul says that "the gospel . . . was preached to every creature which is under heaven" (Col. 1:23). This has been a controversial verse because it seems impossible that the gospel could have been preached to every person in the whole world of Paul's day in just thirty years. However, the phrase "to every creature" can better be translated "in every creation," and this would tell us (as per Ps. 19:1; Rom. 1:20; etc.) that the very nature of creation in its every aspect is bearing witness to the existence and nature of God, and even to his sacrificial love and grace. Furthermore, "in [Christ] are hid all the treasures of wisdom and knowledge" (Col. 2:3).

There then follows a subtle reference to the promised victory of the seed of the woman over the serpent in Genesis 3:15. "Having spoiled principalities and powers, he made a shew of them openly, triumphing over them in it" (Col. 2:15).

Another significant verse refers to Genesis 1:26 and the creation of man in the image of God. Even though Adam sinned and marred that image, it is still there and can be made new by the new birth. "Ye have put off the old man with his deeds; and have put on the new man, which is renewed in knowledge after the image of him that created him" (Col. 3:9, 10).

Unlike the Colossian Epistle, the two letters to the church at Thessalonica have few if any references to creation or other events of pre-Abraham history. These two books, which were probably the first ones written by Paul, address other issues. Interestingly enough, they have more references to the consummation than most of his other epistles, but fewer to the creation.

However, even at this early stage of Paul's ministry, there is no doubt that he believed strongly in the creation. These Epistles place strong emphasis on Christ's resurrection and also on his second coming to complete his redemptive work, both of which uniquely miraculous events require his sovereign power as Creator. Both Epistles also refer to the ministry of his holy angels and the conversion of the Thessalonians from idolatrous evolutionary polytheism.

For example, note the following passages from the first Epistle: "Ye turned to God from idols to serve the living and true God; and to wait for his Son from heaven, whom he raised from the dead, even Jesus, which delivered us from the wrath to come" (1 Thess. 1:9, 10). "We believe that Jesus died and rose again. . . . the Lord himself shall descend from heaven with a shout, with the voice of the archangel, and with the trump of God" (1 Thess. 4:14, 16).

Then, note these from 2 Thessalonians: "The Lord Jesus shall be revealed from heaven with his mighty angels, in flaming fire taking vengeance on them that know not God, and that obey not the gospel of our Lord Jesus Christ: who shall be punished with everlasting destruction from the presence of the Lord, and from the glory of his power" (2 Thess. 1:7–9). "The Lord shall . . . destroy with the brightness of his coming: even him, whose coming is after the working of Satan with all power and signs and lying wonders" (2 Thess. 2:8, 9).

Such power as attributed to Christ in these verses could be true only of the Creator.

The Pastoral Epistles and Their Creation Witness

Paul's two letters to young Timothy, plus one each to Titus and Philemon, are known as the Pastoral Epistles. These also contain a number of references to the early records in Genesis. First, in justifying his instruction that women should not have pastoral or teaching authority over men in a church, Paul refers to the example of Adam and Eve. "For Adam was first formed, then Eve. And Adam was not deceived, but the woman being deceived was in the transgression. Notwithstanding she shall be saved in childbearing, if they continue in faith and charity and holiness with sobriety" (1 Tim. 2:13–15).

This passage is an explicit Pauline confirmation of the historical validity of the account of the creation and fall of Adam and Eve. There is also a somewhat enigmatic reference to the divine curse as it applied to the conception and birth of children through the woman (Gen. 3:16). The promise that she will be saved through childbearing very possibly refers—at least in type—to the prophecy of the coming Savior as the seed of the woman (Gen. 3:15).

In the next chapter, in outlining the qualifications of bishops, Paul cautions against the selection of any new Christian to hold such an office, "lest being lifted up with pride he fall into the condemnation of the devil" (1 Tim. 3:6). Pride, coupled with unbelief, is really the root of every sin and was the occasion of the primeval fall of Satan from his exalted place in the angelic hierarchy in the beginning.

Paul then warns against "seducing spirits, and doctrines of devils" who, in attempting to corrupt God's primeval command regarding marriage, will be "forbidding to marry, and commanding to abstain from meats" (1 Tim. 4:1, 3). The latter command from these demonic spirits opposes God's post-flood instruction to Noah (Gen. 9:3). Both attitudes—rejecting marriage and demanding vegetarianism—are increasingly common in these "latter times" (1 Tim. 4:1). In opposition to forced vegetarianism and legalistic banning of certain foods, Paul reiterates that "every creature of God is good, and nothing to be refused, if it be received with thanksgiving" (1 Tim. 4:4).

In the final chapter of his first Epistle to Timothy, Paul identifies the Lord Jesus Christ as "the blessed and only Potentate, the King of kings, and Lord of lords; who only hath immortality, dwelling in the light which no man can approach unto; whom no man hath seen, nor can see: to whom be honour and power everlasting. Amen" (1 Tim. 6:15, 16). Such a description can apply in its essence only to the great Creator, God the Father, yet it clearly seems in context to refer to God the Son, the Lord Jesus Christ. This paradox is resolved only in the mystery of the Godhead.

The Epistle concludes with a strong exhortation to defend the faith against "profane and vain babblings, and oppositions of science falsely so called" (1 Tim. 6:20). This "pseudo-science" is essentially the gnostic philosophy which, like the philosophies of the Stoics and Epicureans, was strictly based on pantheistic evolution. Then, as now, evolution was "science falsely so called."

In Paul's second letter to Timothy, Paul gives a beautiful exposition of the fulfillment of the primeval prophecies. "[God] hath saved us, and called us with an holy calling, not according to our works, but according to his own purpose and grace, which was given us in Christ Jesus before the world began, but is now made manifest by the appearing of our Saviour Jesus Christ, who hath abolished death, and hath brought life and immortality to light through the gospel" (2 Tim. 1:9–10).

The curse of death, pronounced because of Adam's sin, has been abolished (still potential, but certain) because of the work of God in Christ. And, in the eternal omniscience of God, all was accomplished, even our own personal salvation, even before he created the world.

Paul's letter to Titus makes further reference to the same great truth, speaking of the "hope of eternal life, which God, that cannot lie, promised before the world began" (Titus 1:2). Then, in Titus 2:13, Paul identifies Jesus as God when he writes of "the glorious appearing of the great God and our Saviour Jesus Christ." He calls him "God our Saviour" in Titus 3:4 and "Jesus Christ our Saviour" in Titus 3:6.

The shortest Epistle of the apostle Paul is his one-chapter letter to his friend Philemon. The letter is very personal in tone, so there was no occasion in context to refer to the creation.

Many scholars believe that Paul was also the author of the Epistle to the Hebrews. However, his name is not included in that book, and there are many other scholars who reject the Pauline authorship of the book. Consequently, I shall include it with the General Epistles in the next chapter. In the meantime, it is abundantly certain that Paul, like Matthew, Mark, and Luke, was a strong creationist.

15

Creation and the Flood in the General Epistles

The Strong Testimony of Hebrews

By the term "General Epistles" is meant those attributed neither to Paul nor John. Specifically, these include Hebrews, James, 1 Peter, 2 Peter, and Jude. Hebrews is included because its authorship is unknown, though many attribute it to Paul. The three Epistles of John are not included here because all the writings of John, including the Gospel of John and the Book of Revelation, were composed toward the very end of the first century and are thus conveniently grouped together as representing the final, settled opinions of the apostles and prophets of the New Testament concerning the creation and other primeval events of history.

The Book of Hebrews, whoever its author was, does indeed contain many references to these events. In its very opening verses, we are told that "God . . . hath in these last days spoken unto us by his Son, whom he hath appointed heir of all things, by whom also he made the worlds; who being the brightness of his glory, and the express image of his person, and upholding all things by the word of his power, when he had by himself purged our sins, sat down on the right hand of the Majesty on high" (Heb. 1:2–3). Not only is Jesus heir of all things, but also he created the worlds and is now upholding all things. He is the brightness—or the "out-radiating"—of the glory of God.

The next verses speak of God's angels, but with the assurance that Christ is better than the angels and receives their worship. The writer then quotes the account of the creation of the angels, as found in Psalm 104: "[God] maketh his angels spirits, and his ministers a flame of fire" (Heb. 1:7).

Referring again to Christ as Creator, he also quotes from the 102nd psalm. "Thou, Lord, in the beginning hast laid the foundation of the earth; and the heavens are the work of thine hands: they shall perish; but thou remainest; and they all shall wax old as doth a garment; and as a vesture shalt thou fold them up, and they shall be changed: but thou art the same, and thy years shall not fail" (Heb. 1:10–12).

All that was in the first chapter of Hebrews. In chapter 2 the writer quotes David in the 8th psalm, referring to Adam's dominion mandate and then showing that its ultimate accomplishment and fulfillment will be in the second Adam, the true Son of man.

> But one in a certain place testified, saying, what is man, that thou art mindful of him? or the son of man, that thou visitest him? Thou madest him a little lower than the angels; thou crownedst him with glory and honour, and didst set him over the works of thy hands: thou hast put all things in subjection under his feet. For in that he put all in subjection under him, he left nothing that is not put under him. But now we see not yet all things put under him. But we see Jesus, who was made a little lower than the angels for the suffering of death, crowned with glory and honour; that he by the grace of God should taste death for every man. For it became him, for whom are all things, and by whom are all things, in bringing many sons unto glory, to make the captain of their salvation perfect through sufferings (Heb. 2:6–10).

It is necessary to quote this extended section to see once again how intimately connected is the work of Christ as both our Creator and Redeemer. He is the one "by whom are all things," who gave Adam dominion over the world in the beginning, but who then must also reclaim and exercise that dominion as the ultimate Son of man by dying for every man.

And, in so doing, "as the children are partakers of flesh and blood, he also himself likewise took part of the same; that through death he might destroy him who had the power of death, that is, the devil; and deliver them who through fear of death were all their lifetime subject to bondage" (Heb. 2:14–15). Thus, he fulfilled the great prophecy of Genesis 3:15, crushing the head of the old serpent through whose deceptions sin and death had intruded into God's creation. Those who were under the bondage of the ancient curse, doomed to die, were thereby able to be delivered from their innate fear of death, since he had conquered death by his own death and resurrection.

In the third chapter, there is a passing reference to creation when we are reminded that "he that built all things is God" (Heb. 3:4). Then, in the fourth chapter, there is an important and explicit confirmation that the creation was, indeed, completed at the end of creation week, in a context comparing God's rest after completing his work of creation to the believer's rest in Christ after he ceases trusting in his works for salvation. "The works were finished from the foundation of the world. For he spake in a certain place of the seventh day on this wise, And God did rest the seventh day from all his works" (Heb. 4:3, 4).

This is still further confirmed in Hebrews 4:10. "He that is entered into his rest, he also hath ceased from his own works, as God did from his." God has not ceased from his work of sustaining and saving his creation, of course, but he, long ago, finished his work of creating and making all things. This reminder once again stresses clearly and strongly that no "creation" (that is, no evolution—not even theistic evolution) is going on today. Everything was finished and functioning from the beginning. The weekly rest every seventh day is a worldwide (though often unacknowledged) commemoration of that fact.

The fifth, sixth, and seventh chapters of Hebrews center around the great priest of the most high God, Melchizedek. Although he was a contemporary of Abraham, Melchizedek was considered better even than Abraham (Heb. 7:6, 7) and undoubtedly was much older than Abraham. In fact, since he is said to have had "neither beginning of days, nor end of life; but [was] made like unto the Son of God; abid[ing] a priest continually" (Heb. 7:3), he may even have *been* the Son of God, in a preincarnate theophany.

Contrasting the many and repeated sacrificial offerings of the Levitical priesthood with the one offering of our great High Priest, made after the order of Melchizedek, the author of Hebrews points out that Christ did not have to offer his own blood often, as with the animal sacrifices, "for then must he often have suffered since the foundation of the world; but now once in the end of the [age] hath he appeared to put away sin by the sacrifice of himself" (Heb. 9:26).

Note the implication that animal sacrifices had, indeed, been offered ever since the foundation of the world, which means that sin had been present during the entire age. There were not billions of animals suffering and dying before sin came into the world to necessitate such sacrifices.

Three of the great antediluvian men of faith (Abel, Enoch, Noah) are eulogized in Hebrews 11, considered by most to be the greatest chapter on faith in the Bible. The great works of faith of these and the later patriarchs mentioned in this chapter all illustrate the kinds of works that characterize genuine faith in the true God and his saving grace.

The last two verses of Hebrews 10 (and, remember, there were no chapter divisions in the original Greek Epistles) describe the nature of this faith. "Now the just shall live by [this] faith," and "we are . . . of them that believe [actually, have faith, using the same Greek word] to the saving of the soul" (Heb. 10:38, 39). So the faith of the patriarchs (and matriarchs) of Hebrews 11 was a living faith, and a saving faith!

Therefore, it is significant that the very first, foundational object of this living faith was God's special creation of all things! "Through faith we understand that the worlds were framed by the word of God, so that things which are seen were not made of things which do appear" (Heb. 11:3). In the Greek, "worlds" is *aeons*—that is, the continuum which comprises our complex cosmos of time and space and matter. Furthermore, this cosmos was not produced from some primeval chaos or pre-existing materials of any kind—"things which do appear." It was simply called into being by the omnipotent Word of God! This plain assertion completely refutes any possibility of theistic evolution. It is difficult, therefore, to reconcile belief in evolution—even its theistic variety—with the saving faith of which this passage speaks. At the least, any professing Christian who also believes in evolution needs to follow Paul's advice to the Corinthians: "Examine yourselves, whether ye be in the faith; prove your own selves" (2 Cor. 13:5).

Following this important designation of creation as the foundational object of faith, the three antediluvian examples of the works of saving faith not only confirm the historicity of the three patriarchs but also provide a fitting type of the characteristics of a growing faith in any age.

First: "By faith Abel offered unto God a more excellent sacrifice than Cain, by which he obtained witness that he was righteous" (Heb. 11:4).

Cain offered the fruits he had coerced by his own efforts from the cursed ground, whereas Abel came with the shed blood of an animal sacrifice, knowing that "without shedding of blood is no remission" (Heb. 9:22). Abel's faith in God's word, as shown by his substitutionary sacrifice of an animal, "was imputed to him for righteousness" (Rom. 4:22).

Second: "By faith Enoch was translated that he should not see death; and was not found, because God had translated him: for before his translation he had this testimony, that he pleased God" (Heb. 11:5). This testimony supports the remarkable record in Genesis that the prophet Enoch, who had "walked with God" (Gen. 5:24), was taken direct into heaven without dying. The type suggests that a walk of faith with God follows justification by faith on the basis of a substitutionary sacrifice.

Third: "By faith Noah, being warned of God of things not seen as yet, moved with fear, prepared an ark to the saving of his house; by the which he condemned the world, and became heir of the righteousness which is by faith" (Heb. 11:7). After salvation through faith in the death of an innocent substitute, and then a daily walk of faith with the Lord, comes concern and self-sacrifice for the salvation of one's family. Noah was "moved with fear"—not for himself, but for "his house," who surely would have been engulfed in the wickedness and violence of the ungodly world had not Noah "prepared an ark to the saving of his house." Four times in Genesis we read that Noah obeyed God in everything God told him to do and, as a result, God told Noah: "Come thou and all thy house into the ark; for thee have I seen righteous before me in this generation" (Gen. 7:1).

This record in Hebrews not only asserts the truth of the Genesis account of Noah and the ark but also implies the validity of the fact that there was no rain in the earth (Gen. 2:5) before the flood. Noah believed God even though his word centered on "things not seen as yet."

There is one final passage in Hebrews of significance in this connection. "Ye are come unto mount Sion, and unto the city of the living God, the heavenly Jerusalem, and to an innumerable company of angels, to the general assembly and church of the firstborn, which are written in heaven, and to God the Judge of all, and to the spirits of just men made perfect, and to Jesus the mediator of the new covenant, and to the blood of sprinkling, that speaketh better things than that of Abel" (Heb. 12:22–24).

This beautiful prophetic passage is not a spiritual allegory but an actual description of the great future assembly of all the saved men and women of all the ages when Christ returns. There, in that majestic city, "which hath foundations, whose builder and maker is God" (Heb. 11:10), will be gathered every redeemed soul (from Adam on), as well as the innumerable host of heaven, the holy angels who have been anxiously awaiting this day since the time of their first creation.

And the Lord Jesus will be there, having made it all possible with the sprinkling of his shed blood over the heavenly mercy seat overshadowed by the cherubim (Heb. 9:5). The first human blood shed was that of Abel, whose blood cried out from the ground (Gen. 4:10), but the blood of Jesus spoke, not only of innocent suffering (like that of Abel) but also of eternal salvation for all assembled there in the city of God.

The Key Witness of Peter

It is significant that Peter, that "prince of the apostles," who had been so greatly used by the Lord in the very first days of the Christian church, should also be used (especially in the last chapter of his writings) to prophesy concerning the last days of the church and to understand so clearly the key role of creationism in the church's last-day witness.

Peter, who had walked with Jesus for three years and had acknowledged him to be the Son of the living God, yet had fled and denied even knowing him when he was arrested, experienced a complete transformation of faith and life when he knew Christ had conquered death and risen from the dead. Peter recognized that Christ's substitutionary death on the cross had been planned even before the creation and that he and all believers had now been redeemed "with the precious blood of Christ, . . . who verily was foreordained before the foundation of the world, but was manifest in these last times for you" (1 Pet. 1:19, 20).

Peter was then given the remarkable revelation that, during the period while Jesus' body was resting in Joseph's tomb after the crucifixion, Jesus was "quickened [that is, actively alive] by the Spirit: by which also he went and preached unto the spirits in prison; which sometime were disobedient, when once the longsuffering of God waited in the days of Noah, while the ark was a preparing, wherein few, that is, eight souls were saved by water. . . . [Jesus Christ] is gone into heaven, and is on the right hand of God; angels and authorities and powers being made subject unto him" (1 Pet. 3:18–20, 22).

By Peter we are thus informed that, while Noah was building the ark, he was also calling the people of his day to repentance. But they were all disobedient and perished in the flood, while only eight souls (Noah, Shem, Ham, Japheth and their wives) were saved by its waters from the incurable wickedness and pervasive violence of the antediluvian world.

Then, Christ in his spirit (that is, the Holy Spirit, one with him and the Father in the eternal Godhead) descended into Sheol, the great pit in the heart of the earth, where the souls of all the dead had descended to await the judgment. Those who had died in faith were set free by Christ at that time, since *he* had just borne their judgment on the cross, and were taken with him from Sheol to God's heaven when he returned from Sheol and the tomb.

To the lost "spirits in prison," however, he proclaimed his victory and their doom ("proclaimed" is a better translation in context here than "preached"). However, these "spirits" were not merely the lost souls of Noah's day. All the lost souls of all the ages are there in Sheol, and there must be a special reason why "the days of Noah" are specially mentioned.

The reason must lie in the special circumstances that led to the universal, continual wickedness of that terrible time. The satanic attempt to corrupt all flesh (as recorded in Gen. 6:1–5) had culminated in universal demon possession of the bodies and minds of the (already rebellious against God) people of those dark days. Finally the whole world was ensnared in this evil invasion of demonic spirits, and the only remedy was global cleansing by the great flood. It is most probable, therefore, that these "spirits in prison" were the evil spirits responsible for this calamity. In Peter's second Epistle, it is revealed that "God spared not the angels that sinned, but cast them down to hell [that is, to Tartarus, the lowermost region of *Sheol,* or Hades] . . . to be reserved unto judgment" (2 Pet. 2:4).

The very next verse says, likewise, that God "spared not the old world, but saved Noah the eighth person, a preacher of righteousness, bringing in the flood upon the world of the ungodly" (2 Pet. 2:5). The close succession of these verses strongly suggests that the actions likewise were successive. That is, God cast the angels that sinned—the evil spirits that had corrupted all flesh—down to Tartarus to be bound in dark chains to await their final judgment. Then he proceeded to bring in the flood upon the world of the ungodly.

So it is most likely that the "spirits in prison" to whom Christ proclaimed his victory were those who had long before tried to prevent His coming into the human family by corrupting all the members of that family. Now, as a result of his great triumph on the cross and in the tomb, all "angels and authorities and powers" have been "made subject unto him," in his exalted position "on the right hand of God."

Before continuing with references in Peter's second Epistle, however, we find one other important notice of the Creator in his first Epistle. Much of this Epistle (like that of Job) is taken up with the question of what seems to be unjustified suffering inflicted on those who love and obey God. The solution, as Job learned, is simply to recognize that God, as Creator, knows and does what is right in the scales of eternity. The great truth of creation and divine sovereignty helps us to place our little problems in true perspective. And this is what Peter says, too. "Let them that suffer according to the will of God commit the keeping of their souls to him in welldoing, as unto a faithful Creator" (1 Pet. 4:19).

Turning again to Peter's second Epistle, we read that "we have not followed cunningly devised fables" (2 Pet. 1:16), as the heathen do, with their evolutionary nature myths. He compares our "more sure word of prophecy" to "a light that shineth in a dark place" (2 Pet. 1:19), probably an allusion to the first divine light dispelling the primeval darkness at the creation. This analogy is developed further when he notes that the Scriptures came as "holy men of God spake as they were moved by the Holy Ghost" (2 Pet. 1:21). This answers to the "moving" of the Holy Spirit in the presence of the ancient waters just prior to the entrance of light into the world.

The second chapter of 2 Peter introduces a graphic description of the false teachers of the last days and their baleful influence even among Christians, as well as their eventual damnation. This prompts the comparison with the fallen angels and ungodly world of Noah's day, as discussed above.

In 2 Peter 2:5 the phrase "Noah the eighth person, a preacher of righteousness," is somewhat enigmatic, since "person" is not in the original. Noah is probably called "the eighth preacher of righteousness" because only eight of the ten antediluvian patriarchs had the patriarchal responsibility of leading the family in their testimony for God in their respective generations. That is, Enoch was translated while his father Jared still served as patriarch, and Lamech (father of Noah) died before his father Methuselah. Each of the other eight (Adam, Seth,

Enos, Cainan, Mahalaleel, Jared, Methuselah, Noah) *did* serve a period as family patriarch and keeper of the inspired records for transmission to future generations.

It is also worth noting that the words for "flood" and "world" in this verse are especially graphic. The Greek for "flood" is *kataklusmos*, from which we get our word "cataclysm." In the next verse, speaking of the judgment on Sodom and Gomorrah, which was probably a great earthquake and volcanic outpouring, Peter says that God "condemned them with an overthrow" (2 Pet. 2:6). Here the Greek is *katastrophe*. The point is that a catastrophe, no matter how violent, is only local, whereas a cataclysm is worldwide. The Genesis flood is always, in the New Testament, called *the cataclysm*.

The third and last chapter of Peter's last Epistle is perhaps the most important of all New Testament references to creation and the flood. In fact, it is one of the most important of all messages to the church in the last days.

The chapter begins with an exhortation to believers to "stir up your pure minds" (2 Pet. 3:1)—*not* "stir up your emotions"! But our minds are not to be stirred up with the philosophies of intellectual secularism and humanism, but with the eternally rich and relevant Word of God. "Be mindful," Peter says, "of the words which were spoken before by the holy prophets [that is, the Old Testament Scriptures], and of the commandment of us the apostles of the Lord and Saviour [that is, the New Testament Scriptures]" (2 Pet. 3:2).

This exhortation will be especially relevant in the last days, when sound instruction in the Scriptures will be largely replaced, even in Christian churches, by shallow emotionalism on the one hand and compromising intellectualism on the other—both of which conditions are almost universally prevalent in the "Christian" world today.

Peter then goes on to point out the urgency of his warning. "Knowing this first . . ." he says—that is, "first of all." This tells us that the condition he is about to describe is of absolutely primary importance and critically needs correcting if true biblical Christianity is not to be so diluted in the last days. "When the Son of man cometh, shall he find faith on the earth?" (Luke 18:8).

"There shall come in the last days scoffers," Peter warns, "walking after their own lusts, and saying, Where is the promise of his coming? for since the fathers fell asleep, all things continue as they were from the beginning of the creation" (2 Pet. 3:3, 4).

In Peter's second sermon in Jerusalem, soon after Christ's return to heaven, he had noted that the Lord will remain in heaven "until the times of restitution [or restoration] of all things, which God hath spoken by the mouth of all his holy prophets since the world began" (Acts 3:21). Ever since God's protevangelic promise in Eden, followed by his messages through the prophets Abel, Enoch, Noah, and all the other ancient prophets, and then through the God-called prophets of the New Testament, God has been promising that the lost Paradise will be restored by the coming Redeemer. Christians for almost two thousand years have looked forward to these coming "times of restoration." Once again note that this prophecy has been available from the prophets "since the world began"—not waiting until 4 billion or so years later.

Yet the promise has not yet been fulfilled, so scoffers have now started questioning and even ridiculing this promise, even in those nominally "Christian" lands where "the promise of his coming" has been known and widely preached and believed for centuries. Instead of looking for the return of Christ to save the world, the scientists and educators and liberal theologians are now insisting that man himself can bring about the "new world order" where peace and righteousness will finally prevail.

And the pseudo-intellectual rationale for this arrogant and blasphemous assertion is the doctrine that "all things continue as they were from the beginning of the creation." That is, these scientists and liberal theologians maintain that even "creation" is still continuing, by the same processes that have been "creating" things since the beginning. Since all processes that are now operating can be understood "scientifically" (by which they mean "naturalistically," without any supernatural intervention by some imaginary Creator), there is no reason to think these processes will not continue just the same way in the future. Since, therefore, there was no real *creation* (only naturalistic evolution), there will be no supernatural *re*-creation in the future, so "where is the promise of his coming?"

This premise has, for the past 150 years or so, been called the "principle of uniformitarianism," the assumption being that natural processes have always functioned in the past the same uniform way that they do in the present, so that "the present is the key to the past." It arbitrarily denies—or at least ignores—the possibility that there was ever any miraculous creation or cataclysmic destruction in the past that could have altered these uniform processes of nature.

The uniformitarian premise that "all things continue as they were from the beginning of the creation" has been imposed on all the sciences, but has been of particular importance as applied in historical geology, the study of earth history. It is especially bound to conflict head-on with God's revelation of the six-day creation and the great flood, leading as it does to the concept of long geological ages during which all things were evolving from primordial chaos to their present high complexity. Thus, if these uniformitarian, evolutionary geological ages ever really happened at all, then the Genesis record of creation and the flood is false. Not only so, but the rest of the Bible is also unreliable. Its writers claimed to be divinely inspired, yet *they* all accepted this Genesis record as historically and literally true, and they based all other theological doctrines on this foundation in Genesis.

Consequently, this issue—as Peter says—is of paramount importance in the last days, and we should understand it "first of all." But then he also places it in its true perspective, giving us the answer to it. "For this they willingly are ignorant of, that by the word of God the heavens were of old, and the earth standing out of the water and in the water: whereby the world that then was, being overflowed with water, perished" (2 Pet. 3:5, 6).

The very facts one must deny in order to rationalize the uniformitarian evolutionary assumption—namely, special fiat creation by God's word and the later global deluge—are supported so overwhelmingly by both biblical and scientific evidence that to ignore this evidence is *willful* ignorance! We have been surveying all the biblical evidences for these two "non-uniformitarian" worldwide events in this book, and there are now many other books available which survey the scientific evidence.[1]

These two key verses (2 Pet. 3:5, 6) are of profound importance, and too many Christians have ignored them too long. The heavens and the earth were spoken into existence by God's omnipotent word, not by natural processes. Initially God established the earth in the midst of two great reservoirs of water, one below, one above, the earth standing both "out of," yet "in" (that is, "surrounded by") water, as described in Genesis 1:2, 6–8. Then, later, it was by those same waters that "the world [that is, *kosmos*, the ordered earth/atmosphere system] that then was, being overflowed with water, perished," when both "the fountains of the great deep" and "the windows of heaven" poured forth their waters to cleanse the whole earth. The Greek for "overflowed" is *katakluzo*.

Whenever this word and its cognate *kataklusmos* are used in the New Testament, they always refer explicitly to the Genesis flood in the days of Noah (note, e.g., Matt. 24:39; 2 Pet. 2:5). This was the only true *cataclysm* in world history. There was no "pre-Adamic cataclysm," as some have speculated, or any other—only the watery cataclysm by which the antediluvian cosmos perished.

The world that emerged from the waters of the great deluge, as seen by those who emerged from the ark, was vastly different from the former world. *This* world—"the heavens and the earth, which are now"—"by the same word [is] kept in store[note Heb. 1:3—"upholding all things by the word of his power"], reserved unto fire" (2 Pet. 3:7). Just as the first earth and its heaven were destroyed by water, so this cosmos will one day be destroyed by fire. The present "curse" on the earth affects its very elements, and the earth's crust is laced with the fossil remains of billions of once-living creatures, and all this must be purged by fire in order to "restore all things" as God has promised. Accordingly, when that day comes, "the elements shall melt with fervent heat, the earth also and the works that are therein shall be burned up" (2 Pet. 3:10; also note 3:12).

Then God will create "new heavens and a new earth, wherein dwelleth righteousness," as he has promised "by the mouth of all his holy prophets since the world began" (2 Pet. 3:13; Acts 3:21). Men may ridicule the promise of his coming, but it *will* be accomplished, at the proper time. "The Lord is not slack concerning his promise . . . but is longsuffering to us-ward, not willing that any should perish, but that all should come to repentance" (2 Pet. 3:9). Therefore we should, as we wait for its fulfillment, simply "account that the longsuffering of our Lord is salvation" (2 Pet. 3:15). There is at least an implication here that we can in some way hasten its fulfillment ourselves by earnestly doing all we can to bring others to repentance and salvation (2 Pet. 3:12).

Note also the important implication of 2 Peter 3:8. "Be not ignorant of this one thing, that one day is with the Lord as a thousand years, and a thousand years as one day." Some have distorted the meaning of this verse to argue that the "days" of creation week were actually the 4.6 billion years of the evolutionary geological ages. But "a text without a context is a pretext"! The context of this striking verse has nothing to do with the six days of creation.

Rather, the context is one discussing the last-days conflict between biblical creationism and flood geology, on the one hand, and the long evolutionary geological ages inferred from the false premise of evolutionary uniformitarianism, on the other. Peter is simply reminding us that God can do in one day that for which uniformitarianism would require a thousand years. The great flood, with its abundant evidences of rapid sedimentary and other processes, provides a much better explanation for the earth's fossil beds and other phenomena than uniformitarianism can ever do.

Uniformitarian, naturalistic, atheistic evolutionism is, as Peter says, dominant in the last days. Through most of world history, however, various pantheistic forms of evolutionism have been incorporated in the various anti-God systems of philosophy and religion. Christians have often been tempted, therefore, especially those who are "unlearned and unstable" in their superficial commitment to the Scriptures, to "wrest" the Scriptures in order to try to accommodate the pseudo-scientific theories of the day in God's crystal-clear record of creation, the flood, and the other *real* events of past history. "Christian evolutionists" are also doing this today, in wholesale fashion. But Peter warns that such twisting of the Scriptures may be "unto their own destruction" (2 Pet. 3:16). He urges us not to allow ourselves to be "led away with the error of the wicked," but, rather, to "grow in grace and in the knowledge of our Lord and Saviour Jesus Christ" (2 Pet. 3:18), for he is the true Creator/Redeemer, and his knowledge is truth.

Brothers of Christ

The five-chapter Epistle of James and the one-chapter Epistle of Jude have an interesting feature in common. Both men are believed by many conservative biblical scholars to have been brothers of Jesus. Jude was certainly a brother of James (Jude 1), and James is called "the Lord's brother" in Galatians 1:19. Both James and Judas are said to be "his brethren" in Matthew 13:55. Assuming this identification is correct, one can only imagine—and marvel—at the thoughts of these younger brothers (or half-brothers) of Jesus, who originally did not believe on him (John 7:5), when they later came to realize that they had grown up in the same household with their Creator! In any case, their Epistles give all due homage to him.

James is often considered to be the first-written of the twenty-seven New Testament books. One especially important and beautiful creation reference is in this book. "Every good gift and every perfect gift is from above, and cometh down from the Father of lights, with whom is no variableness, neither shadow of turning. Of his own will begat he us with the word of truth, that we should be a kind of firstfruits of his creatures" (James 1:17, 18).

James not only recognizes God as the Creator, but also gives him the unusual title "Father of lights," probably in reference to his creation of "light" (Gen. 1:3) as the basic entity of omnipresent energy and of the particular "lights" (Gen. 1:14–16) to serve as the particular source of earth's energy.

With God, James says, is no "shadow of turning." The Greek for "turning" is *trope*. This word, combined with the Greek *en*, becomes "entropy," which is the key scientific concept now associated with God's curse on the earth, the "bondage of corruption" (Rom. 8:21). The second law of thermodynamics, as noted before, is also the law of increasing entropy (that is, in-turning). Any system which turns inward to feed on itself, so to speak, will eventually decay and die.

Every system must eventually decay and die unless it can continually incorporate external energy and information. Every system, that is, except God! With him is "no variableness, neither shadow of turning."

He is not only the Father of all energy. He begat *us;* we also are his creations. He created us by his word, just as he did the universe. "Of his own will begat he us with the word of truth, that we should be a kind of firstfruits of his creatures" (James 1:18). James, in fact, also says that men "are made after the similitude of God" (James 3:9). Even though that "image" (Gen. 1:27) has been marred by sin, we are still in his image.

There is also a reference to the permanence of the created kinds. "Can the fig tree, my brethren, bear olive berries? either a vine, figs? so can no fountain both yield salt water and fresh" (James 3:12).

James also confirms the historicity of the patriarch Job, who lived soon after the flood, and whose book contains many references to the events of Genesis 1:11. "Ye have heard of the patience of Job," he writes, "and have seen the end of the Lord; that the Lord is very pitiful, and of tender mercy" (James 5:11). He includes Job, in fact, as one of the prophets of the Lord (v. 10).

The one-chapter Epistle of Jude has much in common with 2 Peter, warning against apostasy in the last days. Like Peter, he writes of "the angels which kept not their first estate, but left their own habitation." God, he says, "hath reserved [them] in everlasting chains under darkness unto the judgment of the great day" (Jude 6). This is referring, of course, to "the sons of God" who took "the daughters of men" (Gen. 6:2) in the days before the flood. They "left their own habitation" among the host of heaven to follow Lucifer in his attempt to corrupt all flesh in the days of Noah, and are now, therefore, in "everlasting chains under darkness."

Jude issues strong warnings against the false teachers who "crept in unawares" into the Christian community, "turning the grace of our God into lasciviousness" (Jude 4). These men "have gone in the way of Cain" (Jude 11). The books of Luke and Hebrews confirmed the historicity of Abel; Jude here indicates that Cain also was a real person, and that, indeed, he is a type of all those who try to supersede God and his word with their own devices.

Jude also reveals that Enoch was, indeed, a great prophet against the ancient apostasy of the antediluvians, and that he even prophesied of the far-off apostasy in the last days before the coming of the Lord in judgment. "Enoch also, the seventh from Adam, prophesied of these, saying, Behold, the Lord cometh with ten thousands of his saints, to execute judgment upon all, and to convince all that are ungodly among them of all their ungodly deeds which they have ungodly committed, and of all their hard speeches which ungodly sinners have spoken against him" (Jude 14, 15).

There are two apocryphal books bearing Enoch's name,[2] but it is doubtful that these are authentic in their present form. Jude's inspired account, however, verifies that at least the above fragment did, indeed, come from Enoch himself. Enoch's prophecy also gives further insight into antediluvian society. Not only was there a multitude of "ungodly sinners" committing "ungodly deeds," but they were also broadcasting "hard speeches" against God, thereby inciting still others to rebel against him. Enoch's courageous preaching of coming judgment against such activities was apparently rejected, and God soon took him into heaven without dying, evidently preserving him for a future ministry.

Jude also refers briefly to Peter's prophecy of the latter-day humanistic scoffers (2 Pet. 3:3), but he does not go further into the uniformitarian conflict, as discussed in the previous section. Here is Jude's statement: "The apostles of our Lord Jesus Christ . . . told you there should be mockers in the last time, who should walk after their own ungodly lusts. These be they who separate themselves, sensual, having not the Spirit" (Jude 18, 19). The adjective "sensual" indicates their philosophy to be materialistic; they are also divisive, attempting to subvert the unity and message of sound churches. Despite their outward profession, they do not have the Spirit, and thus are not born-again Christians. By all means, therefore, Christians should not follow their teachings.

16

The Beloved Disciple and Creation Evangelism

Creation and the Gospel of John

In this chapter we come finally to the writings of the apostle John, Christ's beloved disciple. John was the author of the fourth Gospel, three Epistles, and, last but certainly not least, the closing and climactic book of the Bible, the Book of Revelation. John's books, especially his Gospel and the Book of Revelation, are heavily laced with references to Genesis and the events of primeval earth history.

In fact, the Gospel of John starts with the very same opening words as Genesis: "In the beginning." This is most important in considering the message of this fourth Gospel, written long after the other three and obviously written mainly for Gentiles. It places a strong emphasis on the unique deity of Jesus as the only begotten Son of God. The very purpose of John was to win his readers to Christ. He describes seven great miracles of Christ, all requiring the creative power of God for their accomplishment, and then says, "And many other signs [same word as "miracles"] truly did Jesus in the presence of his disciples, which are not written in this book: but these are written that ye might believe that Jesus is the Christ, the Son of God; and that believing ye might have life through his name" (John 20:30, 31).

Thus John's purpose was evangelistic, and this purpose is apparent throughout the book. It is understandable that Christian evangelists frequently preach from John and that Christian laymen often give Gospels of John to those they are trying to lead to Christ. Since evangelism was John's divinely inspired purpose, we can well assume his approach is the best approach to use in witnessing.

It is thus important to note that *he begins* with creation! It is sad that so many Christians today argue that, since creation is controversial and not very important, talking about creation is a hindrance to "soul-winning." John didn't think so, and his message was inspired by the Holy Spirit. Here is how he begins his evangelistic approach. "In the beginning was the Word, and the Word was with God, and the Word was God. The same was in the beginning with God. All things were made by him; and without him was not any thing made that was made" (John 1:1–3).

The God of Genesis ("In the beginning God") is thus identified as the Word (we read of God *speaking* explicitly at least sixteen times in the creation chapter, Genesis 1). We already know from other passages we have studied in the New Testament that this One by whom God created all things—his Word—is none other than Jesus Christ. But this is made absolutely certain in verse 14: "The Word was made flesh, and dwelt among us, (and we beheld his glory, the glory as of the only begotten of the Father,) full of grace and truth."

Thus the Lord Jesus Christ is the Creator of *"all things."* John considered it vital that those whom he wanted to win to saving faith in Christ should know this first of all—and so, therefore, should we! This is not *all* they need to know, of course, but this is the foundational truth, without which the structure, sooner or later, will collapse.

John goes on to say that "in him was life; and the life was the light of men. And the light shineth in darkness; and the darkness comprehended it not" (John 1:4, 5). Only God can create life, for he is the living God. Only God can conquer darkness, for he is the light that "comprehended" the darkness. Just as his light had pierced the primeval darkness, so light came into a sin-darkened world when he became flesh, but the darkened hearts of men refused to recognize him. The darkness could not comprehend (take in) the light.

"That was the true Light, which lighteth every man that cometh into the world [not just the Jews, note, nor even the elect, but everyone ever conceived in the human family]. He was in the world, and the world was made by him, and the world knew him not. He came unto his own, and his own received him not. But as many as received him, to them gave he power to become the sons of God, even to them that believe on his name" (John 1:9–12).

Although he had created the world and all its inhabitants, its leaders (both Jews and Gentiles) rejected and crucified him. And that is still the way; if he had come at any other time, before or since, its rulers and wise men and religionists would have rejected him and done away with him if they could, just as did those in the first century.

But here and there—both then and now—are individuals who will "believe on his name" when they hear of him and understand who he is and what he has done. These are the ones for whom John was writing, the ones who will become "sons of God," being "born, not of blood, nor of the will of the flesh, nor of the will of man, but of God" (John 1:13). They will believe that Jesus is, indeed, the only begotten Son of God, and therefore they will be "born again" by the Holy Spirit of God.

A remarkable further revelation of what is entailed in the title "the Word," as applied to Christ, is given in verse 18: "No man hath seen God at any time; the only begotten Son, which is in the bosom of the Father, he hath declared him." This tells us that, whenever God has actually *appeared* in some form to anyone, he appeared through the person of the Son. This must apply also to those who have *heard* God, for the Word of God, who "declares" him, is the Son of God.

When telling how Christ turned water into wine at the wedding feast, John makes this comment: "This beginning of miracles did Jesus in Cana of Galilee, and manifested forth his glory; and his disciples believed on him" (John 2:11). This first of the seven "signs" described by John does, indeed, illustrate John's evangelistic purpose, which was to show by his miracles that Jesus was the Son of God, thereby leading men to believe.

No one but the Creator could create wine out of water, directly superseding the law of entropy. In fact, each of the seven miracles described by John was a miracle of special creation, and apparently was selected by John for this reason. Many miracles of the Bible—in fact, most— were miracles of providence, rather than creation. That is, they involved control of process rates or timing of natural events rather than actual creation of matter or energy or higher order. But the seven "signs" in John were all miracles of creation, demonstrating beyond question that Jesus was the Creator and the Christ, the Son of God. This, in fact, was the testimony of "a master of Israel," Nicodemus, when he acknowledged: "No man can do these miracles that thou doest, except God be with him" (John 3:10, 2).

The second miracle was healing a young man at the point of death, six miles away, by a spoken word (John 4:46–54). Then Jesus gave a man perfect limbs, after they had been crippled and atrophied for thirty-eight years (John 5:5–9). Next, he created a great amount of bread and fish to feed a multitude (John 6:5–14), and then created an anti-gravity force to be able to walk on the sea (John 6:16–21). He made new eyes for a man born blind (John 9:1–7). Finally, he restored life to Lazarus, dead and in the grave for four days (John 11:1–44). Each of these seven miracles required creative power, requiring therefore the work of the Creator himself.

Then, of course, he accomplished a greater miracle than all others combined, the greatest miracle since he had created the world in the beginning. He defeated Satan and sin and death on the cross, then descended to Hades, returning with the spirits of all who had died in faith, revived his own dead body in Joseph's tomb, and ascended to heaven. Surely, no one should ever doubt that Jesus is the Creator and the Christ, the Son of God. The thrilling story of his resurrection is the theme of John's 20th chapter, climaxed and concluded with the verses, already quoted (vv. 30, 31), stressing the evangelistic purpose of his Gospel.

In another vein, Jesus put his approval on the writings of Moses, including the Book of Genesis, and rebuked the Jews for not recognizing him: "Had ye believed Moses, ye would have believed me: for he wrote of me. But if ye believe not his writings, how shall ye believe my words?" (John 5:46, 47).

John records many claims made by the Lord Jesus, which amount to claims of deity. In particular, these are the seven great "I am" statements in the Gospel, as follows:

I am the bread of life (John 6:35).
I am the light of the world (John 8:12).
I am the door (John 10:9).
I am the good shepherd (John 10:11).
I am the resurrection and the life (John 11:25).
I am the way, the truth, and the life (John 14:6).
I am the true vine (John 15:1).

The significance of the "I am" claims is especially pointed up in Jesus' statement to the Pharisees: "Verily, verily, I say unto you, Before Abraham was, I am" (John 8:58). This was clearly an assertion that he was self-existent, the eternally pre-existing God, the Creator.

In the same interchange, he accused his Pharisaic opponents of being children of Satan: "Ye are of your father the devil, and the lusts of your father ye will do. He was a murderer from the beginning, and abode not in the truth, because there is no truth in him. When he speaketh a lie, he speaketh of his own: for he is a liar, and the father of it" (John 8:44).

As the father of liars and the father of murderers, Satan had been fighting his Creator since the beginning. The Lord Jesus knew of his lie to Eve and his instigation of Cain, as well as his continued deceptions and killings through all the ages since. And Satan has spiritually sired many other human children, like the Pharisees, to continue and implement his attacks.

In the upper room, with the disciples, Jesus made what appears to be a comment related to the primeval curse on the woman. God had said to Eve "I will greatly multiply thy sorrow and thy conception; in sorrow thou shalt bring forth children" (Gen. 3:16). Referring to this, Jesus said, "A woman when she is in travail hath sorrow, because her hour is come: but as soon as she is delivered of the child, she remembereth no more the anguish, for joy that a man is born into the world" (John 16:21).

In his prayer in the upper room, Christ referred remarkably to the councils within the triune Godhead before the world was created. "Father, I will that they also, whom thou hast given me, be with me where I am; that they may behold my glory, which thou hast given me: for thou lovedst me before the foundation of the world" (John 17:24). The love within the Godhead is therefore the root and source of every other love.

It was this love that led God to create the world, and this love that led the Father to send the Son into the world to redeem the world. There are at least forty references in the Gospel of John to the coming of the Son down from his eternal residence in heaven to live as a man in the world he created. The first is his amazing statement to Nicodemus: "No man hath ascended up to heaven, but he that came down from heaven, even the Son of man which is in heaven" (John 3:13). The last is the charge to his disciples after his resurrection: "As my Father hath sent me, even so send I you" (John 20:21). This commission followed his prayer in the upper room: "As thou hast sent me into the world, even so have I also sent them into the world" (John 17:18).

John's Three Epistles

Many of the emphases in John's Gospel are also repeated in his three Epistles (Word, life, light, truth, etc.). The first Epistle, like his Gospel, goes back to the beginning, thus reflecting the first verse of Genesis. "That which was from the beginning, which we have heard, which we have seen with our eyes, which we have looked upon, and our hands have handled, of the Word of life; (for the life was manifested, and we have seen it, and bear witness, and shew unto you that eternal life, which was with the Father, and was manifested unto us)" (1 John 1:1, 2).

The eternal, uncreated Word of God thus became incarnate, just as John stresses in the first chapter of his Gospel (John 1:1–3, 14). Even though this Epistle, unlike his Gospel, was primarily written for believers, John's soul-winning motivation still is apparent, when he says in the next verse; "That which we have seen and heard declare we unto you, that ye also may have fellowship with us" (1 John 1:3).

He begins his "declaration" by noting "that God is light, and in him is no darkness at all" (1 John 1:5). Therefore, God did not have to *create* light on Day One—he merely had to say, "Let there be light." It was the primeval *darkness* that had to be created (Isa. 45:7), in order to provide the diurnal cycle of day and night for his creation.

The basic truth that "his Son Jesus Christ" (1 John 1:3) actually existed with the Father from eternity is repeated: "Ye have known him that is from the beginning" (1 John 2:13). Also, the truth that the eternal Son was sent into the world, which is so often noted in John's Gospel, is repeatedly emphasized here. For example, note the following: "Ye know that he was manifested to take away our sins; and in him is no sin" (1 John 3:5). "Every spirit that confesseth that Jesus Christ is come in the flesh is of God: and every spirit that confesseth not that Jesus Christ is come in the flesh is not of God" (1 John 4:2, 3). "In this was manifested the love of God toward us, because that God sent his only begotten Son into the world, that we might live through him" (1 John 4:9). "Herein is love, not that we loved God, but that he loved us, and sent his Son to be the propitiation for our sins" (1 John 4:10). "We have seen and do testify that the Father sent the Son to be the Saviour of the world" (1 John 4:14).

John also refers again, as he does in his Gospel, to the primeval sin of Satan and the fact that he led the whole world into captivity to sin and death and that this was from the beginning of the world. "He that committeth sin is of the devil; for the devil sinneth from the beginning. For this purpose the Son of God was manifested, that he might destroy the works of the devil. . . . In this the children of God are manifest, and the children of the devil" (1 John 3:8, 10).

As an example, John notes that this influence of the devil and his children was manifested very early in Cain, the first child born into the world. "Cain . . . was of that wicked one, and slew his brother" (1 John 3:12). Once again, incidentally, the New Testament here confirms the historicity of the Genesis record of Cain and Abel.

John does assure us, however, that "he that is begotten of God keepeth himself, and that wicked one toucheth him not" (1 John 5:18). Nevertheless, it remains true, ever since Eden (and even since Calvary), that "the whole world lieth in wickedness" (1 John 5:19). In these verses, the words "wickedness" and "wicked one" are both the same word in the Greek. Satan is "the prince of this world" (John 12:31) and "the god of this world" (2 Cor. 4:4), and John says here that the entire world *lies in* that wicked one! Yet it still remains true, for the believer, that "greater is he that is in you, than he that is in the world" (1 John 4:4). Then, in his final verse, John issues a last warning to Christians of the dangers in the pagan evolutionism around them. "Little children, keep yourselves from idols. Amen." (1 John 5:21). There are, of course, many other references throughout the Scriptures to idols, even though I have mentioned only a few of them specifically. All of them imply an evolutionary history foundation.

The second and third Epistles of John have only one chapter each and, like Paul's Epistle to Philemon, are highly personal, so have little occasion to refer to the events of ancient times. Second John is written to "the elect lady and her children" (v. 1) and 3 John to "the wellbeloved Gaius" (v. 1), both coming from John as "the elder."

The concept of "the truth" is still strong in both, however, and John warns again that "many deceivers are entered into the world, who confess not that Jesus Christ is come in the flesh. This is a deceiver and an antichrist" (2 John 7). The incarnation of the eternal Creator in the human flesh which he had created, in order to provide salvation for those he had made in his image, by his atoning death and resurrection, is such basic truth that John commands: "If there come any unto you, and bring not this doctrine, receive him not into your house, neither bid him God speed" (2 John 10).

Creation Restored and the Book of Revelation

We come finally to John's last Epistle and, indeed, the last book of God's written Word, the Book of Revelation. As Genesis is the foundational book of the Bible, so Revelation is its consummational book. Paradise is lost in Genesis; paradise is regained in Revelation. Interestingly, although there are numerous allusions to Genesis (more than to any other book of the Old Testament), there are no direct quotations from Genesis (nor from any other book of the Bible) in the Book of Revelation; yet the whole narrative is so saturated with Old Testament figures, allusions, and fulfillments that one could never make sense out of Revelation without a thorough understanding of the Old Testament, *especially Genesis.*

Although the Book of Revelation is given through John, it is actually "the Revelation of Jesus Christ, which God gave unto him" (Rev. 1:1). He is introduced by John with an emphasis on his eternal preexistence; "him which is, and which was, and which is to come" (Rev. 1:4). Then he introduces himself in the same vein: "I am Alpha and Omega, the beginning and the ending, saith the Lord, which is, and which was, and which is to come, the Almighty" (Rev. 1:8). And again: "I am Alpha and Omega, the first and the last" (Rev. 1:11). And yet again, as John fell down before him in his glorified body: "Fear not; I am the first and the last. I am he that liveth, and was dead; and, behold, I am alive for evermore, Amen; and have the keys of hell and of death" (Rev. 1:17, 18).

The Lord Jesus Christ is, therefore, both Creator and Restorer of all things. He has defeated sin and death and the curse.

He writes through John, first of all, about "the things which thou hast seen, and the things which are"; then, later, he shows to John "the things which shall be hereafter" (Rev. 1:19). The apostolic age is about over (John was the last remaining apostle), but there is a long church age coming, so the Lord sends letters to seven churches, representing all the churches that will be formed throughout the world during the church age. In these letters there are various allusions to the original creation, which is soon to be restored.

To the faithful ones in such a church as Ephesus, Jesus promises: "To him that overcometh will I give to eat of the tree of life, which is in the midst of the paradise of God" (Rev. 2:7). Thus Eden and the tree of life in its midst really existed and someday will be restored.

Ephesus is the first church of the seven. To the last, at Laodicea, Jesus introduces himself as "the faithful and true witness, the beginning of the creation of God" (Rev. 3:14). That is, he is both the Creator and, through his Word, the witness of, and the witness about, that creation of his. This suggests that those churches represented by Laodicea are harboring doubts about creation, and need to have its truth reemphasized to them. There are, of course, multitudes of such churches today.

Following the letters to the churches, the Lord proceeds to show John (and us) "things which must be hereafter" (Rev. 4:1). Immediately we are, as it were, ushered into the heavenly throne room, where God is seated on his throne, with "a rainbow round about the throne" (Rev. 4:3).

This is the first mention of the rainbow in the New Testament, and it must remind us of its first mention in the Old Testament (Gen. 9:14), where it was given by God as a sign of his covenant with all nations after the flood. Its presence here suggests that the scene in heaven concerns all nations, not just Israel. To Noah and his family, the rainbow spoke of mercy and deliverance even in the midst of judgment. Similarly, the rainbow surrounding God's throne, just prior to the unleashing of great convulsive judgments on the earth, again promises deliverance to God's people in the midst of judgment.

Around the throne also are seen four "beasts" or "living ones" (Rev. 4:6). From the descriptions, these are the same as the cherubim, the angelic beings who guarded the entrance to the Garden of Eden and the presence of God in Adam's day (Gen. 3:24) and that accompanied God's presence in Ezekiel's day (Ezek. 10).

The cherubim continually recognize the One on the throne with the same ascription applied by the glorified Son of Man to himself. "Holy, holy, holy, Lord God Almighty, which was, and is, and is to come" (Rev. 4:8). There also are twenty-four "elders" around the throne, clearly representing all redeemed men and women through the ages, and they worship him, saying, "Thou art worthy, O Lord, to receive glory and honour and power: for thou hast created all things, and for thy pleasure they are and were created" (Rev. 4:11). This is one of the greatest, as well as most familiar, doxologies in the Bible, and it is significant that it centers on the work of God as Creator. Perhaps we should infer that we, with the elders, will join in this same doxology as soon as we see our Lord on his throne. If so, we should also infer that, if we are going to honor him as our Creator *then,* we should also do it *now.*

The profound question as to *why* God created all things is also answered in this doxology. He created all things for his own pleasure—that is, it simply pleased him to do so. And that's all we need to know! "Pleasure" is the same word in the Greek as "will." Even if we do not understand the divine reasons behind his will, we can know that they are good and right, for whatever God does is right, by definition!

Next, John sees the great scroll representing the ownership deed to the creation—a seven-sealed scroll inscribed both inside and out, in the manner of ancient land records. Only the Lamb, the rightful owner, has authority to break the seals and claim ownership of heaven and earth. As he does, the elders, and then the whole creation, join in the great new song of redemption. "Thou art worthy . . . for thou wast slain, and hast redeemed us to God by thy blood. . . . Worthy is the Lamb that was slain to receive power, and riches, and wisdom, and strength, and honour, and glory, and blessing" (Rev. 5:9, 12).

This is always the proper sequence. Creation, then redemption. Jesus Christ is both our Creator and our Redeemer, and he must be believed and praised as both, for neither is complete alone.

The great theme of divine ownership of the creation appears again in chapter 10, where Christ appears as the mighty angel of the Lord, "come down from heaven clothed with a cloud: and a rainbow was upon his head, and his face was as it were the sun, and his feet as pillars of fire: and he had in his hand a little [scroll] open: and he set his right foot upon the sea, and his left foot on the earth, and cried with a loud voice, as when a lion roareth" (Rev. 10:1–3).

Standing astride land and sea, again with his rainbow (this time as his crown), he proclaims his ownership and his intent shortly to reclaim full possession of his world from the one who has usurped it. "The angel which I saw stand upon the sea and upon the earth lifted up his hand to heaven, and sware by him that liveth for ever and ever, who created heaven, and the things that therein are, and the earth, and the things that therein are, and the sea, and the things which are therein, that there should be time [i.e., delay] no longer" (Rev. 10:5, 6).

In the 11th chapter of Revelation is the remarkable account of God's two witnesses, who will prophesy and call down God's judgments on the earth for three and a half years. Although John does not identify them by name, the strong probability is that these two men will be Enoch and Elijah, who have been in heaven in their mortal bodies for thousands of years. They will be sent back to earth to complete their prophetic ministries—Elijah to Israel, Enoch to the Gentile nations. Both were transported to heaven without dying when their ancient work was only half completed, and they were the only men in all history so privileged. Enoch's ministry was at the approximate midpoint of the Gentile era, between Adam and Abraham, while Elijah prophesied at the midpoint of the age of Israel, from Abraham to Christ.

That Elijah is to return in the last days is assured from Malachi's prophecy at the very end of the Old Testament. "Behold, I will send you Elijah the prophet before the coming of the great and dreadful day of the LORD" (Mal. 4:5). Christ himself confirmed it. "[Elijah] truly shall first come, and restore all things" (Matt. 17:11). Since one of the two witnesses must certainly be Elijah, it almost certainly follows that the other must be Enoch. Enoch, who prophesied long ago of the Lord's final coming in judgment (Jude 14, 15), will prophesy again just prior to that coming. Then he and Elijah will finally be slain, after three and a half years, only to be raised and glorified (like the Lord of whom they had prophesied) three and a half days later (Rev. 11:7–11).

The 12th chapter of Revelation deals explicitly with Satan's rebellion and the age-long conflict between him and the seed of the woman, as prophesied by God immediately after Adam's fall (Gen. 3:15). The conflict is shown symbolically by two great signs in heaven.

> And there appeared a great wonder in heaven, a woman clothed with the sun, and the moon under her feet, and upon her head a crown of twelve stars: and she being with child cried, travailing in birth, and pained to be delivered. And there appeared another wonder in heaven; and behold a great red dragon, having seven heads and ten horns, and seven crowns upon his heads. And his tail drew the third part of the stars of heaven, and did cast them to the earth: and the dragon stood before the woman which was ready to be delivered, for to devour her child as soon as it was born. And she brought forth a man child, who was to rule all nations with a rod of iron and her child was caught up unto God, and to his throne (Rev. 12:1–5).

The Book of Revelation, like all other books of the Bible, should be taken literally unless the context clearly requires a figurative interpretation, as is the case here.

However, when symbolic interpretations are indicated, the interpretation is always to be found in the Scriptures themselves—either in the immediate context or in the broader context of the prophetic Scriptures as a whole. In this case, the interpretation is right at hand, in the following: "And there was war in heaven: Michael and his angels fought against the dragon; and the dragon fought and his angels, and prevailed not; neither was their place found any more in heaven. And the great dragon was cast out, that old serpent, called the Devil, and Satan, which deceiveth the whole world: he was cast out into the earth, and his angels were cast out with him" (Rev. 12:7–9).

Thus, we are told plainly that the great dragon in the heavens is none other than the Devil, or Satan. He is also identified as the ancient serpent who tempted Eve in the garden and caused the entrance of sin and death into the world.

The stars which his tail draws with him to the earth are likewise identified as the fallen angels, evidently a third of the angelic multitude, those who followed Satan in his primeval rebellion against God. These now constitute the evil principalities and powers of the air, the wicked spirits in the atmospheric heavens, with whom Christians must continually wrestle (note Eph. 2:1, 2; 6:11–12), putting on the whole armor of God. At this future time, all these evil spirits will be cast permanently to the earth, with no further access to God, as our accusers before him.

The sign of the woman in the heavens is not specifically explained except by context. The manchild is certainly Jesus Christ, for he is to "rule all nations with a rod of iron," and this was long before given as a specific messianic prophecy, a promise made by the Father to the Son (see Ps. 2:7–9). This identification is made even more certain by the fact that he is delivered from the jaws of the dragon, being caught up to God and his throne.

By inference this would seem at first to identify the woman as his mother, Mary, whose virgin conception satisfied the ancient prescription that the coming conqueror of Satan must be the seed of the woman, rather than man. Looking into the context further, however, it seems that the prophecy involves a multiple fulfillment. The woman is "clothed with the sun, and the moon under her feet, and upon her head a crown of twelve stars." This description could hardly apply specifically to Mary, or to Mother Eve, but it might apply to that "Jerusalem which is above . . ., the mother of us all" (Gal. 4:26). The nation Israel is often presented in the Old Testament as a woman, the wife of Jehovah, and Joseph's prophetic dream did include his father Israel and his mother and his brothers under the symbolic representation of sun, moon, and stars (Gen. 37:9, 10). Thus the woman of the great sign in the heavens could represent *both* the human *mother* of whom Christ was born supernaturally and the *nation* of whom he was also born miraculously.

In this case, the man child who is "caught up unto God, and to his throne" may well prefigure not only Christ at his resurrection as its primary interpretation, but also all those Old Testament saints whose bodies also were raised at the time of his resurrection (Matt. 27:52, 53) and who were apparently taken with him into heaven (Eph. 4:8–10).

It may even include the resurrected and raptured saints at the time of his future return. Like Christ, the overcomers in the representative church at Thyatira are given his promise that they also will be given "power over the nations" and will "rule them with a rod of iron" (Rev. 2:26, 27).

Whether or not we can, at this time, discern the full scope of these two great prophetic signs (the woman with her man child and the great red dragon), it is at least obvious that they are describing the outworking of the great protevangelic prophecy in Genesis 3:15, when God told the old serpent, Satan, "I will put enmity between thee and the woman, and between thy seed and her seed; [he] shall bruise thy head, and thou shalt bruise his heel."

When the dragon is cast out of heaven to the earth and finds he is unable to destroy the woman and her man child, he is "wroth with the woman" and goes forth "to make war with the remnant of her seed, which keep the commandments of God, and have the testimony of Jesus Christ" (Rev. 12:17). At this point, the seed of the woman seems broadened to include not only Christ himself but also all those in whom his Spirit dwells, especially during the coming period of judgment.

In the next chapter, we immediately confront the primary seed of the serpent, in the form of a great "beast [rising] up out of the sea, having seven heads and ten horns," thus partaking of the nature and power of the dragon (compare Rev. 13:1 and 12:3). Although in a sense there are many "children of God" and "children of the devil" (1 John 3:10), beginning with Abel and Cain, there is one primary Son of God and seed of the woman, and one primary Son of Perdition and seed of the serpent, and the climactic battle of the ages will be fought between them.

As the dragon is said to be "that old serpent, called the Devil, and Satan" (Rev. 12:9), so this Beast is said to be "a man" (Rev. 13:18), but he is possessed and controlled by Satan. Eventually, the world will capitulate to Satanism, under the influence and persecutions of the Beast. "They worshipped the dragon which gave power unto the beast: and they worshipped the beast" (Rev. 13:4). Thus will Satan finally realize his age-long goal of being recognized by the world of mankind as its god. It will be only for a brief period, however, for he will only be worshiped by those "whose names are not written in the book of life of the Lamb slain from the foundation of the world" (Rev. 13:8).

All this and more is involved in the great prophecy of Genesis 3:15, but we need not discuss it further here.[3] This is sufficient for our immediate purpose of showing the close correlation between Genesis and Revelation.

All of these events will occur in the coming period of judgment called by Jesus the time of "great tribulation" (Matt. 24:21). It will become so difficult for the believers of those days to preach the gospel that God will finally send an angel to do this. The gospel proclamation of the angel is described in a very important passage. "I saw another angel fly in the midst of heaven, having the everlasting gospel to preach unto them that dwell on the earth, and to every nation, and kindred, and tongue, and people, saying with a loud voice, Fear God, and give glory to him; for the hour of his judgment is come: and worship him that made heaven, and earth, and the sea, and the fountains of waters" (Rev. 14:6, 7).

This mighty angel, flying back and forth around the world, crying out to every nation with a voice so loud that all can hear, is preaching the *everlasting gospel!* This gospel, being everlasting, has always been the same. It must be the same gospel of grace preached by the apostle Paul, for he warned the Galatian legalizers that if even "an angel from heaven, preach any other gospel unto you than that which we have preached unto you, let him be accursed" (Gal. 1:8).

And the essence of the gospel as preached by the angel is: "Worship him who made all things!" This should be enough to correct forever those who object to the preaching of creation and who say we should just "preach the gospel." One does not preach the gospel at all unless he, like God's angel, calls men to worship their Creator first of all.

The gospel of Christ includes more than the creation, of course, for it incorporates the whole scope—past, present, and future—of the person and work of the Lord Jesus Christ. But it *does include* his work of creation, for this is the foundation of all the rest. A person who professes to believe the gospel without believing in creation is trusting in "another gospel," one which has no foundation, and therefore cannot endure, and cannot save.

Undoubtedly the reason why the proclaiming angel stresses the creation component of the gospel is that the world government of the Beast will be a humanistic, pantheistic, Satanist government, founded on the premise of evolution and on the denial of the authority of God the true Creator.

By the same token, it would seem that those in the present time whose faith in evolution, or any of its religious fruits, is keeping them from salvation in Christ need to hear the angel's message first of all. They must be brought to faith in their Creator before they can be brought to understand their need of him as their sin-bearing, death-defeating Redeemer.

Then follows another angel, saying, "Babylon is fallen, is fallen, that great city, because she made all nations drink of the wine of the wrath of her fornication" (Rev. 14:8).

This is the first reference to Babylon in the Book of Revelation, though it is mentioned more frequently in the Bible as a whole than any city except Jerusalem. The city of Babylon was the great enemy of the people of God throughout the entire history of Israel through the time of their exile in Babylon. But this prophetic proclamation of the angel must refer to more than that. Ancient Babylon fell to the Medo-Persians over five hundred years before Christ, yet the angel proclaims its fall as yet to come.

Even more significant is the identification of Babylon as the city which has intoxicated *all nations* with "the wine of the wrath of her fornication." That could not be said of the Babylon of Nebuchadnezzar or the Babylon of Hammurabi. It could only be true of the Babylon of Nimrod, for Babel did indeed infect all nations with Nimrod's spiritual fornication. This age-long drunkenness of the nations, and its end-time climax, is examined in detail in chapters 16—18 of Revelation.

In the 16th chapter, "the great river Euphrates," flowing through Babylon, "dried up" (Rev. 16:12), in preparation for the movement of great armies past Babylon on their way to Armageddon. Then, soon after, occurs the greatest earthquake in history, "and great Babylon [comes] in remembrance before God, to give unto her the cup of the wine of the fierceness of his wrath" (Rev. 16:19).

The 17th and 18th chapters are devoted altogether to Babylon, first its age-long influence for the devil, then its ultimate destruction. First, John is shown another sign, this time another great woman. This one, however, is great in wickedness. She is called "MYSTERY, BABYLON THE GREAT, THE MOTHER OF HARLOTS AND ABOMINATIONS OF THE EARTH" (Rev. 17:5).

This symbolic harlot is more than the literal city of Babel, or Babylon as it was later called, of course, but she received her name from the literal city where she was born. It was there at Babel that Nimrod founded the world's first great kingdom, centered at Babel and Nineveh, later to develop into the powerful and incredibly violent and cruel Assyro-Babylonian empire. It was at Babel that Nimrod fomented and led the first post-flood rebellion against God, and it was from there that God scattered the tribes throughout the world, after confounding their tongues so they could no longer organize their proposed anti-God world government.

From there the various nations carried with them the system of pantheistic (and, therefore, evolutionistic) religion evidently introduced by Satan through Nimrod in the zodiacal shrine dedicated to the host of heaven at the apex of Babel's tower. This religio-cultural complex was carried in varied, but essentially equivalent, form throughout the world by the scattering tribes. The Babel religion, rejecting God as Creator, was essentially the evolutionistic, humanistic, pantheistic, polytheistic, spiritistic, astrological, animistic, idolatrous system that identifies ultimate reality with the eternal space/mass/time universe, instead of with its Creator.

Such a system of religion inevitably leads to moral evil of all kinds, as well, and such has been the history of most of the nations of the world in every age. No wonder that this "Mystery, Babylon" has been called by God "the Mother of Harlots and Abominations [that is, immoral idolatrous practices] of the earth."

This vast religious system is shown to John as sitting upon (that is, controlling) the great Beast and his confederation of the world's nations. This suggests that the ecumenical and syncretistic movements being promoted by the different religions of the world will eventually prove successful and a "world religion" (which has long been the goal of the United Nations and its UNESCO division, as well as of all the modern New Age cults and movements) will be adopted as their official religion by the nations of the world. It will, of course, be based on evolution and will be some form of pantheistic humanism which attempts to incorporate the appropriate features of Hinduism, Buddhism, and all the other world religions, including liberal and ritualistic forms of Christianity. Eventually, as noted above, it will become full-fledged Satanism, but probably only after the kings of the various nations decide to eliminate all other religious vestiges from any control over their people. "These shall hate the whore, and shall . . . burn her with fire" (Rev. 17:16). No other authority will be countenanced for long by the Beast and his satanic master. Nimrod's ancient rebellion and goal of world government opposing God will eventually be realized, and all will be compelled, under penalty of death, to worship Satan and obey his man of sin. But this will not be for long, for the next chapter describes the final and complete destruction of Babylon.

Babylon is not only the world religious system of the last days; it will also become an actual city again, probably the world capital of the Beast. The 18th chapter of Revelation describes the city and its destruction in such detail that it could only refer to a real city, a city that is the most influential, and most evil, city on earth.

We have already noted that this was prophetically indicated in Zechariah 5:5–11. Although Babylon gradually drifted into relative oblivion about a century after Christ, it was never completely abandoned (as the prophets Isaiah and Jeremiah had predicted would eventually happen), and it has actually been partially restored in recent years by the Iraqi government as a potential tourist and cultural attraction. It is ideally situated, both geographically and politically, to become the capital of a world government. And it is ironically appropriate that the great city which was the world's first great center of apostasy should become the final center of world opposition to God.

In any case, it is doomed. "With violence shall that great city Babylon be thrown down, and shall be found no more at all. . . . for thy merchants were the great men of the earth; for by thy sorceries were all nations deceived. And in her was found the blood of prophets, and of saints, and of all that were slain upon the earth" (Rev. 18:21, 23, 24).

Then, in short order, the seed of the serpent—that is, the Beast—will be taken and "cast alive into a lake of fire burning with brimstone" (Rev. 19:20), followed quickly by "the dragon, that old serpent, which is the Devil, and Satan," who will be cast "into the bottomless pit" for "a thousand years" (Rev. 20:2, 3). Then, after the thousand years, Satan will be freed to deceive the nations once more. This rebellion of the serpent and his seed will be his last, for "the devil that deceived them was cast into the lake of fire and brimstone, where the beast and the false prophet are, and shall be tormented day and night for ever and ever" (Rev. 20:10).

At last, the seed of the woman will have crushed forever the head of the old serpent, and sin and death will be no more!

The present cursed earth and its atmospheric heaven will be burned up (2 Pet. 3:10), and God will finally make it new and young again, forever. In the beginning God created the heaven and the earth, but John records that at this time: "I saw a new heaven and a new earth: for the first heaven and the first earth were passed away; and there was no more sea. And I John saw the holy city, New Jerusalem, coming down from God out of heaven, prepared as a bride adorned for her husband" (Rev. 21:1, 2).

The next two chapters—which are, in fact, the final two chapters of God's inspired Word—contain the most glorious words ever written, describing the new heaven and the new earth and the beauties of the New Jerusalem. Even though, as we have seen, the sun and moon were created to last forever, the heavenly city "had no need of the sun, neither of the moon, to shine in it; for the glory of God did lighten it, and the Lamb is the light thereof" (Rev. 21:23).

In the first earth there was a division between day and night, but in the new earth "there shall be no night there" (Rev. 21:25), for there will be no further need of the darkness. The first earth initially had a global ocean and was again covered with the sea when the great flood destroyed the world in Noah's day, but in the new earth there will be "no more sea" (Rev. 21:1).

And, most important, there will be no more sin and evil. "There shall in no wise enter into it any thing that defileth" (Rev. 21:27), for all the unsaved of all the ages will have been resurrected from their prison in Hades and taken for final judgment before God's great white throne. "The sea gave up the dead which were in it; and death and hell [that is, Hades] delivered up the dead which were in them. . . . And death and hell were cast into the lake of fire. This is the second death. And whosoever was not found written in the book of life was cast into the lake of fire" (Rev. 20:13–15).

The special mention of the dead who are in the sea seems enigmatic, but it probably represents the multitudes who perished in the waters of the great flood.

The New Jerusalem, the home of all those who are saved, will be the eternal reality of that for which man's original home in the Garden of Eden was only the type. In Eden a river from an artesian spring "went out of Eden to water the garden" (Gen. 2:10). In the New Jerusalem "a pure river of water of life" will flow "out of the throne of God and of the Lamb" (Rev. 22:1).

In the garden there was "every tree that is pleasant to the sight, and good for food; the tree of life also [grew] in the midst of the garden" (Gen. 2:9). In the holy city, "on either side of [the] river, was there the tree of life, which bare twelve manner of fruits, and yielded her fruit every month: and the leaves of the tree were for the healing of the nations" (Rev. 22:2). As noted already, the New Jerusalem is called "the paradise of God," and the promise is given: "To him that overcometh will I give to eat of the tree of life, which is in the midst of the paradise of God" (Rev. 2:7).

Actually, the English word "paradise" is transliterated from the Greek *paradecsos*, which is taken in turn from the Hebrew *pardes*, meaning "forest" or "orchard." It is clear that it was a term applicable to the beautiful home of Adam and Eve when God was present with them. It is used in the New Testament by Christ (Luke 23:43) and by Paul (2 Cor. 12:4) to refer to the place of God's presence in heaven—which, in fact, is the place Christ went to prepare for his redeemed ones.

The gate to the garden had to be guarded by the cherubim to keep sinners from the tree of life (Gen. 3:24). As for the New Jerusalem, however, "the gates of it shall not be shut at all by day: for there shall be no night there" (Rev. 21:25), and the leaves of the tree will be for healing the nations.

More important than any of these features, however, is the fact that sin, and the curse, and death, which entered that first garden, will all be gone from the beautiful city. "There shall in no wise enter into it any thing that defileth" (Rev. 21:27). "There shall be no more curse" (Rev. 22:3). "And there shall be no more death" (Rev. 21:4).

It is significant that each of the four main aspects of the curse will be specifically removed in the new world: "God shall wipe away all tears from their eyes; and there shall be no more death, neither sorrow, nor crying, neither shall there be any more pain: for the former things are passed away" (Rev. 21:4). When the curse was pronounced, it specifically incorporated *sorrow* ("in sorrow shalt thou eat of it all the days of thy life"), *crying* ("in the sweat of thy face shalt thou eat bread"), and *pain* ("thorns also and thistles shall it bring forth to thee"), in addition to *death* ("unto dust shalt thou return" [Gen. 3:17–19]). The Lord Jesus, again calling himself "Alpha and Omega, the beginning and the end," promises to "make all things new" again and stresses that "these words are true and faithful" (Rev. 21:5, 6). All of his primeval purposes in creation, interrupted for a little season by the entrance of sin into the world (but allowed by God so that he could be known and understood and loved as Redeemer and Savior, as well as Creator), will be finally accomplished and will endure forever.

"There shall be no more curse . . . and his servants shall serve him: and they shall see his face. . . . and they shall reign for ever and ever" (Rev. 22:3–5). This is the best of all! For a little while, Adam and Eve walked and talked with God in the garden, trying to serve him in exercising dominion over his creation as he had commanded. But men and women have failed in this mandate ever since they disobeyed God's Word and ate the forbidden fruit. With the curse removed, however, they will finally be enabled to serve their Lord in exercising this dominion over the creation effectively, and they shall do so forever and ever.

"And they shall see his face," in perfect fellowship with their Lord forever, as they "do his commandments, that they may have right to the tree of life, and may enter in through the [pearly] gates into the city" (Rev. 22:14). Through all the ages to come, we shall live and serve in the presence and fellowship of our great Creator and loving Savior, our Lord Jesus Christ.

17

The Biblical Doctrine of Creation

Creation in All the Bible

If nothing else, this excursus through the Scriptures has shown conclusively that creationism is a *biblical* doctrine, not just a Genesis story. There are references to creation and to God as Creator in practically every one of the sixty-six books of the Bible. Even in those few books where the doctrine is not explicitly mentioned (as in the one-chapter, very personal Epistles of Paul and John), it is certainly implied in the very attitudes of the writers.

The other events of the early chapters of Genesis—the fall, the curse, the murder of Abel, the translation of Enoch, the flood, the ark, etc.—are also mentioned in later books of the Bible, especially in the New Testament. And wherever they are mentioned, it is crystal clear that the writers invariably regarded them as literally, historically true. There is never a hint that the Genesis records are merely allegories or legends or anything other than sober histories of the early days of the earth and its inhabitants.

The chief characters are all mentioned by name in the New Testament—Adam, Eve, the serpent, the cherubim, Cain, Abel, Enoch, Noah—not to mention the complete genealogy from Adam to Christ, as given in Luke's Gospel. There can be no legitimate doubt whatever, that not only Moses, but all the other divinely inspired writers of the books of the Bible, and even Christ himself, believed and taught that the Genesis record, from its very first verse onward, must be received as absolutely factual and foundational to all the rest of the Bible. To question this is to question the veracity and knowledge of the omniscient Creator himself, and this may come dangerously close to rejecting the warning of Revelation 22:19.

In all the many, many references to creation, there is not the slightest hint that any process of "evolution" could ever be regarded as God's method of creation. This was not because the writers were unfamiliar with evolutionism, because all the ancient religions and philosophies of men in those days (except for those based on the Genesis account) were based on some form of evolution.

Nor is there any hint in the Bible of great ages of past time. The biblical writers took the record in Genesis at face value, including the revealed truth that God had created and made all things in heaven and earth in six solar days. And, again, this was not because of ignorance of the "old-earth" concept. The pagans of the day all believed in the eternal preexistence of the space time universe, and in endless ages of prehistory. The idea of a recent creation and young earth was a radically new concept to people of that day who did not know or believe the Word of God, just as it is in our day.

It is also important to emphasize that the Lord Jesus, as well as the apostle Peter and the writer of Hebrews, regarded the flood as a worldwide cataclysm, not as either a local or tranquil flood, as many modern evangelicals do today. These evangelicals do this solely in order to accommodate the evolutionary geological ages, hoping thereby to appease their non-Christian academic colleagues.

This book, therefore, is an urgent plea to our Christian brethren to come back to simple faith in the plain words of Scripture, as they deal with the vital doctrine of creation. God is surely able to convey, through his holy apostles and prophets, exactly what he means, and we would do well to assume he means exactly what he says.

In this chapter I will try to collect and organize the most important and currently relevant aspects of the teachings of the whole Word of God on these vital themes first set out in the first eleven chapters of Genesis. In going though the whole Bible to collect all these reference, I have followed essentially a chronological, progressive revelation type of approach, trying to understand each new revelation in the context of what those who first received it already knew.

Now that we have gone all through the Bible, however, we have God's *complete* revelation on creation and related events. It is, therefore, appropriate to codify and analyze all of it for these latter days in which we live.

The Creator

The Bible teaches unequivocally that the Creator is a great person who created the entire universe of space and time, as well as matter and energy and all the systems and personalities that exist in the space/time universe. The Creator is neither the "Mother Earth" of the ancient pagan pantheists nor the "cosmic consciousness" of modern pantheists, and certainly not the light of "Evolution" as promoted by New-Age philosophers. The Creator is God, *Elohim,* the uni-plural God set forth in the most profound and probably most ancient words ever written: "In the beginning God created the heaven and the earth" (Gen. 1:1).

God in his essence is omniscient, omnipresent, omnipotent, and eternal. He is "the King eternal, immortal, invisible, the only wise God" (1 Tim. 1:17). He had no beginning himself, for he *created* time, in the beginning. Being present everywhere he cannot be directly *seen* or *heard* anywhere. "No man hath seen God at any time" (1 John 4:12). As Jesus said: "Ye have neither heard his voice at any time, nor seen his shape" (John 5:37). "God is light, and in him is no darkness at all" (1 John 1:5). He is perfect in holiness, impeccable in judgment, absolute in truth. "O the depth of the riches both of the wisdom and knowledge of God? how unsearchable are his judgments, and his ways past finding out! . . . For of him, and through him, and to him, are all things" (Rom. 11:33, 36).

Yet, although no man has seen him or heard him or comprehended him, "the only begotten Son, which is in the bosom of the Father, he hath declared him" (John 1:18). "He that hath seen me hath seen the Father," said Jesus (John 14:9). Therefore, his disciples could say, "That which was from the beginning, which we have heard, which we have seen with our eyes, which we have looked upon, and our hands have handled, of the Word of life . . . that which we have seen and heard declare we unto you" (1 John 1:1, 3).

The true God of creation, therefore, is not the inscrutable Allah of the Muslims, but is the God/Man, Jesus Christ. "The Word was made flesh, and dwelt among us, (and we beheld his glory, the glory as of the only begotten of the Father,) full of grace and truth" (John 1:14). God is, indeed, absolute in light and holiness and truth, beyond the comprehension of sinful men. But, also "God is love" and "in this was manifested the love of God toward us, because that God sent his only begotten Son into the world, that we might live through him" (1 John 4:8, 9).

Thus, the very Creator of heaven and earth is none other than the Lord Jesus Christ! He who is "the image of the invisible God" (Col. 1:15) is the one by whom God "created all things" (Eph. 3:9). In probably the greatest of all Christological passages, Paul says "For by him were all things created, that are in heaven, and that are in earth, visible and invisible, whether they be thrones, or dominions, or principalities, or powers: all things were created by him, and for him: and he is before all things, and by him all things consist" (Col. 1:16, 17).

We also have the exalted testimony of the incomparable prologue to the Gospel of John. "In the beginning was the Word, and the Word was with God, and the Word was God. The same was in the beginning with God. All things were made by him; and without him was not any thing made that was made" (John 1:1–3).

That Word later became flesh, manifest as the only begotten of the Father. God became man, incomprehensible as this may seem; in fact he became *perfect* man—man as God had intended man to be, but as all other men have failed to be. Thus, God "was in the world, and the world was made by him, and the world knew him not" (John 1:10). The world, in fact, rejected him and "crucified the Lord of glory" (1 Cor. 2:8).

But even this was in God's plan, for thereby he became our Redeemer as well as our Creator. He who was "equal with God . . . became obedient unto death, even the death of the cross. Wherefore God also hath highly exalted him, and given him a name which is above every name" (Phil. 2:6, 8, 9). He died for our sins and then conquered sin and death and Satan in his resurrection, and has thereby "obtained eternal redemption for us" (Heb. 9:12).

Some (Jews, Moslems, and others) may acknowledge God as Creator, but reject him as their redeeming Savior. Many Christians profess to accept him as their "personal" Savior, but reject him as the mighty

God and Creator of all things, opting instead to believe that the process of evolution created all things.

But if we would know and honor and believe on Christ *as he really is* (not "another Jesus, whom we have not preached," says Paul [2 Cor. 11:4], then we should acknowledge him and trust him as both mighty Creator and gracious Redeemer. We should praise him as our great Creator and love him as our saving Redeemer.

We may not (in fact, *cannot*) completely understand how Christ could be both God and man, or how God could be both Father and Son, but Christ has fully vindicated his right to make such a claim—by his miraculous conception, his miracles, his sinless life, his perfect words, his self-controlled sacrificial death, and his glorious resurrection. We may not understand, but we can readily believe *him!*

In fact, although God is one, yet he has revealed himself as a tri-une God—one God, yet three persons, Father, Son, and Holy Spirit. Each person is equally, fully God—*one* God! The universe God created is a tri-universe, thus reflecting its Creator. It is a *uni*-verse, not a *poly*-verse, but it is a *tri*-universe of space, matter, time ("heaven, earth, beginning" [Gen. 1:1]), with each pervading the entire universe and each existing only in concert with the other two. And, specifically, it was "by Christ" that the Father through the "moving" Spirit (Gen. 1:2) created this great tri-universe.

The Process of Creation

There was no actual *process* of creation, although people often speculate as to *how* God created. Usually, when this question is raised, the questioner has in mind some supposed process of evolution as God's method of creation.

The fact is, however, that creation was altogether miraculous, not capable of being described in terms of natural processes at all. When God created (Hebrew *bara*), it was instantaneous, accomplished simply by his omnipotent Word. Some have called this "fiat creation." God said: "Let there be . . . ," and there it was! This fact is noted in several Scriptures in addition to the creation chapter in Genesis. For example:

> By the word of the LORD were the heavens made; and all the host of them by the breath of his mouth. . . . For he spake, and it was done; he commanded, and it stood fast (Ps. 33:6, 9).

Praise ye him, sun and moon: praise him, all ye stars of light. Praise him, ye heavens of heavens, and ye waters that be above the heavens. Let them praise the name of the LORD: for he commanded, and they were created. He hath also stablished them for ever and ever: he hath made a decree which shall not pass (Ps. 148:3–6).

Through faith we understand that the worlds were framed by the word of God, so that things which are seen were not made of things which do appear (Heb. 11:3).

It is significant that, whenever the Bible speaks of the creation of the world, it is always in the past tense. For example: "Thou hast made heaven, the heaven of heavens, with all their host, the earth, and all things that are therein, the seas, and all that is therein, and thou preservest them all" (Neh. 9:6). And: "[God] created heaven, and the things that therein are, and the sea, and the things which are therein" (Rev. 10:6). Never does any passage suggest that God is still "creating" the world, as evolutionism would require.

In fact, the work of creation is so uniquely supernatural that the verb "create" never has any subject except "God," for only God can create. This is not the case with such verbs as "make" (Hebrew *asah*) and "form" (Hebrew *yatsar*), however. Men can make things and form things out of preexisting materials, but only God can create the basic materials themselves. Furthermore, God can also make things and form things out of preexisting materials and can do so much more rapidly and perfectly than men can do.

This distinction is significant in the two creation chapters, Genesis 1 and 2. Three acts of fiat creation are recorded, as follows:

(1) "In the beginning God created the heaven and the earth" (Gen. 1:1). Space and time were called into existence, along with the elements of matter, or "earth."
(2) "God created great whales, and every living creature that moveth" (Gen. 1:21). Here God called biological, conscious, moving *life* into existence.
(3) "God created man in his own image . . . ; male and female created he them" (Gen. 1:27). The elements of man's body were created on Day One; the entity of life (Hebrew *nephesh*, translated "creature" in Genesis 1:21, is translated "soul" in Genesis 2:7, when Adam became a "living soul") was created on Day Five.

Finally, God created his own image—a spiritual nature—in man and woman on Day Six. Thus, man alone, out of all God's creation, is body, soul, and spirit.

Only three acts of creation (calling entities into existence *ex nihilo*) are mentioned, but these entities were then used by God to "make" and "form" all other systems. Seven acts of "making" are mentioned, as follows:

(1) "God made the firmament" (Gen. 1:7).
(2) "God made two great lights" (Gen. 1:16).
(3) "He made the stars also" (Gen. 1:16).
(4) "God made the beast of the earth . . . and cattle . . . and every thing that creepeth upon the earth" (Gen. 1:25).
(5) "Let us make man in our image" (Gen. 1:26).
(6) "Out of the ground made the LORD God to grow every tree that is pleasant to the sight, and good for food" (Gen. 2:9).
(7) "The sea is his, and he made it" (Ps. 95:5).

These seven basic things that God "made" out of the elements he had "created" constitute a representative list only, for Genesis 2:4 tells us that "the LORD God made the earth and the heavens," and Genesis 1:31 says that "God saw every thing that he had made, and, behold, it was very good." These are evidently comprehensive statements meant to apply to all physical and biological systems in heaven and earth.

Furthermore, God's "making" acts were instantaneous, just as were his "creating" acts (note Ps. 33:6, as discussed above). Both were altogether miraculous, the only difference being that God "made" things out of basic entities he had already "created." Both his "creating" and "making" works were finished in the six days and are not going on today, as theistic evolution would imply. The creation chapter concludes with the dictum that God "rested from all his work which God created and made" (Gen. 2:3).

The "forming" work of God implies something more personal and care-taking than either his "creating" or "making." Here God works like a potter forming clay into a particular vessel. In particular, "the LORD God formed man of the dust of the ground" (Gen. 2:7). Although the word is not repeated, it is obvious that God also formed woman, for he built Eve out of flesh and bone from Adam's side (Gen. 2:21–23).

It is also noteworthy that "out of the ground the LORD God formed every beast of the field, and every fowl of the air" (Gen. 2:19), implying that he is especially interested in at least these higher animals.

Two later passages of interest tell us that "his hands formed the dry land" (Ps. 95:5) and that "I form the light" (Isa. 45:7). He neither created nor made "light," of course, because God *is* light, but he did "create darkness," and then formed day and night, dividing the light from the darkness.

As far as the dry land is concerned, God took special care in its structure and composition, for he "formed the earth and made it; he hath established it, he created it not in vain, he formed it to be inhabited" (Isa. 45:18). The sea is only temporary (Rev. 21:1), but the renewed earth will be the home of his people forever (Rev. 22:5).

Thus God has created, made, and formed the earth, just as he both created and made man and woman in his image, and carefully formed their bodies.

In all of this, there is no hint whatever of any slow process of evolution being used by God for any part of his creating, making, or forming work. None of these are going on now (except in rare miracles), for "the works were finished from the foundation of the world," and God "hath ceased" from all his works" (Heb. 4:3, 10).

The Time and Duration of Creation

The fact of fiat creation has, as shown in the foregoing, been conclusively documented in Scripture, as has the fact that all of God's work of creating and making was finished and completely functioning (pronounced "very good" by God) by the end of the six-day creation period described in chapter 1 of Genesis.

There is, nevertheless, a widely held opinion, even among those evangelical Christians who do not believe in evolution, that the earth is about 4.6 billion years old and the universe perhaps 15 billion years old. The reasons for holding such an opinion, however, cannot be derived from Scripture, for the Bible clearly teaches that all things were made in six solar days, not over several billion years.

While occasionally the word for "day" in Genesis (Hebrew *yom*) can be used to mean "time" in general, it is never used in the Old Testament (in over a thousand occurrences) to mean a definite period of time, with a beginning and an end, unless that period is either a literal day or the daylight part of the day/night cycle. Furthermore, it can mean "time" instead of a literal day only if the context requires it. The context certainly does *not* require it here in Genesis; the only reason for suggesting such a thing is the supposed necessity of finding 4.6 billion years of earth history in the Genesis record of creation.

In fact, the context in Genesis 1 completely precludes any such interpretation, as though the writer anticipated future attempts to do this and was trying specifically to guard against it. God defines his terms, and the very first time the word "day" was used, he was careful to do just this. "God divided the light from the darkness. And God called the light Day, and the darkness he called Night. And the evening and the morning were the first day" (Gen. 1:4, 5).

"Day," therefore, was defined by the Lord as the light period in the light/darkness cycle which he initiated on that first day and which has continued every day since. There is no way it could mean anything like a geological age in this context.

The terminology "evening and morning" as bounding each day, and the numbering of the successive days as "first day," "second day," etc., both add further contextual restrictions guarding the literal use of "day" here, for both usages are always applied in the Old Testament only to literal days.

The "days," therefore, are regular solar days, and the divine acts of creating and making on each day were all accomplished and finished during six of these days. Each verse in the chapter begins with "and," using the Hebrew conjunction *waw*, indicating continuing and successive action. There is no room in the narrative for time gaps of any consequence, certainly not billions of years.

If any uncertainty still remains on this question, however, it should be forever dispelled by the divinely inscribed (as well as inspired) words of the fourth commandment. "Remember the sabbath day, to keep it holy. Six days shalt thou labour, and do all thy work: but the seventh day is the sabbath of the LORD thy God . . . For in six days the LORD made heaven and earth, the sea, and all that in them is, and rested the seventh day: wherefore the LORD blessed the sabbath day, and hallowed it" (Exod. 20:8–11).

It could hardly be clearer than this. Man's six days of work followed by one day of rest were specifically patterned after God's primeval week, and this is the very reason why people all over the world have kept time in weeks ever since. In fact, Jesus said that "the sabbath was made for man" (Mark 2:27). There should no longer be any doubt that God created and made everything in the universe in a week of six days followed by a day of rest, exactly like our week. Otherwise, language itself is meaningless, and God cannot communicate with those he created in his image. Yet these words were inscribed on "tables of stone, written with the finger of God" (Exod. 31:18), and God considered them so important that disobedience to them by an Israelite was punishable by death.

In addition to these explicit statements, the absolute silence of the entire Bible with respect to great ages of time before man is very significant. On the other hand, there are several passages that indicate quite definitely that people have been living on earth since its very beginning.

For example, Zacharias the priest, father of John the Baptist, in his prayer of thanksgiving for the coming of the Messiah in fulfillment of prophecy, noted that God had been speaking "by the mouth of his holy prophets, which have been since the world began" (Luke 1:70). Similarly, the apostle Peter, during his sermon in the porch of the temple, said that Christ had returned to heaven "until the times of restitution of all things, which God hath spoken by the mouth of all his holy prophets since the world began" (Acts 3:21).

Thus, both Zacharias and Peter affirmed that God's prophets had been promising Christ's coming since the very first age of the world, not just since the end of some previous geological age.

Similarly, Jesus spake of "the blood of all the prophets, which was shed from the foundation of the world" (Luke 11:50). The first such prophet was Abel (Luke 11:51), the son of Adam. Cain slew his brother right at the beginning of world history, not 4 billion years later.

One of the most clear-cut references of this type (and others could be cited) is found in the answer of the Lord Jesus to the hypocritical question of the Pharisees about marriage and divorce. "Jesus answered and said unto them, For the hardness of your heart [Moses] wrote you this precept. But from the beginning of the creation God made them male and female. For this cause shall a man leave his father and mother, and cleave to his wife" (Mark 10:5–7).

Here the Lord Jesus (who was *there* when Adam and Eve were created, for he was their Creator!) was quoting from "both" accounts of creation (as the liberals would call them) in the same context (quoting from Gen. 1:27 and Gen. 2:24), without the slightest acknowledgment of the liberals' claim that the two accounts are contradictory. He regarded them both as divinely inspired and of such authority that he based his teaching on marriage, the most important of all human institutions, on them.

But note in particular his understanding of the time of this definitive event. It was at "the beginning of the creation" that "male and female created he them" (Gen. 1:27), not—as theistic evolutionists and progressive creationists assert—some billion years after the beginning of the creation that bisexual reproduction evolved, and then over 3.5 billion years later still that men and women evolved (or "were created").

We must conclude, in view of all the above, if we are honest with God's Word, that the whole universe was made in six literal days.

Furthermore, there is no place in the Bible for geological ages either *before* the six days of creation (as per the so-called gap theory) or *after* them. "In six days the LORD made heaven and earth, the sea, and *all that in them is*" (Exod. 20:11). All the stars in the heaven, all the deep core and mantle and crust of the earth, all the waters of the sea, were made in the six days of creation week. There was *nothing* before that, except God, for God himself said so, inscribing this comprehensive summary of creation with his finger on tables of stone (Exod. 31:18).

As far as chronology after the creation week is concerned, no one has ever imagined that the supposed billions of years of earth history could be placed after man's creation! It is barely possible that slight gaps might be found in the genealogies of Genesis 5 or Genesis 11, but nothing comparable to a billion years! As a matter of fact, there is no evidence in the context of Scripture itself that any gaps exist at all. These chapters appear to be intended as sober genealogical records, with additional data inserted at each name to yield chronological records as well. Essentially the same genealogy is inserted in 1 Chronicles 1:1–28 and Luke 3:34–38, so that neither Old Testament writers nor New Testament writers ever suggested or suspected that the Genesis genealogies were incomplete.

If we are going to rely solely on Scripture, as I am trying to do in this book, we have to conclude that God created all things in six literal days about six thousand or so years ago.

The Impossibility of Evolution

It may seem redundant at this point to note further biblical evidence against evolution, since the Scriptures already discussed clearly teach that God created and made all things in six literal days. The Bible also stresses, several times in Genesis 2:1–3 and elsewhere, that he ceased all the creating and making works thereafter, so that all "the works were finished from the foundation of the world" (Heb. 4:3).

Nevertheless, evolutionists will continue to believe in evolution, regardless of the evidence. "For this they willingly are ignorant of," says Peter, "that by the word of God the heavens were of old, and the earth . . ." (2 Pet. 3:5). "The invisible things of him from the creation of the world are clearly seen," says Paul, "being understood by the things that are made, . . . so that they are without excuse" (Rom. 1:20).

Consequently, it is well to point out some of the negative evidences against evolution, as well as the positive evidences for creation. For example, the plants and animals made by God during creation week were given reproductive systems that enabled them to reproduce only "after their kinds," never after some other kind. This phrase, or its equivalent, occurs no less than ten times in the first chapter of Genesis. The same truth is re-emphasized in the New Testament. "God giveth it a body as it hath pleased him, and to every seed his own body" (1 Cor. 15:38).

Although modern forms of evolutionism, such as Darwinism, were unknown in biblical days, the various pagan religions of the Gentile nations were all based on polytheistic pantheism, which was merely another form of evolutionism, denying or ignoring the existence of the one transcendent God and Creator of all things. Pagan religions attributed the development of the world, including its living creatures, to the "gods" and "goddesses" who were, in essence, mere personifications of the forces and systems of nature. The only ultimate, eternal, non-evolved, reality was the space time universe itself, rather than the Creator of the universe. The Gentiles "worshipped and served the creature more than the Creator" (Rom. 1:25). These various forms of ancient pantheistic evolutionism are being revived today in the so-called New-Age movement.

Consequently, the pervasive biblical condemnations of idolatry are, in effect, directed against the philosophy which today would be called evolutionism. This whole system has been transmitted throughout the world from the first civilization after the flood, from the religion of the first Babylonians, the Sumerians. This was all brought about by Nimrod (the founder of Babel) when he led the whole world population of the time to rebel against God, building a great tower dedicated to the worship of the "host of heaven." This involved worship of both the stars and the fallen angels, who soon became identified as the gods of the nations and the components of the creation which they purportedly controlled. The rebellion was thwarted by God's miraculous confusion of the people's languages and enforced worldwide dispersion, as described in Genesis 10 and 11. But they all carried their idolatrous evolutionary religion with them, and it is this system which God repeatedly rebuked, especially because his chosen people, Israel, repeatedly compromised with it.

> As the thief is ashamed when he is found, so is the house of Israel ashamed; they, their kings, their princes, and their priests, and their prophets, saying to a stock, Thou art my father; and to a stone, Thou hast brought me forth: for they have turned their back unto me (Jer. 2:26, 27).
> When they knew God, they glorified him not as God, neither were thankful; but became vain in their imaginations, and their foolish heart was darkened. Professing themselves to be wise, they became fools, and changed the glory of the uncorruptible God into an image made like to corruptible man, and to birds, and fourfooted beasts, and creeping things (Rom. 1:21–23).

In the apostolic period, this religion had been "intellectualized" into Greek philosophy, and it was this evolutionary philosophy that Timothy was warned about by Paul when he wrote: "O Timothy, keep that which is committed to thy trust, avoiding profane and vain babblings, and oppositions of science falsely so called" (1 Tim. 6:20). Evolution is, indeed, a pseudo-science, and Paul's warning is more needed today than ever.

The Worldwide Flood

The truth of the worldwide flood in the days of Noah is a vital component of the biblical doctrine of creation, for the flood marked the transition from the primeval world to the present world. It makes impossible the evolutionary assumptions made by the "last days scoffers" who argue that "all things continue as they were from the beginning of the creation" (2 Pet. 3:3, 4). Furthermore, the flood assures us that God did not forget his created world after he imposed the curse on the ground and all man's dominion. He cleansed the earth of its violence and wickedness by water, and this is an implicit promise that one day he will purify it completely by fire, even purging the curse from its very elements (2 Pet. 3:10).

The Lord Jesus, in fact, used the worldwide judgment of the flood as a type of the worldwide effects of his second coming. "But as the days of Noe were, so shall also the coming of the Son of man be. For as in the days that were before the flood they were eating and drinking, marrying and giving in marriage, until the day that Noe entered into the ark, and knew not until the flood came, and took them all away; so shall also the coming of the Son of man be" (Matt. 24:37–39).

Peter also confirmed the universality of the flood in three passages in his Epistles. Note the following: "When once the longsuffering of God waited in the days of Noah, while the ark was a preparing, wherein few, that is, eight souls were saved by water" (1 Pet. 3:20). "[God] spared not the old world, but saved Noah the eighth person, a preacher of righteousness, bringing in the flood upon the world of the ungodly" (2 Pet. 2:5). "The world that then was, being overflowed with water, perished" (2 Pet. 3:6).

Similarly, the writer of Hebrews (the apostle Paul?) recognized the unique nature of the flood. "By faith Noah, being warned of God of things not seen as yet, moved with fear, prepared an ark to the saving of his house" (Heb. 11:7).

These New Testament passages make it certain that Christ and the apostles knew the flood was worldwide, unique in all history, destroying all the world's wicked and spiritually indifferent inhabitants, sparing only the eight people of Noah's family.

Some have suggested in the past (though few do today, in view of modern evidences of human antiquity in every continent) that the flood was "worldwide" only in the sense of reaching as far as human migrations had extended. There can be no question, however, that in the 1,656 years after God's command to Adam to "be fruitful, and multiply, and [fill] the earth" (Gen. 1:28), the rapidly growing populations had, indeed, essentially filled the whole earth. For God said, "The earth is filled with violence through them; and, behold, I will destroy them with the earth" (Gen. 6:13). Thus "the earth" itself had to be destroyed in order to destroy "them."

The account of the flood in Genesis 6–9 explicitly requires the global character of the flood. How else could one interpret the statement that "the same day were all the fountains of the great deep broken up, and the windows of heaven were opened. And the rain was upon the earth forty days and forty nights" (Gen. 7:11, 12)?

Or how could one derive a local flood from the statement that "the waters prevailed exceedingly upon the earth; and all the high hills, that were under the whole heaven, were covered. Fifteen cubits upward did the waters prevail; and the mountains were covered" (Gen. 7:19, 20)? The draft of the ark was evidently fifteen cubits when loaded (its height was thirty cubits), so this statement indicates that the ark could float freely over all the mountains of the pre-flood world. The waters "prevailed upon the earth an hundred and fifty days" (Gen. 7:24), and only then were the "fountains of the deep" and the "windows of heaven" stopped so the waters could begin to go down (Gen. 7:24–8:2).

And what about the fact that "all flesh died that moved upon the earth, both of fowl, and of cattle, and of beast, and of every creeping thing that creepeth upon the earth, and every man: all in whose nostrils was the breath of life, of all that was in the dry land, died. . . . and Noah only remained alive, and they that were with him in the ark" (Gen. 7:21–23). No one could possibly read a local flood into such events unless he were blinded by his need to believe in the geological ages—any evidences of which a worldwide flood would certainly have destroyed. Furthermore, such a flood would have deposited the very rock units which today are misinterpreted as evidence for the geologic ages.

Then there was the covenant God made with Noah and all the animals after the flood: that never "shall all flesh be cut off any more by the waters of a flood; neither shall there any more be a flood to destroy the earth" (Gen. 9:11). This covenant was sealed by the sign of the rainbow, visible in the sky for the first time with the precipitation of the vapor canopy, "the waters above the firmament." If the flood was only a local flood, God has broken his covenant countless times in the many centuries of destructive local floods that mankind has experienced subsequently.

The animals preserved in the ark were released after the flood to "breed abundantly in the earth, and be fruitful, and multiply upon the earth" (Gen. 8:17). There certainly would have been no need of an ark "to keep them alive" on the earth (Gen. 6:19, 20) if the flood had been only a local flood, for migration to a region not to be reached by the flood would have been a far easier solution. The same would have applied to Noah and his family, but the fact is that from the three sons of Noah "was the whole earth overspread" (Gen. 9:19) after the flood. Only these lived through the global flood.

Writers of the Old Testament concur with those of the New that the flood was a worldwide cataclysm. Job said concerning it that God "sendeth [the waters] out, and they overturn the earth" (Job 12:15). David said that "the LORD is upon many waters. . . . The LORD sitteth upon the flood; yea, the LORD sitteth King for ever" (Ps. 29:3, 10). In the 104th psalm, clearly speaking of the flood, the psalmist wrote that God "coveredst [the earth] with the deep as with a garment: the waters stood above the mountains" (v. 6). Then he spoke of the mountains rising and sea basins opening to receive the drain waters from the flood, "that they turn not again to cover the earth" (vv. 5–9).

Isaiah the prophet referred to the flood when he reminded Israel that God had sworn that "the waters of Noah should no more go over the earth" (Isa. 54:10).

Thus Job, David, Isaiah, Peter, Paul (or whoever wrote Hebrews), and the Lord Jesus Christ himself all confirmed the primeval testimony of Noah and his sons, preserved and edited by Moses, that the antediluvian age ended with the worldwide cataclysm of the great flood. There is no suggestion anywhere in the Bible that this flood was either a local flood or a tranquil flood that left no evidence, just as there is not a scintilla of evidence of evolution or of an ancient pre-Adamic earth in Scripture. Christians who reject the strong testimony in God's Word of a recent creation and a global hydraulic cataclysm must do so for personal reasons, not biblical reasons.

The Foundational Importance of Biblical Creationism

There seem to be a considerable number of Bible-believing Christians who agree that the Bible does teach a recent six-day creation and worldwide flood, but who do not consider these truths very important, and so rarely preach or teach them. This is a tragedy, because there is no doctrine of Scripture more vital or important than the doctrine of creation. It is nothing less than the foundation of all Christian doctrine and of true biblical Christianity. That is why God placed it first in the Bible. Consider the following brief summaries of doctrines based on creation.

(1) Foundation of True Christology

Jesus Christ was our Creator before he became our redeeming Savior. "For by him were all things created" (Col. 1:16). "And without him was not any thing made that was made" (John 1:3). "By [him] also [God] made the worlds; who being the brightness of his glory, and the express image of his person, and upholding all things by the word of his power, when he had by himself purged our sins, sat down on the right hand of the Majesty on high" (Heb. 1:2, 3). Unless, therefore, we base our presentation of the person and work of Christ on his role as Creator, we are actually teaching "another Jesus" (2 Cor. 11:4).

(2) Foundation of True Gospel

The gospel of Christ includes his substitutionary death, burial, and bodily resurrection, but its foundation is his work of creation. The final, climactic biblical reference to the gospel calls it the "everlasting gospel," so it has always been the same. "I saw another angel fly in the midst of heaven, having the everlasting gospel to preach unto them that dwell on the earth, . . . saying with a loud voice, . . . worship him that made heaven, and earth, and the sea, and the fountains of waters" (Rev. 14:6, 7). Creation must be included if we truly "preach the gospel."

(3) Foundation of True Faith

The first object of a "living faith" and "saving faith" (Heb. 10:38, 39) is given in the greatest "faith chapter" in the Bible, Hebrews 11. "Through faith we understand that the worlds were framed by the word of God, so that things which are seen were not made of things which do appear" (Heb. 11:3). This verse clearly negates theistic evolution, which assumes the present earth and its creatures were made out of previous materials. It also indicates that meaningful faith to live by must be built first on faith in special creation.

(4) Foundation of True Evangelism

The purpose of John's Gospel was to help men "believe that Jesus is the Christ, the Son of God; and that believing ye might have life through his name" (John 20:31). This divinely inspired purpose of evangelism was implemented first of all by the divinely inspired approach in initiating this testimony. "In the beginning was the Word, and the Word was with God, and the Word was God. . . . All things were made by him; and without him was not any thing made that was made" (John 1:1, 3). John's evangelistic witness began, like Genesis, "In the beginning."

(5) Foundation of True Missions

In carrying out Christ's Great Commission, Paul preached to the polytheistic evolutionists at Lystra: "Ye should turn from these vanities unto the living God, which made heaven, and earth, and the sea, and all things that are therein" (Acts 14:15). Then, when he preached to the atheistic evolutionists (Epicureans) and pantheistic evolutionists (Stoics) at Athens, he again began with the Creator. "God that made the world and all things therein . . . is Lord of heaven and earth" (Acts 17:24). But, on the other hand, when he preached to those who already knew and believed the Scriptures, including the truth of creation (i.e., the Jews), he began immediately with the Scriptures foretelling the saving work of Christ. This two-pronged procedure provides an ideal guide for our own witness in missions and evangelism.

(6) Foundation of True Bible Teaching

Here Christ gave us his own example. After his resurrection, speaking with his two disciples on the way to Emmaus, "beginning at Moses [and, therefore, in Genesis] and all the prophets, he expounded unto them in all the scriptures the things concerning himself" (Luke 24:27).

(7) Foundation of True Fellowship

Since creation is the foundation of all true doctrine, particularly the doctrines of Christ and salvation, it should also be the foundation of true church fellowship. Paul touched on this when he said his goal was "to make all men see what is the fellowship of the mystery, which from the beginning of the world hath been hid in God, who created all things by Jesus Christ: to the intent that now unto the principalities and powers in heavenly places might be known by the church the manifold wisdom of God" (Eph. 3:9, 10). Our Christian fellowship, founded on the work of Christ in creation and redemption, is thus a testimony even to the angels.

(8) Foundation of True Marriage and Family Relationships

When asked about the most basic of all human institutions, marriage and family, the Lord Jesus merely referred to the record of creation. "Have ye not read, that He which made them at the beginning made them male and female, and said, For this cause shall a man leave father and mother, and shall cleave to his wife: and they twain shall be one flesh? Wherefore they are no more twain, but one flesh. What therefore God hath joined together, let not man put asunder" (Matt.19:4-6).

(9) Foundation of All Human Vocations

"God blessed them, and God said unto them, Be fruitful, and multiply, and replenish [i.e., fill] the earth, and subdue it: and have dominion over the fish of the sea, and over the fowl of the air, and over every living thing that moveth upon the earth" (Gen. 1:28). "God said, . . . let [man] have dominion . . . over all the earth" (Gen. 1:26). This primeval dominion mandate to "subdue" the earth implies all honorable human occupations—science to understand the earth, technology to develop it, commerce to utilize it, education to transmit its knowledge, humanities to glorify it, all through which to honor God and serve as stewards of the earth, under him.

(10) Foundation of Christian Life

When a person becomes a believing Christian, he is made "a new creature" (2 Cor. 5:17) in Christ by the Holy Spirit. He puts on "the new man, which is renewed in knowledge after the image of him that created him" (Col. 3:10). The image of God in man has been marred by sin, but when he is created again by the new birth, he can then begin to live the kind of life for which God created man in the beginning. Once he has adopted the biblical worldview, including a proper understanding of creation and redemption, the Christian will rightly relate to other Christians, society around him, and the Creator/Redeemer himself.

Many other illustrations of the foundational importance of the doctrine of creation could be given, but these ten should make the point. Creation is not an incidental or peripheral doctrine, by any means, but is foundational to everything else in Christian faith and practice.

This concludes our through-the-Bible study of creation and other events of primeval history. I have tried to search out and discuss every passage dealing with these themes, and there are many indeed, as we have seen.

This, of course, has been strictly a study in *biblical* creationism. Other books, some of which are listed in Appendix C, deal strictly with *scientific* creationism, and still others with the sociological and historical *rel-*

evance of creationism. Every honorable field of study or practice is ultimately based on God's work and purpose in creation, so the data in each field, rightly understood, will give further evidence of creation. The most important evidences of all, however, are the revelations in God's written Word, and *these* have constituted the theme of *this* book.

Appendix A

Creation in Extra-Biblical Writings

The Apocrypha

The fourteen books, or parts of books known as "the Apocrypha" (a term meaning "hidden things"), are believed by most Roman Catholics, as well as some others, to be part of the canon of inspired Scriptures. Most Christians, however (including myself), recognize them as valuable historical and instructional documents but not as divinely inspired.

It is not as important, therefore, to examine *their* teachings regarding primeval history as it is for the sixty-six books of the standard canon of Scripture. Nevertheless, such references do have considerable value in showing what the Jews of that period (generally the four hundred "silent" years between the Old and New Testaments) believed concerning the authenticity and historicity of the Genesis record. With this limitation in mind, I shall survey them briefly, rather than in the same detail as applied to the canonical Scriptures.

And when we do this, it soon becomes apparent that these writers of the Apocrypha, as well as the inspired writers of Scripture, regarded the Genesis accounts to be completely factual and authoritative. Nowhere do they make any concessions to the pagan evolutionism of the Gentile nations around them. There can be no doubt that the Jews of the interTestamental period were committed to strict creationism (six literal days, the fall, the worldwide flood, etc.).

The fourteen books of the Apocrypha are generally listed in the following order

(1) 1 Esdras (the Greek form of Ezra)
(2) 2 Esdras
(3) Tobit
(4) Judith
(5) Insertions in the O.T. Book of Esther
(6) Wisdom of Solomon
(7) Ecclesiasticus (also called "The Wisdom of Jesus, Son of Sirach")
(8) Baruch (supposedly to be added to Jeremiah, and including an "Epistle of Jeremiah")
(9) Song of the Three Holy Children (supposed insertion in Daniel)
(10) History of Susanna (also supposedly added to Daniel)
(11) Bel and the Dragon (another supposed addition to Daniel)
(12) Prayer of Manasses (supposed insertion in 2 Chronicles)
(13) 1 Maccabees
(14) 2 Maccabees

The following quotations are merely samplings from the various apocryphal books, not a complete list. They are taken from the Authorized King James Version of 1611, with only the spellings modernized.

1 Esdras 6:13

"So they gave us this answer: We are the servants of the Lord which made heaven and earth."

2 Esdras 3:4–11

"O Lord, who bearest rule, thou spakest at the beginning, when thou didst plant the earth (and that thyself alone) and commandest the people, and gavest a body unto Adam without soul, which was the workmanship of thine hands, and didst breathe into him the breath of life, and he was made living before thee. And thou leddest him into paradise, which thy right hand had planted, before ever the earth came forward. And unto him thou gavest commandment to love thy way, which he transgressed; and immediately thou appointedst death in him, and in his generations, of whom came nations, tribes, people, and kindreds out of number. And every people walked after their own will, and did wonderful things before thee, and despised thy commandments. And again in process of time thou broughtest the flood upon those that dwelt in the world, and destroyedst them. And it came to pass in every one of them, that as death was to Adam, so was the flood to these. Nevertheless one of them thou leftest, namely Noah with his household, of whom came all righteous men."

2 Esdras 6:38–54

"And I said, O Lord, thou spakest from the beginning of the creation, even the first day, and saidst thus, Let heaven and earth be made: and thy word was a perfect work. And then was the Spirit, and darkness, and silence were on every side; the sound of man's voice was not yet formed. Then commandest thou a fair light to come forth of thy treasures, that thy work might appear. Upon the second day thou madest the spirit of the firmament, and commandedst it to part asunder, and to make a division betwixt the waters, that the one part might go up, and the other remain beneath. Upon the third day thou didst command that the waters should be gathered in the seventh part of the earth: six parts hast thou dried up and kept them, to the intent that of these some being planted of God, and tilled, might serve thee. For as soon as thy word went forth, the work was made. For immediately there was great and innumerable fruit, and many and diverse pleasures for the taste, and flowers of unchangeable color, and odors of wonderful smell: and this was done the third day. Upon the fourth day thou commandedst that the Sun should shine, and the Moon give her light, and the stars should be in order, and gavest them a charge to do service unto man, that was to be made. Upon the fifth day, thou saidest unto the seventh part, where the waters were gathered, that it should bring forth living creatures, fowls and fishes: and so it came to pass. For the dumb water, and without life, brought forth living things at the commandment of God, that all people might praise thy wondrous works. Then didst thou ordain two living creatures, the one thou calledst Behemoth, and the other Leviathan, and didst separate the one from the other: for the seventh part (namely where the water was gathered together) might not hold them both. Unto Behemoth thou gavest one part which was dried up the third day, that he should dwell in the same part, wherein are a thousand hills. But unto Leviathan thou gavest the seventh part, namely the moist, and hast kept him to be devoured of whom thou wilt, and when. Upon the sixth day thou gavest commandment unto the earth, that before thee it should bring forth beasts, cattle, and creeping things:

and after these, Adam also whom thou madest lord of all thy creatures, of him come we all, and the people also whom thou hast chosen.

Tobit 8:6

"Thou madest Adam, and gavest him Eve his wife for an helper and stay: of them came mankind: thou hast said, It is not good that man should be alone, let us make unto him an aide like unto himself."

Judith 16:13–14

"I will sing unto the Lord a new song, O Lord, thou art great and glorious, wonderful in strength and invincible. Let all creatures serve thee: for thou spakest, and they were made, thou didst send forth thy Spirit, and it created them, and there is none that can resist thy voice."

Additions to Esther 13:10, 11

"For thou hast made heaven and earth, and all the wondrous things under the heaven. Thou art Lord of all things, and there is no man that can resist thee, which art the Lord."

Wisdom of Solomon 10:1–4

"[Wisdom] preserved the first formed father of the world that was created alone, and brought him out of his fall, and gave him power to rule all things. But when the unrighteous went away from her in his anger, he perished also in the fury wherewith he murdered his brother. For whose cause the earth being drowned with the flood, Wisdom again preserved it, and directed the course of the righteous, in a piece of wood, of small value."

Ecclesiasticus 17:1–4

"The Lord created man of the earth, and turned him into it again. He gave them few days, and a short time, and power also over the things that are therein. He endued them with strength by themselves, and made them according to his image, and put the fear of man upon all flesh, and gave him dominion over beasts and fowls."

Ecclesiasticus 44:16–18

"Enoch pleased the Lord, and was translated, being an example of repentance, to all generations. Noah was found perfect and righteous, in the time of wrath, he was taken in exchange [for the world]; therefore was he left as a remnant unto the earth when the flood came. An everlasting Covenant was made with him, that all flesh should perish no more by the flood."

Ecclesiasticus 49:14

"But upon the earth was no man created like Enoch, for he was taken from the earth."

Baruch 3:32–34

"But he that knoweth all things, knoweth her, and hath found her out with his understanding: he that prepareth the earth for evermore, hath filled it with fourfooted beasts. He that sendeth forth light, and it goeth: calleth it again, and it obeyeth him with fear. The stars shined in their watches, and rejoiced: when he calleth them, they say, Here we be, and so with cheerfulness they shewed light unto him that made them"

Song of the Three Holy Children 3:60

"O ye waters that be above the heaven, bless ye the Lord: praise and exalt him above all for ever."

Bel and the Dragon 1:5

"[Daniel] answered and said, Because I may not worship idols made with hands, but the living God, who hath created the heaven, and the earth, and hath sovereignty over all the earth."

Prayer of Manasses (no verse structure)

"O Lord, Almighty God of our fathers, Abraham, Isaac, and Jacob, and of thy righteous seed: who hast made heaven and earth, with all the ornament thereof: who hast bound the sea by the word of thy commandment: who hast shut up the deep, and sealed it by thy terrible and glorious Name, whom all men fear, and tremble before thy power."

1 Maccabees 2:61–63

"And thus consider ye throughout all ages, that none that put their trust in him shall be overcome. Fear not then the words of a sinful man, for his glory shall be dung and worms. Today he shall be lifted up, and tomorrow he shall not be found, because he is returned into his dust, and his thought is come to nothing."

2 Maccabees 7:23

"But doubtless the Creator of the world, who formed the generation of man, and found out the beginning of all things, will also of his own mercy give you breath, and life again, as you now regard not your own selves for his Law's sake."

2 Maccabees 7:28

"I beseech thee, my son, look upon the heaven, and the earth, and all that is therein, and consider that God made them of things that were not, and so was mankind made likewise."

2 Maccabees 7:4

"And when they said, There is in heaven a living Lord, and mighty, who commanded the seventh day to be kept."

These quotations from the Apocrypha by no means exhaust the references therein to creation and other primeval events. There is a much greater number that have not been quoted. These are representative, however, and do clearly indicate that the Jews of the period between Malachi and the coming of Christ did, indeed, regard the Genesis record as divinely inspired and authoritative. They believed in *ex nihilo* creation, in the six literal days and the Genesis account of the creation events of those days, in the placing of Adam and Eve in the Garden of Eden, in the fall and entrance of death, in the curse, in the Cain-and-Abel story, in the translation of Enoch, in the worldwide flood, in the Noahic covenant, and in all the other great events as reported in Genesis 1–11.

Sometimes the accounts are embellished with new insights, or perhaps just interpretive comments, but nowhere does any writer in the Apocrypha ever question or reject any statement of the Genesis record. Never is there the slightest suggestion that these records are not precisely historical, just as they stand.

Furthermore, there is no evidence of any tendency toward any kind of evolution, atheistic or pantheistic or theistic. This is especially remarkable in view of their long contact with the evolutionary paganism of the Canaanites and other idolaters. Presumably their sad exile into the midst of Babylon's sophisticated idolatry had purged them of such tendencies. No doubt there was some knowledge by this time of the evolutionary philosophies of the Greeks but, if so, no intimation of its influence appears in the apocryphal books. Though they were often disobedient to God, they did, at least believe in him as transcendent Creator of all.

Creationism in the Pseudepigrapha

In addition to the Apocrypha, there exist many ancient books collectively known as the Pseudepigrapha, or "falsely ascribed writings," so called because many of them were attributed by their authors (who are believed to have lived in the first or second centuries before Christ) to ancient biblical patriarchs (Adam, Noah, the twelve sons of Jacob, Solomon, etc.). There is no need to discuss all of these here, except to note that all of them assumed the authenticity and historicity of Genesis, as well as the other canonical books of the Old Testament. They added to them in great measure, but did not question them.

The additions were often fanciful and probably fictional, but always intended piously, not destructively. It is possible that some of these writings were embellishments of ancient traditions handed down over the centuries from the pre-Abrahamic patriarchs. The Bible indicates, for example, that both Abraham and Job had access to ancient records of divinely given laws long before Moses received the Law on Mount Sinai (note Gen. 26:5; Job 23:12). Since "the book of the generations of Adam" (Gen. 5:1) was definitely a written document, it is certain that the antediluvian patriarchs all had a written language and undoubtedly many books and other documents existed in those ancient days. Most of these were destroyed in the great flood, but it surely is reasonable—indeed, highly probable—that Noah took many such documents with him into the ark.

There is, of course, the inspired New Testament Epistle of Jude, which asserts that a book written (at least in part) by Enoch still existed in his time (see Jude 14, 15).

Therefore, we should not dismiss these pseudepigraphal writings out of hand, as some may have actually preserved ancient traditions of real historical events. At the same time, internal evidence seems to indicate quite conclusively that they have at least been extensively embellished by unknown writers in the centuries just before Christ. They have generally been considered "pious forgeries" and cannot be accepted as divinely inspired histories, but they may possibly contain segments of ancient traditions of real events and are therefore worthy of study in this context.

The most important of these writings are the two books attributed to Enoch. These (or at least some portion of them) were accepted as canonical for a while by some of the church fathers. The apostle Jude, as noted above, actually incorporated a brief segment from Enoch in his own inspired Epistle.

The first Book of Enoch has been translated into English from its only extant ancient manuscript (a translation from the Greek into Ethiopic). It incorporates portions of another writing known as the Book of Noah, and evidently was first written in Hebrew, or possibly Aramaic. A number of scholars believe it is a compilation of several writings from different authors and times.

Be all that as it may, the author or authors attribute it to Enoch, and much of the book is presented as a vision received by him from God. It has been divided into 118 chapters, and the fragment quoted by Jude appears in its very first chapter as follows: "And behold! He cometh with ten thousands of his holy ones, to execute judgment upon all, and to destroy all the ungodly: and to convict all flesh of all the works of their ungodliness which they have ungodly committed, and of all the hard things which ungodly sinners have spoken against him" (1 Enoch 1:9).

Since Jude, by divine inspiration, placed the stamp of authenticity on this particular prophecy of Enoch, as given right at the very beginning of his book, it seems reasonable at least to take the rest of the book seriously, though this does not at all imply accepting it as true in all respects.

Consequently, we can note a few of the points made by Enoch (or whoever may have been the author) as at least of some interest with respect to the Genesis record. There is a lengthy section, for example, on the angelic intrusion into human affairs through cohabiting with earthly women, resulting in a population of giants—giants in both size and wickedness (compare Gen. 6:1–4). This, plus the evil influence of these angels in general, resulted in worldwide wickedness and the resulting decision of God to send the flood and to bind the fallen angels in the "valley" of the earth to await the final judgment (compare Jude 6).

Enoch also says that, once the giants were slain, their spirits (partaking of both angelic and human natures) became the evil spirits that roam the earth (1 Enoch 15:8–12), afflicting men "unto the day of the consummation."

There are references to Cain and Abel, to the coming flood, to the building of the ark, to the new covenant after the flood, to behemoth and leviathan, and to many other aspects of the ancient world, all consistent with the Genesis record, but going beyond it.

There are also "prophecies" relating to the history of Israel and the coming Messiah, including many references to the "Son of Man." A large portion of the book deals with the final judgments and the eternal kingdom.

The second Book of Enoch, also called "The Secrets of Enoch," is known essentially only from a Slavonic translation rediscovered in recent times in Russia and Serbia. It was, however, probably known and used by the early Christian church. Like the first Book of Enoch, it also is in the form of an autobiographical narrative by the ancient prophet, in particular consisting of visions along with angelic translations.

In chapters 25 through 30 of 2 Enoch, God is shown rehearsing to Enoch the events of creation week. The order and events in general agree with those in Genesis, though with many imaginative embellishments. One interesting addition is the story of God creating angels on the second day, followed by the fall of Satan on the same day. The fall of Adam and Eve is narrated in chapters 31 and 32.

Then, in chapter 33, appears a recurring theme in ancient Jewish apocalyptic literature—that there would be just seven thousand years of history, evidently to correspond to the seven days of creation week, followed by endless time not counted by years. God's warning of the future deluge appears in chapter 34, and the final translation of Enoch into heaven is described in chapter 67.

The Book of Jubilees is also one of the more significant of these pseudepigraphal writings of the intertestamental period. The title is derived from the unknown author's calendrical scheme, as he attempts to develop the history of the world, beginning with the creation, into multiples of jubilee periods (the Mosaic prescription of a "jubilee" year following forty-nine normal years). It was originally written in Hebrew, translated into Greek, and from Greek into Ethiopic, which is the form in which it has been preserved until the present. It was translated from Ethiopic into English by Professor George Schodde, of Capital University in Ohio.

Much of the book seems intended as a commentary on Genesis, with many imaginative extensions, some of which might represent authentic traditions from antiquity. Note, for example, the following:

> And the angel of the face spoke to Moses by the command of the Lord, saying: "Write all the words of creation, how in six days the Lord God finished all the works which he created, and rested on the seventh day and sanctified it for all the years and established it as a sign for all his works." For on the first day he created the heavens above and the earth and the waters and all the spirits that serve before him, and the angels of the face and the angels that cry "holy," and the angels of the spirit of fire . . . (Jubilees 2:1).

The account continues with the work of the rest of the days of creation week, following the Genesis order, but much amplified (Jubilees 2:3–17).

There is one very interesting variation. It is said that Adam's naming of the animals took place in the first five days of the *second* week. Then Eve was made from Adam's rib on the sixth day of *that* week! Then they worked in the garden for seven years before the temptation of Eve and the resultant fall of Adam. The account also indicates that all the animals in Eden could speak until the curse (Jubilees 3:1-6; 3:24).

Adam and Eve had many sons and daughters, with both Cain and Seth marrying sisters (Jubilees 4:9, 10, 11). There are also references to the sins of the angels, the warning of the coming deluge, and the translation of Enoch (Jubilees 4:23, 24, 25; also Jubilees 5).

The ark and the great flood are described, with the ark coming to rest "upon the top of Lubar, one of the mountains of Ararat." Then, later, "all the mouths of the deep of the earth were opened, and the water began to descend into the deep below" (Jubilees 5:26, 27).

The story of the Tower of Babel " in the land of Sinaar" and the resulting confusion of tongues and dispersion is given in Jubilees 10:16–21.

Another book of this sort, of even more doubtful authenticity, is the so-called Book of Jasher. An ancient book of this name is mentioned in Joshua 10:13, as confirming the amazing miracle of Joshua's long day. It is mentioned once again, in II Samuel 1:18, in a strange parenthetical reference introducing David's lamentation over the death of Saul and Jonathan. This verse reads: "(Also he bade them teach the children of Judah the use of the bow: behold, it is written in the book of Jasher.)."

"Jasher" is believed to mean "the Upright," rather than a man's name. Thus the original book of Jasher is supposed to have been a sort of continuing saga of the deeds of the great men of God of the earliest ages. It was long believed to have been lost, though no one knew when or how.

In later centuries, however, a few manuscripts purporting to be copies of the Book of Jasher, began to turn up. These are believed by most authorities, to be pious fiction. One such manuscript does, however include so many fascinating details of the lives of the ancient patriarchs, that one wonders whether it may, after all, be based in part on records of true history, preserved over the centuries by Noah, Moses and others. Even if this is true, there are so many embellishments in it that the book certainly could not have been divinely inspired. At worst, it is pure forgery: at best it is based on genuine historical records, but encrusted with many imaginative additions and distortions.

This particular manuscript was first published in English in Vancouver, Canada in 1840, after being translated by an unidentified Hebrew scholar in England. It is said to have been transported to the Jewish community in Spain after the destruction of Jerusalem in the first century. It was eventually taken to Venice after the invention of the first printing press, and published in Hebrew in 1613. The Venice printer had transcribed it from this very old and almost illegible manuscript.

The Book of Jasher, as presently available via this long and circuitous process, is a strange mixture of what appears to be true history with many fanciful—even mythological—embellishments. Many passages seem to come straight out of the canonical Hexateuch, with the English translation sounding much like the King James Version. But then there are a multitude of details added to the Biblical accounts, plus narrations of many events not found in the Bible at all, many of these involving miraculous events which are questionable at best (e.g., the angel Gabriel teaching Joseph to converse in 70 languages just before he was to meet Pharaoh).

Jasher does include the two references mentioned in the Bible. The "long day" quotation of Joshua 10:13 appears in Jasher 88:63, 64. David's mention of Jasher in the introduction to his lament over Saul and Jonathan (2 Sam. 18) is taken from Jacob's dying instructions to Judah as recorded in Jasher 56:9.

The book covers essentially the same ground as Genesis through Joshua, the Hexateuch, but with many deletions and many detailed additions and modifications. It makes fascinating reading, considered as a possible running history and commentary kept by a succession of unknown reporters throughout the early ages, centered around the "upright" patriarchs from Adam down to Joshua. The numerous incredible segments could have been inserted by later scribes. Or the entire book could have been fictional re-telling of ancient history by some unknown scribe.

Whatever its true origin, this Book of Jasher, like the other books of the Pseudepigrapha, accepts the Biblical record of creation and the flood, as well as the other events recorded in Genesis 1–11, as true history. It may enlarge and embellish them but it never questions them. There is never a suggestion that the people of God should compromise with the idolatrous pagan evolutionism of the other nations of the world.

However, according to Jasher, the "sons of men" began to serve other gods as early as in the days of Enos, son of Seth and grandson of Adam. When Enoch came, he led in a great revival, for a time, but then finally was translated to heaven "in a whirlwind, with horses and chariots of fire," as Elijah would be, many centuries in the future.

Jasher also describes graphically the terror of those who refused the preaching of Noah and were left behind when the Flood came. It also says that a third part of the earth's population had been destroyed previously in the days of Enos by a tremendous flooding of the river Gihon. When the great Flood itself began, and the Ark was closed, the account says that 700,000 men and great hordes of animals were clamoring unsuccessfully to get into the ark.

The book noted that, in the days of Peleg, "the sons of men were divided, and in the latter days, the earth was divided." It also notes that Nimrod was "more wicked than all the men that were before him, from the days of the Flood until those days." Another surprising account told how Abram was hidden by Terah in a cave from the wrath of Nimrod, and that later he spent much time with Noah and Shem to learn about the Lord and His ways.

When God judged the people for their building the Tower of Babel, those who had said that "we will ascend to heaven and place our gods there and serve them" were made to become "like apes and elephants," whatever that means. At that time, "all the sons of men were dispersed into the four corners of the earth."

According to Jasher, Nimrod continued to rule Babel and Shinar after the dispersion of the others, and became known as Amraphel, king of Shinar (note Gen. 14:1). Terah, Abram's father, was captain of Nimrod's armies, serving his idols, until after Abram was born. It had been prophesied that Abram would defeat Nimrod, so Nimrod tried to slay Abram when he was still a child, and Terah hid him in a cave. When he was grown, Abram rebuked both Nimrod and Terah for serving other gods. The king sought unsuccessfully to kill Abram, and eventually Abram and Terah left the land of the Chaldees to escape his wrath. Nimrod himself was later slain by Esau, grandson of Abram, while both, known as great hunters, were out hunting.

Before this, Amraphel (Nimrod) and three other kings invaded Canaan and were defeated by Abram. At that time Jasher says Adonizedek—evidently the same as Melchizedek—who was "King of Jerusalem" met and blessed Abram, and Abram gave him tithes of the spoil, as "a priest before God." A most interesting note is added parenthetically, that "the same was Shem."

The entire book is full of fascinating historical details supplementing the Biblical records. These often sound authentic and illuminating.

Yet there are also many events narrated which seem quite incredible. The book remains an enigma.

There are thus many imaginative details in these Pseudepigrapha added to all the simple biblical narratives of these great events of primeval history. Some may reflect authentic traditions, but most are surely nothing but pious fiction. The important point, however, is that these and all other ancient writings of the Pseudepigrapha are at least based on strong belief in the historicity of the Genesis account. These ancient writers may have added to the accounts, but they never thought of doubting them. To them the Genesis record was sober history.

Josephus and the Ancient Books

Flavius Josephus, the Jewish historian, may be the most important of the extra-biblical writers. Born in A.D. 37, he lived during the Apostolic period, dying in A.D. 100. He was well educated, born in a priestly family, and held an important position in the Jewish community before the fall of Jerusalem in A.D. 70. He was later on good terms with the Roman emperors Vespasian and Titus, spending much of his mature years in Rome, as an honored and influential citizen. He was also given extensive properties in Judaea.

He was a very learned man and undoubtedly had access to many ancient records which are no longer available today, especially with all the resources of the mighty Roman empire at his disposal. With his intense indoctrination in Jewish religion, he must have been familiar with all the traditions of the fathers, now long forgotten, and he was vitally interested in the history of his people. Furthermore, his writings were intended as serious histories not tales attributed to the ancient patriarchs, like most of the apocalyptic literature.

Consequently, although his writings are not inerrant or divinely inspired in any sense, they are recognized by most scholars as excellent historical studies, at least as reliable as any other writings of ancient times. Thus it is significant that, just as the writers of the Apocrypha and Pseudepigrapha did, Josephus accepted all the records of Genesis as true and accurate history.

The first six chapters of Book I of his *Antiquities of the Jews* cover the history of the world from creation through the dispersion of the nations of the world and the confusion of the languages at Babel. He follows the order and events of Genesis, except that he adds a number of interesting items of information not contained in Genesis. Some of these may have been derived from other ancient writings or traditions which he believed were authentic. On the other hand, many of his comments seem to be mere arbitrary—perhaps Pharisaical—interpretations of the Genesis records.

He does say that Adam had "many other children" (*Antiquities* 2:3)[1] besides Cain and Abel. In a footnote the translator, William Whiston, an early eighteenth-century scholar, says: "The number of Adam's children, as says the old tradition, was thirty-three sons and twenty-three daughters."

Josephus also accepts the old tradition that, before the curse, all the animals could talk and the serpent was able to walk upright (1:4). He writes at some length about the wickedness of Cain and his descendants (2:2) in contrast to the godliness of Seth and his posterity (2:3). He says the latter "were the inventors of that peculiar sort of wisdom which is concerned with the heavenly bodies, and their order" (2:3). He says that Adam predicted two future destructions of the world—one by fire, one by water (2:3).

After seven generations, however, even the descendants of Seth became wicked. This resulted, at least in part, when "many angels of God accompanied with women, and begat sons that proved unjust and despisers of all that was good." Their deeds, he says, "resembled the acts of those whom the Grecians call giants" (3:1). The result was God's warning of the coming flood, indicating that these giants would only live for 120 years.

Josephus notes that the ancient patriarchs (Adam through Noah) were heads of "governments," evidently of the Sethite descendants. He also makes the significant observation that their records—dates of birth and death, dates of the birth of the sons succeeding each in turn, etc.—were actually written down and transmitted from father to son. "The time is written down in our sacred books, those who then lived having noted down, with great accuracy, both the births and deaths of illustrious men" (3:3). The dates—including even those of Enoch's translation and the coming of the flood—all agree with those in the standard Hebrew text of Genesis. This affirmation strongly confirms the internal evidence of Scripture that Genesis is based on the written records of the ancient patriarchs, not on verbal traditions.

With respect to the flood, Josephus surely considered it to be world-wide. "When God gave the signal, and it began to rain, the water poured down forty days, till it became fifteen cubits higher than the earth, which was the reason why there was no greater number preserved, since they had no place to fly to" (3:5).

Josephus discusses the continued existence of the ark thus: "However, the Armenians call this place *The Place of Descent;* for the ark being saved in that place, its remains are shewn there by the inhabitants to this day" (3:5). He then notes similar reports from the Babylonian historian Berosus, Hieronymus the Egyptian, Nicolaus of Damascus, Mnaseas, "and a great many more" (3:5). Whiston, in his translator's footnote, adds the following; "Whether any remains of this ark be still preserved, as the people of the country suppose, I cannot tell. Mons. Tournefort had, not very long since, a mind to see the place himself, but met with too great dangers and difficulties to venture through them."

Josephus makes a special point of affirming that the ancients did, indeed, live to great ages, citing as confirming witnesses all the great historians of antiquity—Berosus, Hesiod, Hieronymus, and many others—saying that they all "relate that the ancients lived a thousand years" (3:9).

Josephus also recounts the rebellion of Nimrod against God, climaxed by the building of the Tower of Babel and the final confusion of tongues and dispersion. For confirmation, he notes the following: "The Sibyl also makes mention of this tower, and of the confusion of the language, when she says thus: 'When all men were of one language, some of them built a high tower, as if they would thereby ascend up to heaven; but the gods sent storms of wind, and overthrew the tower, and gave every one his peculiar language; and for this reason it was that the city was called *Babylon.'* But as to the plain of Shinar, in the country of Babylonia, Hestiaeus mentions it, when he says thus: 'Such of the priests as were saved, took the sacred vessels of Jupiter Enyalius, and came to Shinar of Babylonia.'"

The sixth chapter of Josephus's *Antiquities of the Jews* corresponds to the "Table of Nations" in Genesis 10, giving much valuable supplementary ethnological information. We need not review all these names and connections here, but the following examples may be of some interest. Gomer, one of the sons of Japheth, is said to be the ancestor of the Galatians, or Galls. The Scythians were descendants of Magog. The Greeks came from Javan, and the Medes from Madai. Tiras founded the Thracians, Meshech the Cappadocians, and Tubal the Iberes. Three sons of Gomer are also mentioned: Ashkenaz was ancestor of the Rheginians, Riphath of the Paphlagonians, and Togarmah of the Phrygians. These nations, of course, are given names as they were known in Josephus's day. There has been much additional migration and mixing since then.

Of the children of Ham, Josephus notes that Cush was the ancestor of the Ethiopians, Mizraim of the Egyptians, Phut of the Libyans, and Canaan of the Canaanites.

The descendants of Shem included Elam, whose descendants, the Elamites, eventually became the Persians. Aram founded the Syrians. Ashur lived at Nineveh and was father of the Assyrians. Arphaxad was ancestor of the Chaldeans, according to Josephus. Lud became the Lydians.

Heber, a grandson of Arphaxad, gave his name to the Hebrews. One of Heber's sons was Peleg, and Josephus makes the following important point concerning him. "He was called Phaleg, because he was born at the dispersion of the nations to their several countries: for Phaleg, among the Hebrews, signifies *division*" (6:4). Josephus thus offers no support to certain recent ideas suggesting that there was an actual splitting of the continental land mass at the time of Peleg.

It is also important to note, in view of modern controversies, that Josephus takes the genealogies and chronologies of the standard Hebrew text of Genesis 5 and 11 at face value. He never suggests any "gaps" or other mistakes in these records. At the most, he allows less than 5,000 years from the beginning to his own times.

Appendix B

Special Studies in Biblical Creationism

The topics discussed in this Appendix have already been mentioned in connection with my expositions of the relevant texts of Scripture. However, the subjects are so significant as to warrant special discussion as independent topics. These discussions are based on articles originally written many years ago for *Acts and Facts*, the monthly newsletter of the Institute for Creation Research, and thus are not conveniently available otherwise. Hence, with certain modifications, they are reprinted for ease of reference in this Appendix.

Creation and the Seven-Day Week

An often-overlooked testimony to the fact of creation is the phenomenon of the seven-day week. Almost universally observed in both the present world and the ancient world, it is so deeply rooted in human experience and so natural physiologically that we seldom think about its intrinsic significance. The structure of man's daily existence—the time framework in which he conducts his activities—continually bears witness that the Word of God is sure and can be ignored only at the peril of losing all meaning to life.

The Unique Week

All the other important time markers in human life are clearly based on astronomical and terrestrial constants. The day, for example, is the duration of one rotation of the earth on its axis; the year is the duration of one orbital revolution of the earth about the sun; the month is the approximate interval between new moons as the moon orbits the earth; the seasons are marked by the equinoxes and solstices.

But the week has no astronomical basis whatever! Yet we order our lives in a seven-day cycle, doing certain things on Monday, certain other things on Tuesday, and so on through the week. Furthermore, the common pattern is one of six normal working days, then a day of rest or change, then six normal days again, and so on, with the special day regarded as either the last of the seven preceding it, or the first of the seven following it.

How could such a system ever have originated? Most encyclopedias and reference books treat the subject very superficially, if at all. Most of the discussions that do try to deal with it attribute the origin of the week to the use of "market days," pointing out also that the interval between market days was different in different nations, though rarely varying more than a day or so above or below seven days. With the exception of an occasional biblical scholar, almost none of these writers even consider the obvious explanation—namely, that the seven-day week was established by God himself, at the beginning!

Every effect must have an adequate cause, and the only cause which is truly able to account for such a remarkable phenomenon as the week is that it was established at creation and has been deeply etched in our common human consciousness ever since. Even if the week is noted in some cultures in terms of regular market days, this still does not explain how the market days happened to cluster around every "seventh" day, instead of every fifteenth day or nineteenth day or something else. Besides, there were various ancient nations whose weeks were quite unrelated to any marketing customs.

A related phenomenon, equally remarkable, is the almost universal significance attached to the number "seven" as a number speaking of completeness, usually with special religious overtones. This number is not "natural" in any physical way. It would be more natural to use the number "ten" (the number of a man's fingers), or the number "twelve" (the number of months in the year), or perhaps the number "365," to represent fulness. Why "seven"? Yet "seven" is everywhere the number of completeness.

The Origin of Sabbath Observance

Many people believe that the custom of a weekly day of rest began with Moses, when he incorporated Sabbath observance into the Ten Commandments. Such an explanation is superficial. Not only is there considerable evidence that Sabbath observance existed in both Israel and in other nations long before Moses, but the Word of God makes it plain that it was established by God himself, in commemoration of his completed creation, and that it has been observed as a special day, at least by some, ever since. Here is the record: "Thus the heavens and the earth were finished, and all the host of them. And on the seventh day God ended his work which he had made; and he rested on the seventh day from all his work which he had made. And God blessed the seventh day, and sanctified it: because that in it he had rested from all his work which God created and made" (Gen. 2:1–3).

God "rested" after finishing his work of creating and making all things in the universe in the six days just completed. His rest was not because of fatigue (note Isa. 40:28), but was simply a cessation of his creative activity.

And then God *blessed and sanctified* the seventh day! He declared it to be a holy day, a day peculiarly the Lord's Day. The six days had been occupied with his creation; *one* day should be occupied with the Creator. He frequently referred later to the day as "my Sabbath" (e.g., Exod. 31:13).

From Adam to Moses

It is clearly implied in the story of Cain and Abel that the children of Adam continued to regard every seventh day as a day of rest and worship, even after the expulsion from Eden. "And in process of time it came to pass, that Cain brought of the fruit of the ground an offering unto the LORD. And Abel, he also brought of the firstlings of his flock and of the fat thereof" (Gen. 4:3, 4).

On this particular day, Cain was not tilling the ground, as he normally did, nor was Abel tending his sheep. On this day, they met with the Lord and brought him an offering.

And what day was that? The phrase "in process of time" is, literally, "at the end of the days" ("process" = Hebrew *gets* = "end"; "time" =

Hebrew *yamin* = "days"). The day on which they brought their offerings was the day "at the end of the days," and this clearly can be nothing but the seventh day, the day which God had blessed and hallowed.

The story of Noah contains many allusions to the seven-day week. Note the following in chapters 7 and 8 of Genesis:

1. "For yet seven days, and I will cause it to rain upon the earth" (7:4).
2. "And it came to pass after seven days, that the waters of the flood were upon the earth" (7:10).
3. Forty weeks later (280 days—compare 7:11; 8:3–6) Noah sent forth the dove and the raven (8:7, 8).
4. "And he stayed yet other seven days; and again he sent forth the dove" (8:10).
5. "And he stayed yet other seven days; and sent forth the dove" (8:12).
6. Noah and his family left the ark exactly 371 days, or 53 weeks, after they had entered it (compare verses 7:11; 8:3, 4; 8:14).

Whether these repeated references to actions taken every seven days imply that they all took place on God's rest day is not stated, although it does seem probable. In any case, it is clear that both God and Noah were ordering events in terms of a seven-day cycle.

During the centuries from Noah to Moses, there was little occasion to refer to the week as such. However, there seem to be at least two allusions to it—in the story of Jacob and Leah ("fulfil her week," Gen. 29:27, 28) and in the story of Jacob's burial (Gen. 50:10).

Whatever form of Sabbath observance might have been practiced by the early patriarchs, it is probable that the long servitude in Egypt caused many to forget its religious significance, even though the weekly cycle was followed. When the time came for God to redeem his people, however, he began to remind them of its importance. In preparation for the great Passover deliverance, he commanded: "Seven days shall ye eat unleavened bread. . . . And in the first day there shall be an holy convocation, and in the seventh day there shall be an holy convocation to you; no manner of work shall be done in them, save that which every man must eat, that only may be done of you" (Exod. 12:15, 16). In this preparation for the incorporation of the Sabbath into the Ten Commandments, it is interesting to note that both the *first day* and the *seventh day* were days of rest and worship!

The Ten Commandments

Soon after this, the Israelites were strongly reminded that a seventh day each week was intended to be a day of rest, as God illustrated with the manna (Exod. 16:4, 5, 25–30), which fell for six days each week and was withheld by God on the seventh. They were instructed to collect only what they needed for each day. Anything that was left over spoiled before the next day—but not the extra that they kept over from the day before the Sabbath, when God would send no manna. Finally, Sabbath observance was incorporated as the fourth in the array of Ten Commandments recorded for Israel by the very finger of God on tables of stone (Exod. 31:18). "Remember the sabbath day, to keep it holy. Six days shalt thou labour, and do all thy work: but the seventh day is the sabbath of the LORD thy God: in it thou shalt not do any work . . . (Exod. 20:8–10).

It should be stressed again that the Sabbath observance was by no means established here for the first time. The Israelites, however, were now commanded to *remember* the Sabbath and to *keep it holy,* as it should have been since God so pronounced it following the creation. The Lord's holy day may have been neglected by God's chosen people, or even forgotten altogether by most other nations, but it was still God's primeval commandment. At this time, God stressed again that the basis for the commandment was not regional but universal, relating to the entire creation. "For in six days the LORD made heaven and earth, the sea, and all that in them is, and rested the seventh day: wherefore the LORD blessed the sabbath day, and hallowed it" (Exod. 20:11). A commandment intended for *all* people should certainly be obeyed by the *chosen* people!

Christ, the Lord of the Sabbath

With the passing of the centuries, the Sabbath eventually became almost exclusively associated with the religious ceremonies of the nation of Israel, even though the Creator had hallowed it originally for all men. When that Creator eventually became man, however, in the person of Jesus Christ, he stressed that it had never been intended as a mere Jewish religious ritual, as the Pharisees had distorted it, but for the good of all men. "The sabbath was made for man, and not man for the sabbath" (Mark 2:27). All men needed to have a day of rest (for their own *physical* good) and worship, and to regularly remind themselves of the great truth of creation (for their *spiritual* good). And they needed to remember continually that the one who came to redeem them was also the one who had created them. "The Son of man is Lord even of the sabbath day," he said (Matt. 12:8).

It was appropriate, therefore, that after Christ's death and resurrection, Christians from every nation soon began once again to observe one day in every seven as a day of rest, as they heard and believed the gospel of Christ. Now, however, there were two great works of God to commemorate, the completion of creation and the completion of redemption. As Christ had long ago finished the work of creation (Col. 1:16), so he could now report once again to the Father: "I have finished the work which thou gavest me to do" (John 17:4). This work was climaxed with the great victory cry from the cross: "It is finished" (John 19:30).

For a time, Jewish Christians continued to participate both in the synagogue services on the seventh day each week (e.g., Acts 17:2) and also in Christian services on the first day of the week (Acts 20:7). Eventually, as they were more and more excluded from the synagogue, they observed only the Lord's day, on the first day of the week (1 Cor. 16:2), thereby honoring Christ simultaneously as both Creator and resurrected Savior.

The Lord's Day

There was discussion for a long time (continuing in some degree even today) as to whether Christian churches, once they were completely separated from the Jewish assemblies, should observe the Lord's day on the seventh day of the week, as the Jews did, or on the first day of the week, as the day of Christ's resurrection. Without entering into this particular discussion, we note here the important point that Christians never even questioned the necessity for a weekly "rest day" on which especially to honor the Lord. That need was taken for granted, regardless of whether the "Sabbath" was to be observed on Saturday or Sunday. ("Sabbath" in Hebrew means neither Saturday nor Sunday, neither seventh day nor first day, but *rest* day!) In view of the chaotic state of ancient chronology, there is obviously no way of knowing which day of the modern week is an exact multiple of seven days since God's first rest day. The Muslims, in fact, observe it on our Friday.

Those Christians who worship on Saturday believe that the Sabbath cycle has been kept intact ever since the creation and so they follow the practice of today's orthodox Jews, who make the same assumption. Other Christians, however, point out that the present Jewish calendar was not established until the fourth century A.D., so there is neither historical nor scientific basis for insisting that our present Saturday was the primeval Sabbath. Some Christian writers have argued that our modern Sunday was the ancient Sabbath, and others have maintained that the day of the week on which the Sabbath fell actually changed from year to year, being affected by Sabbaths other than the weekly Sabbath, including one which extended for two days each year. The "long day" of Joshua (Josh. 10:12–14) also must have affected the weekly cycle in some as yet uncertain fashion. In any case, the important consideration is the *fact* of a weekly "Lord's day," rather than the particular day of the modern weekly cycle on which it is observed.

It is significant that the Ten Commandments, representing God's ineffable and unchanging holiness as they do, even though specifically written down in the Mosaic law for Israel's sake, are also written in the consciences of all men (Rom. 2:14, 15). Consequently, these commandments were accepted and applied in the New Testament, as well (e.g., Rom. 13:9; Eph. 6:2; etc.).

This affirmation is clearly implied for the Sabbath commandment in particular. "he spake in a certain place of the seventh day on this wise, And God did rest the seventh day from all his works. . . . There remaineth therefore a rest to the people of God" (Heb. 4:4, 9). In this passage in Hebrews (vv. 1–11), the English word "rest" occurs nine times. All except one of these are translations of essentially the same Greek word *(katapausis)*, implying rest from labor. The exception is verse 9: "There is yet reserved therefore a Sabbath rest (Greek *sabbatismos,* derived from *sabbaton,* "Sabbath") to the people of God." This is the only occurrence of this particular word in the New Testament.

In context, the writer is showing that the ultimate "rest" for God's people, which was typically portrayed by God's rest after creation and which was therefore typified by every weekly Sabbath observance, was not attained in Canaan under either Joshua or David, and was still reserved for the future even after Christ had returned to heaven and the Christian era had begun. Since the *antitype* is yet future, therefore, the *type* must still be in operation, just as the animal sacrifices in the temple did not cease until Christ "had offered one sacrifice for sins for ever" (Heb. 10:12). This fact, combined with the evident fact that all the early Christians continued to observe a weekly "Lord's day," and that nowhere in the New Testament is it stated that Sabbath observances should cease, makes it clear that this commandment, like all the Ten Commandments, applies in the Christian dispensation, as well as in the Mosaic dispensation, though not with the same applications and penalties that related specifically to the Mosaic ordinances. As a matter of fact, God's people will continue to observe a weekly Sabbath even in the coming kingdom age (note Isa. 66:23, Ezek. 46:3).

All of this is the tremendous testimony of the seven-day week and, especially, of the day of rest which marks its boundaries. *Its very existence can only be explained by the reality of a primeval six-day completed creation!* God desires that we never forget that he is both our Creator and Redeemer, and also that we continually look forward to the eventual fulfillment of all his creative and redemptive purposes, when they are finally consummated in that eternal Rest for all the people of God in the ages to come.

Creation and the Birth of Christ

The Mystery of the Incarnation

The incarnation of Jesus Christ, in which the transcendent Creator actually entered his own creation, and God became man, is such an important doctrine of the New Testament that without it there can be no true Christianity. "Every spirit that confesseth that Jesus Christ is come in the flesh is of God: and every spirit that confesseth not that Jesus Christ is come in the flesh is not of God" (1 John 4:2, 3).

But how could the one who "was God" (John 1:1) from the beginning be the same one who "was made flesh, and dwelt among us" (John 1:14)? How could he truly be "Emmanuel, which being interpreted is, God with us" (Matt. 1:23)? How could the infinite, eternal God become finite and temporal?

Perhaps the most amazing aspect of the incarnation is that a God who is absolute holiness could reside in a body of human flesh. Is it not true that "they that are in the flesh cannot please God" (Rom. 8:8)? Our human bodies have been formed through many generations of genetic inheritance from Adam himself, and "in Adam all die" (1 Cor. 15:22).

The paradox is partially resolved, of course, when it is realized that Jesus Christ came in a body which was not of sinful flesh. His body was truly "in the flesh," but only in "the likeness of sinful flesh" (Rom. 8:3).

But even this doesn't resolve the dilemma completely, for how could his body be of flesh (carbon, hydrogen, amino acids, proteins, etc.), received by the normal process of reproduction of the flesh of his parents, without also receiving their genetic inheritance, which is exactly what makes it *sinful* flesh? "Behold, I was shapen in iniquity; and in sin did my mother conceive me" (Ps. 51:5). "Man that is born of a woman is of few days, and full of trouble . . . . Who can bring a clean thing out of an unclean? not one" (Job 14:1, 4).

The Problem of Inherited Physical Defects

Not only is there the problem of inherent sin, but also that of inherent physical defects. Over many generations, the human population has experienced great numbers of genetic mutations, and these defective physical factors have been incorporated into the common genetic pool, affecting in some degree every infant (except Jesus) ever born. Yet the Lamb of God, to be an acceptable sacrifice for the sins of the world, must be "without blemish and without spot" (1 Pet. 1:19). The very purpose of the incarnation was that God could become the *Savior* of men as well as their *Creator,* but this required that in his humanity he must be "holy, harmless, undefiled, separate from sinners" (Heb. 7:26), and this would have been absolutely impossible by the normal reproductive process.

The solution could only have been through a mighty miracle! He could not have been conceived in the same manner as other men, for this would inevitably have given him both a sin-nature and a physically defective body, and each would have disqualified him as a fit Redeemer. And yet he had to become truly human. "Wherefore in all things it behoved him to be made like unto his brethren, that he might be a merciful and faithful high priest in things pertaining to God, to make reconciliation for the sins of the people" (Heb. 2:17).

It is not surprising, therefore, that the Christian doctrine of the virgin birth of Christ has always been such a watershed between true Christians and either non-Christians or pseudo-Christians. Without such a miraculous birth, there could have been no true incarnation and therefore no salvation. The man Jesus would have been a sinner by birth and thus in need of a Savior himself.

On second thought, however, one realizes that it was not the virgin birth which was significant, except as a testimony of the necessity of the real miracle, the supernatural conception. The birth of Christ was natural and normal in every way, including the full period of human gestation in the womb of Mary. In all points, he was made like his brethren, experiencing every aspect of human life from conception through birth and growth to death. He was true man in every detail, except for sin and its physical effects.

The miracle was not his birth but his conception. And here we still face a mystery. Conception normally is the result of the union of two germ cells, the egg from the mother and the seed from the father, each carrying half the inheritance and thus each, of course, sharing equally in the transmission of the sin-nature, as well as all other aspects of the human nature. Each parent thus also makes an equal contribution of defective physical and mental characteristics, due to inherited mutations. Both mental and physical traits are inherited in this way.

Some writers have tried to make the virgin birth appear more amenable to human reason by comparing it to parthenogenesis, by which process the female egg begins to divide and grow into a mature animal without ever being fertilized. This has been known to occur in some insects and even in some mammals. Others have compared the virgin birth to the process of artificial insemination, by which the sperm is artificially introduced into the egg without actual copulation.

In addition to the rather crude concept of the work of the Holy Spirit which such suggestions involve, neither solves the problem of how the inherent defects contained in the *mother's* germ cell could have been kept from the developing embryo. If genetic inheritance in any degree is received from either parent, there seems to be no *natural* way by which the transmission of the sin-nature, as well as physical defects, could have been prevented.

The Necessity of Special Creation

Therefore, even though Jesus was nurtured in Mary's womb for nine months and born without her ever knowing a man, it was also necessary for all this to have been preceded by supernatural intervention, to prevent his receiving any actual genetic inheritance through her. The body growing in Mary's womb must have been specially created in full perfection, and placed there by the Holy Spirit, in order for it to have been free of inherent sin damage. Christ would still have been "made of the seed of David according to the flesh" (Rom. 1:3), because his body was nurtured and born of Mary, who was herself of the seed of David. He would still have been the Son of man, sharing all universal human experience from conception to death, except sin. He would have been truly the seed of the woman (Gen. 3:15), his body having been formed neither of the seed of the man nor the egg of the woman, but having grown from a unique Seed planted in the woman's body by God himself.

That is, God directly formed a body for the second Adam just as he had for the first Adam (Gen. 2:7). This was nothing less than a miracle of creation, capable of accomplishment only by the Creator himself. "That holy thing which shall be born of thee shall be called the Son of God" (Luke 1:35).

Surely God would have devoted no more attention to the design and construction of the body of "the first man [, who] is of the earth, earthy" than he would have to that of "the second man [,who] is the Lord from heaven" (1 Cor. 15:47)!

The Marvel of Inheritance and Prenatal Growth

For that matter, the formation of every human body is a marvelous testimony to the power and wisdom of the Creator of the first human body, and so is his provision for its reproductive multiplication into the billions of bodies of distinctive individuals who have lived through the ages. "I will praise thee; for I am fearfully and wonderfully made" (Ps. 139:14).

The 139th psalm contains a remarkably beautiful and scientifically accurate description of the divine forethought in the processes of heredity and embryonic growth. Verses 15 and 16 of this psalm (with explanatory comments interspersed) are as follows:

> My substance [literally, my frame] was not hid from thee, when I was made in secret, and curiously wrought [literally, embroidered—probably a foregleam of the intricate double-helical structure of the DNA molecule as it carries out its function of template reproduction of the pattern provided by the parents] in the lowest [or, least seen] parts of the earth [God originally made the dust of the earth—the basic elements— then man's body from those elements, and then the marvelous ability to multiply that body]. Thine eyes did see *my substance, yet being unperfect* [all one word, meaning "embryo," in the original; note the embryo is not *imperfect*, but *unperfect*, still in the process of being completed]; and in thy book all my members were written, which in continuance [literally, which days—that is, all the days of development and growth were planned from the beginning] were fashioned [same word as "formed,"

used in Gen. 2:7 for the formation of Adam's body] when as yet there was none of them [the whole amazing process was written into the genetic code even before actual conception].

The Body of Christ

With such careful divine care and attention given to the development of every one of the billions of human bodies conceived since the days of Adam and Eve, how much greater must have been the extent of the divine preparation of the body of God's own Son? As a matter of fact, the design for his body was prepared before the very foundation of the world itself (1 Pet. 1:20; Heb. 10:5). It is probable that, in some degree at least, God had this very body in mind when he undertook to make Adam "in our image, after our likeness" (Gen. 1:26). That is, God formed for Adam a body patterned after that perfect body which had already been planned for the divine incarnation, when the time would come.

Then, "when the fulness of the time was come, God sent forth his Son, made of a woman . . . that we might receive the adoption of sons" (Gal. 4:4, 5).

"Wherefore when he cometh into the world, he saith, Sacrifice and offering thou wouldest not, but a body hast thou prepared me" (Heb. 10:5). The verb "prepared" in this verse is striking. It is the same word in the Greek (i.e., *katartizo*) as is used in the next chapter in Hebrews, in one of the greatest of all those verses in the Bible describing the creation. "Through faith we understand that the worlds were framed by the word of God, so that things which are seen were not made of things which do appear" (Heb. 11:3).

The "preparation" of Christ's body by God was the same process as the "framing" of the worlds by God. As the latter were created *ex nihilo* ("not made of things which do appear"), so must have been the former. The word is also translated "make perfect" (Heb. 13:21, etc.).

To the possible question as to whether such a specially created human body could be a truly *human* body, the conclusive answer is that the *first* Adam had a specially created human body, and he was true man—in fact, the very prototype man. It is entirely gratuitous to say that God could not create a second human body which would be truly human in every respect (except for the inherent defects associated with the sin-nature). Furthermore, nothing less than a true miracle of creation could really accomplish the formation of a true human body which would not be contaminated with sin and its marks.

Thus, the body of Christ was prepared by the great Creator, with no dependence on prior materials, and was made in total perfection, ready to receive him as its occupant. In that perfect body, which would one day be "made . . . to be sin" and would bear "our sins . . . on the tree (2 Cor. 5:21; 1 Pet. 2:24), he would dwell forever after its resurrection and glorification (Rev. 1:13–18).

When God created the world, it was only a little thing (Isa. 40:15–17), but the formation of any human body required the special planning of divine omniscience, eliciting the inspired testimony, "How precious also are thy thoughts unto me, O God? how great is the sum of them!" (Ps. 139:17).

The greatest of all creations, however, was that of the body in which his Son would take up his eternal abode. Miraculously created and conceived, then virgin-born, God's eternal Son became the perfect Son of man.

There is yet another "body of Christ," of which all believers become members, now in process of formation, with Christ the head (Eph. 4:15, 16). This body also is being supernaturally formed by the Holy Spirit (1 Cor. 12:13), with no genetic inheritance from sinful flesh. Its members are "born, not of blood, nor of the will of the flesh, nor of the will of man, but of God" (John 1:13), so that when complete it also will be a body "not having spot, or wrinkle,or any such thing; but . . . [will] be holy and without blemish" (Eph. 5:27).

Here is another mighty act of special creation, repeated again and again whenever a new member is added to Christ's body, when a new son of God is born. "As many as received him, to them gave he power to become the sons of God, even to them that believe on his name" (John 1:12). "If any man be in Christ, he is a new *creature*" (2 Cor. 5:17). These new members have "put on the new man, which after God is *created* in righteousness and true holiness" (Eph. 4:24). "Ye have put off the old man with his deeds; and have put on the new man, which is renewed in knowledge after the image of him that *created* him" (Col. 3:9, 10). "We are his workmanship, *created* in Christ Jesus unto good works" (Eph. 2:10).

The virgin birth of Jesus Christ thus testifies of the marvelous creation of his human body, which then speaks symbolically of the marvelous member-by-member creation of his spiritual body.

The Miracle of God in Man

Some, however, may still believe that such a miracle of creation would somehow dilute the doctrine of the true humanity of the Lord Jesus. They may feel that Jesus would have to have possessed Mary's genes in order to be really human. If his body had been specially created, then how could he really have been "touched with the feeling of our infirmities" and "in all points tempted like as we are" (Heb. 4:15)?

Such doubts, however, are merely due to our limited confidence in God's ability to *create*. To say that God could not have created a truly human body for the Lord Jesus is to deny his omnipotence. Was the body which he created for Adam not a human body? Adam had no genetic inheritance from either mother or father, but he was surely a man. Why could this not have been as true of the second Adam as of the first Adam?

That God did indeed in some miraculous way form such a human body (perfectly human, in fact) is evident from the Scriptures. "In all things it behoved him to be *made like* unto his brethren . . ." (Heb. 2:17). He "was *made* in the likeness of men" (Phil. 2:7). "The Word was *made* flesh" (John 1:14).

Note, however, that this flesh was not *sinful* flesh. Rather, it was "in the *likeness* of sinful flesh" (Rom. 8:3). In every other way, it was real human flesh. Prior to the entrance of sin into the world and prior to the curse on the ground, Adam's divinely formed body needed food and rest, and this was true of the divinely formed body of the second Adam as well. Furthermore, since all of the very elements of the earth later came under the curse (Gen. 3:17; Rom. 8:22), that curse must have affected those atoms and molecules which were gradually added to Jesus' body as it grew from the embryonic state into maturity, as well as the food he ate and air he breathed. He was, indeed, "touched with the feeling of our infirmities."

It is certain, however, that these infirmities did not include sin— either acts of sin or a sin-nature. He "did no sin," he "knew no sin," and "in him is no sin" (1 Pet. 2:22; 2 Cor. 5:21; 1 John 3:5). Neither can we allow even the bare possibility that he *could* have sinned. Though he was true man, he also was very God, and he did not in any wise relinquish his deity when he became man. He was not part man and part God, or sometimes man and sometimes God. Once He became incarnate in human flesh, he became eternally the God-man—all man and all God! Since "God cannot be tempted with evil" (James 1:13), the temptation of Christ (though a real *testing*, in the sense that his impeccability had to be demonstrated to all creation as genuine) could not possibly have resulted in sin on his part. For if he *could* have sinned, then God *might* indeed have been defeated by Satan. But this is unthinkable to one who truly believes in God as the omnipotent Creator of all things.

It was absolutely essential, therefore, that his human body be free of an inherited sin-nature, and even from mental or physical defects resulting from inherited mutations. Biologically and genetically, there is no way this could have been assured except by a miraculous conception, accomplished in such a way that none of the sinful and defective attributes of *either* parent could be transmitted to him.

The question is, how could this have been done? All who believe in the virgin birth recognize that a miracle was required—but what kind of miracle? Could it have been merely a providential statistical juggling of Mary's genes so that those which carried the "sin-factor," as well as specific physical and mental defective mutations were somehow screened out? Hardly, because *all* of Mary's genes (no less than those of Joseph) would have been carriers of sin. There is neither biological nor theological basis for thinking that sin affects only certain genes and chromosomes and not others.

No, a miracle was absolutely required, a miracle of creation. Some suggest that this miracle was performed on Mary herself, so that all her genes were made immaculate. Others suggest that the miracle was performed only on the genes in the particular egg cell which the Holy Spirit "artificially inseminated" with an immaculate sperm cell of his own creating. Still others think that Mary's egg cell was somehow purified by the Holy Spirit of all inherent sin and defects and then caused to grow by a process of parthenogenesis.

Actually, any or all of these amount to the same thing as direct creation. Either the body formed in Mary's womb must have been specially created or else all of the genes in Mary's egg must have been specially re-created; one or the other. In either case, there could have been no direct transmission of physical, mental, or spiritual characteristics (all of which, in every man and woman, are contaminated by sin) from Joseph or Mary or David or Adam. To say otherwise is to imply that the Lord Jesus Christ received a sin-nature by inheritance, and this would disqualify him as Savior.

But this wonderful miracle of creation in no way detracts from his full humanity. He experienced the same complete human life experienced by every other person, from the moment of conception to the moment of death—*except for sin!* Furthermore, he still occupies his human body, now resurrected and glorified. He is "holy, harmless, undefiled, separate from sinners, and made higher than the heavens." "Wherefore he is able also to save them to the uttermost that come unto God by him" (Heb. 7:26, 25).

Creation and the Gospel

Before his return to heaven, after his resurrection, the Lord Jesus Christ gave the Great Commission to all his disciples: "Go ye into all the world, and preach the gospel to every creature" (Mark 16:15).

In order to obey this most important commandment, believers must understand exactly what the gospel is. The word itself (Greek *euaggelion*), as applied to the true gospel, occurs 74 times in the New Testament, and a related word *(euaggelizo)* is translated "preach the gospel" 22 times and "bring glad (or good) tidings" 5 times. The word means "the good news" and in all 101 of the above occurrences is applied to the good news concerning the Lord Jesus Christ.

It seems very significant that, of these 101 references to the gospel of Christ the *central* reference is 1 Corinthians 15:1. First (1 Cor. 15:1–4) is, above all others, the *definition* passage for the gospel. It is here defined as the good news "that Christ died for our sins according to the scriptures; and that he was buried, and that he rose again the third day according to the scriptures." Thus, the central focus of the true gospel is the substitutionary death, physical burial, and bodily resurrection of Jesus Christ.

Note also four vital facts concerning this gospel: (1) it is something to be "received" and "believed" by faith, once for all; (2) it is the means by which we are "saved," continually and forever; (3) it is the fact upon which we firmly "stand"; (4) it is emphatically to be defined, understood, and preached "according to the scriptures."

Although this is the central and key verse for the gospel, all other 100 occurrences are likewise important, if it is truly to be preached "according to the scriptures." It is especially important to study its first and last occurrences.

The first occurrence is in Matthew 4:23, which speaks of Jesus himself "preaching the gospel of the kingdom." Thus it is vital that those who believe and preach the gospel stress its final consummation, when Jesus Christ will finally be acknowledged by every creature to be "KING OF KINGS, AND LORD OF LORDS" (Rev. 19:16).

The last occurrence of the word is in Revelation 14:6, which says the gospel is "the everlasting gospel" that must be preached to all nations. Furthermore, its greatest emphasis must be to "worship him that made heaven, and earth, and the sea, and the fountains of waters" (Rev. 14:7). Thus, the first occurrence of "gospel" looks ahead to the consummation of all things, and the last occurrence stresses the initial creation of all things. As the consummation approaches, it is increasingly important that men look back to the creation. But the creation was saved and the consummation assured when the great Creator and Consummator paid the infinite price for the world's redemption, when he died on the cross and rose again.

The gospel thus entails the full scope of the work of Jesus Christ, from creation to consummation, involving the whole sweep of his redemptive purpose in history. Only this is the gospel "according to the scriptures." One does not truly preach the gospel without emphasizing both the initial special creation of all things by the omnipotent Word of God and also the final consummation of God's purpose in creation itself, as well as the central core of the gospel, the atoning death and triumphant victory over death achieved by the incarnate Creator and Redeemer.

The same threefold work of Christ is expounded in Colossians 1:16–20. "By him were all things created." Then, "by him all things consist [or, are saved]." Finally, by him all things are reconciled. Similarly, in Hebrews 1:2, he "made the worlds," is "upholding all things," and ultimately becomes "heir of all things." "For of him, and through him, and to him, are all things: to whom be glory for ever. Amen" (Rom. 11:36).

The gospel of the Lord Jesus Christ therefore encompasses the threefold work of Christ—creation, conservation, consummation—past, present, and future. One preaches a gospel with no foundation if he neglects or distorts the creation, a gospel with no power if he omits the cross and the empty tomb, and a gospel with no hope if he ignores or denies the coming kingdom. He preaches the gospel "according to the scriptures" only if all three are preached in fullness.

In light of these facts, how sadly mistaken are the great numbers of "evangelicals" (a word meaning "those who preach the gospel") who oppose or neglect the doctrine of creation. They tell us not to "waste time on peripheral controversies such as the evolution-creation question—just to preach the gospel," not realizing that the gospel includes creation and *precludes* evolution! They say we should simply "emphasize saving faith, not faith in creation," forgetting that the greatest chapter on faith in the Bible (Heb. 11) begins by stressing faith in the *ex nihilo* creation of all things by God's Word (v. 3) as preliminary to meaningful faith in any of his promises (verse 13). They advise us merely to "preach Christ," but ignore the fact that Christ was the Creator before he became the Savior, and that his finished work of salvation is meaningful only in light of his finished work of creation (Heb. 4:3–10). They may wish, in order to avoid the offense of the true gospel, to regard creation as an unimportant matter, but God considered it so important that it was the subject of his first revelation. The first chapter of Genesis is the foundation of the Bible; if the foundation is undermined, the superstructure soon collapses.

Furthermore, in light of Revelation 14:6, 7, it becomes more important to emphasize creation with every day that passes. Satanic opposition intensifies as the end approaches. The anti-gospel of Antichrist can be effectively corrected only by the true gospel of the true Christ.

Creation and the Churches

The Command to Preach Creationism

In view of all the foregoing considerations, surely true Christian pastors and teachers in churches everywhere should preach and teach frequently the doctrine of creation—not merely by incidental references in messages on other topics, but systematically and fully expounding this great truth, as revealed both in Scripture and in God's world. There are many reasons for emphasizing creation, but there are three especially urgent commands of Scripture to this effect.

1.Guard the Faith!

These are days in which many in Christendom, even professing Christians, are departing from the Christian faith, which was "once delivered unto the saints" (Jude 3). Some have departed in the direction of cultism and occultism (1 Tim. 4:1), others in the direction of liberalism, humanism, and general ungodliness (2 Tim. 3:1–7). These trends will eventually become so widespread that the Lord Jesus asked the rhetorical question, "When the Son of Man cometh, shall he find [the] faith on the earth?" (Luke 18:8).

Now if one studies carefully the history of such apostasies, in all ages, he will find they always begin with the undermining of this doctrine of special creation. There is always an evolutionary cosmogony of some sort opposing the true Genesis record of the Creator and his creation, attractively presented by the currently dominant philosophies in the name of "science." This was as true with the ancient pagan philosophies as with the modern Darwinian philosophies. The Genesis record is the *only* cosmogony which begins with the transcendent God creating the very universe itself. This recurring tension between revelation and philosophy is inevitably followed by those in the Christian world who seek to compromise. Compromise on special creation, however, is soon followed by compromise on special incarnation, and so on; *eventually this road of compromise ends in a precipice!*

It is urgent, therefore, that each generation of pastors and teachers carefully transmit the full Christian faith to the next generation (2 Tim. 2:2), especially its foundational doctrine of creation. The apostle Paul commanded, "Keep [literally guard] that which is committed to thy trust, avoiding profane and vain babblings [that is, ungodly and empty philosophies] and oppositions of science falsely so called" (1 Tim. 6:20). The command to *avoid* such things does not mean to hide from them, but rather to keep the Christian faith utterly free from their contaminating influence! This can best be done by an informed and regular emphasis on biblical creationism from both pulpit and classroom.

2. Give the Answer!

In our day and age, when practically everyone has been indoctrinated in evolutionary philosophy most of his life, the Christian worker quickly finds that some application or other of this philosophy is the greatest obstacle to winning educated people to an intelligent and lasting conversion to biblical Christianity. Most people realize that, if the first chapter of the Bible is unreliable or vague, there is no reason to take the rest of the Bible very seriously.

The command of the apostle Peter is clear. "Be ready always to give an answer [literally, an apologetic—a systematic, logical, scientific defense] to every man that asketh you a reason of the hope that is in you" (1 Pet. 3:15). Whatever problem an unbeliever may have with respect to the Christian faith, there is an answer! The Christian has not been asked to follow cunningly devised fables. He must be saved by faith, of course, but that faith is a *reasonable* faith, founded on facts. It is not a credulous faith, like that of the evolutionist.

The Christian witness will *not* be ready always to give the answer, of course, unless he *knows* the answer. And he won't know it unless someone teaches it to him. This is the scriptural function of the pastor and teacher (Eph. 4:11–14).

3. Preach the Gospel!

This command is the Great Commission, given by Christ to the church and to every believer. The commission incorporates also the obligation to teach *all* things (Matt. 28:20) that Christ had taught (which obviously includes special creation), but it is even more important to realize that the gospel itself must include the doctrine of creation.

The word "gospel" means "good news," and it refers specifically in the New Testament to the glad tidings of all that Jesus Christ has done for mankind. This necessarily includes the entire scope of his work—past, present, and future, from the creation of all things (Col. 1:16) to the reconciliation of all things (Col. 1:20).

It is significant that the final reference to the gospel in the Bible is found in Revelation 14:6, 7, in a context just prior to his glorious second coming. There it is called the "everlasting gospel" (thus stressing that it will be the same then as it is now), and the essential injunction is that men should "worship him that made heaven, and earth, and the sea, and the fountains of waters." The everlasting gospel thus always stresses recognition of God as Creator, as well as Savior. (The reference to "the fountains of waters" is probably a reference even to his sovereign judgment on sin during the great flood—note Gen. 7:10, 11.)

The command to "preach the gospel to every creature" (Mark 16:15) therefore includes not only the substitutionary atonement and bodily resurrection of Christ (1 Cor. 15:1–4), but also—as a necessary foundational preparation (especially in the last days when there will be widespread denial of creation)—the great truth that God in Christ is the supernatural and omnipotent Creator of all things—not by some imaginary process of evolution, but by the power of his Word!

Ecumenical Creationism

One of the most significant aspects of the study of creation is that men from every type of denominational background recognize its vital importance and are concerned about its relevance to their own denominational doctrines. For example, the writer has been invited at one time or another to speak on this subject in the churches and schools of over sixty-five different religious denominations.

There are multitudes of people and churches in practically every denomination that have been harmfully affected by evolution. At the same time, there are some in each denomination who are vitally concerned about the problem and are doing what they can to restore or to retain special creation as a basic doctrine in their system. Furthermore, although there are still large numbers in each group who are indifferent, it is encouraging that more and more people are getting involved all the time.

This common concern about creationism is drawing together from all these backgrounds people who have heretofore been kept apart by other theological differences. Special creationists, of course, no matter what their denomination, generally share certain other basic beliefs, such as belief in the God of the Bible and belief in the divine inspiration and authority of the Bible. Evolutionists in all denominations, on the other hand, also tend to share certain beliefs among themselves, including a rather loose concept of biblical inspiration and even of the nature of God.

Lest anyone misunderstand, creationists are not advocating ecumenicalism or church union as the concept is usually promoted today. The church union movement is unrealistic when it proposes that Christians of strong Bible-based convictions give them up for the sake of a superficial unity. Each church is to teach "the whole counsel of God" to its members, as it understands that counsel, and it must not reject that responsibility.

However, although there is no doctrine that is *not* important, surely there are some that are *more* important, and special creation is the most basic of all, except the doctrine of God himself. It is amazing that so many churches, schools, and other institutions have very detailed and explicit "statements of faith," comprising what they believe to be their fundamental doctrines, but almost none of these include a specific statement regarding the special creation of all things in the beginning. This tragic oversight has directly resulted in the defection of great numbers of such institutions to the evolutionary world-view, and then inevitably later to liberalism and finally to humanism.

Church unification on any basis short of spiritual unity on *all* the essential doctrines and practices taught in the Bible is probably impossible to attain before the Lord returns. In the meantime, however, it is quite practical to enjoy a genuine fellowship among believers in such truly *basic* doctrines as the existence of an omnipotent, personal God, special creation of all things by God, the reality of Satanic and human rebellion against God, the necessity of salvation provided through God, the future consummation of all things in God, and authoritative biblical revelation from God. In each case, of course, Christians understand by "God" the personal, omnipotent God of the Bible, manifest fully in Jesus Christ (Col. 2:9).

At the practical level, all such believers can work effectively together in public movements and institutions to revive recognition of God as Creator, the doctrine which is the foundation of all other truth. All believers ultimately are in a warfare not *against* each other, but *with* each other, against Satan and his purposes (Eph. 6:12). The creation-evolution issue is at the very center of this warfare. Is God really the sovereign Creator of this universe, or is he somehow limited by eternal matter or by other beings in the universe? Is his Word true and clear or is it tentative and vague, subject to man's shifting opinions? These are the ultimate issues, and genuine believers ought to be united on them.

Unfortunately, man is an inconsistent creature, often governed by emotion and temporal things rather than by sound reasoning and eternal truths. Not all evolutionists are "bad guys"; some are highly moral and spiritual in their personal relations. By the same token, not all creationists are "good guys"; some are opinionated cranks and some even self-seeking charlatans.

Such inconsistencies in human belief and behavior, however, do not invalidate the consistency of the immutable God and his infallible Word. The character of God demands the doctrine of special creation and the Word of God clearly reveals it. The fundamental truths of this doctrine constitute the only sound foundation for the development of all other doctrines. Unity in this doctrine is, therefore, prerequisite to any true unity in other doctrines. It is exciting that just such unity is developing today among godly creationist Christians in all denominations.

"Thou art worthy, O Lord, to receive glory and honour and power: for thou hast created all things, and for thy pleasure they are and were created" (Rev. 4:11).

Appendix C

Supplementary Studies by the Writer

Introduction

During recent decades creationist books, once rather sparse in both scope and number, have proliferated so rapidly that it would be impractical to attempt a complete listing in this brief appendix.

Consequently, I will refer only to a number of my own books here. These are all developed within the framework of literal creationism derived in *this* book, so the message of each is consistent with all the others. Since I have been involved in this field for almost fifty years, I have had opportunity to study just about every important aspect and application of creationism, so the coverage in these books is reasonably comprehensive.

In any case, I trust the books listed below will provide an adequate introduction to the broad fields of scientific creationism and creation relevance, as well as general discussions of both fields in relation to each other and to biblical creationism.

Books on Scientific Creationism

Since the God who made the world also wrote the Word, the data of true science, as obtained by men under the proper use of the dominion mandate (Gen. 1:26–28), must agree with the testimony of Scripture. The books listed in this section show that scientific data do, indeed, support the facts of special creation, the worldwide flood and other events of primeval history as recorded in the Bible and as expounded in this book.

The Genesis Flood (with John C. Whitcomb). Phillipsburg, N.J.: Presbyterian and Reformed, 1961. 518 pages.

Most authorities view this book as the catalyst that initiated the creationist revival of recent decades. It still contains the most extensive discussion of "flood geology" in print, as well as an introduction to many other key concepts of modern creationism.

Scientific Creationism. 2d ed. El Cajon, CA: Master Books, 1985., 281 pages.

Probably the most comprehensive discussion in print of all aspects of modern "creation science." Widely used as a textbook in both Christian and secular schools, it also contains an extensive bibliography of creationist and anti-Darwinian books, as well as thorough indexes of names and subjects.

What Is Creation Science? (with Gary E. Parker). 2d ed. El Cajon, CA: Master Books 1987. 356 pages.

Also a comprehensive coverage of the various aspects of scientific creationism, but with greater weight on the biological aspects. Illustrated.

Science, Scripture and the Young Earth (with John D. Morris). El Cajon, CA: Institute for Creation Research, 1989. 95 pages.

An answer to the main scientific objections (as well as a brief refutation of compromising biblical interpretations) to the biblical doctrine of recent creation and the worldwide flood.

Creation Relevance

In addition to evidences from science and the Bible, the creation-evolution issue can be evaluated by Christ's "fruit test." He pointed out that "a good tree cannot bring forth evil fruit, neither can a corrupt tree bring forth good fruit. . . . Wherefore by their fruits ye shall know them" (Matt. 7:18, 20). The books listed below show that the fruit of evolution's tree is always evil, whereas creationism is the tree of good fruit.

The Long War against God. Grand Rapids: Baker, 1989. 344 pages.

The most extensive treatment in print of the history and impact of evolutionism, this book thoroughly documents the long history of evolutionary philosophy as the basis of every non-biblical religion and as the root of every harmful philosophy and practice in the modern world, as well as the continued witness of the true gospel through the ages and its ultimate triumph. Thoroughly indexed for reference use.

The Remarkable Record of Job. Grand Rapids: Baker, 1988. 146 pages.

This unique approach to the ancient Book of Job shows clearly the vital importance of creationism in the sight of God and in dealing with the most difficult of human problems, the problem of evil.

The God Who is Real. Grand Rapids: Baker, 1988. 85 pages.

This is a small book demonstrating the importance of creationism in evangelism and missions, whether on the foreign field or in American universities. It is also intended for use as an actual evangelistic tool, a small book to place in the hands of interested but skeptical inquirers.

Creation and the Second Coming. El Cajon, CA: Master Books, 1991. 194 pages.

A small book showing the necessity of a creationist approach to an understanding of the prophecies related to the imminent return of Christ, when he will complete and implement all his purposes in creating the world in the first place. Exciting and up-to-date in its prophetic outlook.

Books on General Creationism

The books listed below deal mainly with biblical creationism and earth history. They assume the Bible to be inerrant throughout and of divine authority on every subject with which it deals. They are primarily biblical expositions (as is this present book), but also show how the Bible correlates with true science and true history.

The Biblical Basis for Modern Science. Grand Rapids: Baker, 1986. 516 pages.

The most thorough coverage in print of the harmony of science and the Bible, with a chapter on each of the major sciences and scientific themes in relation to all the relevant Scriptures. A special chapter is included refuting in detail the various theories attempting a compromise with evolution.

The Genesis Record. Grand Rapids: Baker, 1976. 716 pages.

The most widely used commentary on the whole Book of Genesis, scientific in emphasis and also devotional and Christ-centered in exposition. A basic textbook in the modern creation movement, it also contains many useful appendices.

Science and the Bible. Chicago: Moody, 1986. 154 pages.

An evangelistic exposition of the scientific and prophetic insights of the Bible, with answers to difficulties. Previous editions of this book have been continuously in print for over forty-five years and have been used to win many to Christ.

Many Infallible Proofs. El Cajon, CA: Master Books, 1974. 381 pages.

Perhaps the most comprehensive modern text and reference book on practical Christian evidences and popular evangelistic apologetics. This book provides evidences for the absolute truth of Scripture, the deity of Christ, and the great plan of God, in addition to creation, the flood, and other scientific issues, with answers to difficulties and apparent contradictions.

Notes

Chapter 1: *The Genesis Record of Creation*

1. The archaeologist P. J. Wiseman was apparently the first to call attention to this "tablet theory" of the original writing of the records in Genesis that were eventually compiled and edited by Moses. A number of later Old Testament scholars (e.g., David L. Cooper, founder of the Biblical Research Society) have adopted it, and I consider it the only theory that fits all the facts. For a summary of the evidence for this theory, see my commentary, *The Genesis Record* (Baker, 1976), pp. 22–30.

Chapter 2: *The Lost World*

1. See Appendix A.

Chapter 7: *Creation in the Works of David and Solomon*

1. *Sampling the Psalms.* 2d ed. (San Diego: Master Books, 1991).

Chapter 14: *Creation and the Fall in Paul's Epistles*

1. See Henry Morris, *The Biblical Basis for Modern Science* (Grand Rapids: Baker, 1986), 54–66.

Chapter 15: *Creation and the Flood in the General Epistles*

1. For a free descriptive list of books and audiovisual materials on these evidences, write the Institute for Creation Research, P.O. Box 2667, El Cajon, CA 92021.

2. See Appendix A for a discussion of the creation references in these and other ancient extra-biblical writings.

Chapter 16: *The Beloved Disciple and Creation Evangelism*

1. For a verse-by-verse exposition of the Book of Revelation, all in the foundational context of God's creative purpose and its ultimate fulfillment, see my commentary, *The Revelation Record* (Wheaton, Ill.:Tyndale, 1983).

Appendix A: *Creation in Extra-Biblical Writings*

1. All quotes from Josephus are from Book I of his *Antiquities of the Jews.*